TABLE OF CONTENTS

SETTING THE MIND FREE

SETTING
THE MIND
FREE

Releasing
Cult Thinking
To Rejoin Reality

FEATURING TWO CLASSIC WORKS BY

ARTHUR J. DEIKMAN M.D.

FEARLESS BOOKS

NAPA • CALIFORNIA

Fɪʀsᴛ Eᴅɪᴛɪᴏɴ

This volume is a compilation of two previous books by
Arthur Deikman MD: *The Wrong Way Home: Uncovering Patterns
of Cult Behavior in American Society* (Beacon Press, 1994) and *Personal
Freedom: On Finding Your Way to the Real World* (Viking Press, 1976).
This is the first edition of the compilation.

FEARLESS BOOKS
www.fearlessbooks.com

Cᴏᴘʏʀɪɢʜᴛ © 2021 ʙʏ Eᴛᴛᴀ Dᴇɪᴋᴍᴀɴ

ISBN: 978-0-9822799-7-7

Eᴅɪᴛɪɴɢ, Dᴇsɪɢɴ & Tʏᴘᴏɢʀᴀᴘʜʏ:
D. Patrick Miller • Fearless Literary Services
www.fearlessbooks.com/Literary.html

PUBLISHER'S NOTE

THIS IS the second volume of "collected works" by the late Arthur Deikman, MD that I have published under the imprint of Fearless Books.

The first was entitled *Meditations on a Blue Vase,* comprising a number of academic papers and magazine articles that Dr. Deikman had amassed in his significant career as a psychiatrist and a pioneer at the forefront of transpersonal psychology. I met Arthur once, briefly, with his wife Etta to plan the publication of that anthology. However, he had been rendered mute and paralyzed by Parkinson's, and was obviously in a terminal process. But we were all hoping to have the book in print in time for his 84th birthday in 2013.

Sadly, Arthur passed about three weeks before that date, while I was still pulling the anthology together from a small mountain of professional journals, magazines, and even a few mimeographed originals. While *Blue Vase* was thus published as a legacy book, it still sells steadily today to a worldwide audience interested in Arthur's radical thought and paradigm-breaking clinical work. That work included the memorable episode in which Arthur turned the administration of a psychiatric hospital ward over to the patients, accepting their challenge to let them lock the entire staff in a padded room during a Halloween party. (As it turned out, the patients let the staff out "for good behavior" after twenty minutes.)

This volume follows upon the suggestion of a Deikman scholar in India who wanted to know if Arthur's three trade books might be brought back into print. As it turned out, one of them is still in circulation from its original publisher, Beacon Press: *The Observing Self*: *Mysticism and Psychotherapy.* The other two comprise this volume and have a piercing relevance to our times.

When *The Wrong Way Home: Uncovering the Patterns of Cult Behavior in American Society* was initially published in 1994, most Americans were concerned about cultism only its most extreme group manifestations such as the Moonies and People's Temple. But Arthur understood that cult thinking was endemic not only to the American way of life, but to human nature itself. The extended story of "Hugh and Clara Robinson", reprinted in full in this volume, shows how even the most intelligent and sophisticated adults can fall prey to the oppressed, regimented thinking that cults and their charismatic leaders demand.

Despite all his foresight, Arthur could not have anticipated the highly contagious "groupthink" effect of electronic social media. At this writing, the so-called "QAnon cult" has poisoned the thinking of millions, threatening the future of American democracy and culture. Thus, understanding the roots of a cultic mentality has never been more important.

In *Personal Freedom: On Finding Your Way to the Real World*, published nearly two decades earlier than *Wrong Way*, Arthur deftly transits from psychology to mysticism and back again in his highly original exposition on what it means to think freely as an individual. Together, these two works deserve a perennial second life as an indispensable reference on the variant expressions of cultism vs. authentic freedom of thought. I'm proud to be the guardian of most of Dr. Deikman's literary legacy.

In combining these two books I applied a minimal editing hand, removing only the most dated references and eliminating footnoting throughout for the ease of reading. There were no rewrites, major deletions or rearrangement of text, and the original chapter titles and progression in each book have been preserved.

— D. PATRICK MILLER
Publisher, Fearless Books

FOREWORD

I FIRST read *Personal Freedom* in 1977 while completing my doctorate in psychology. I continued to read Arthur Deikman's work in the ensuing years, including *The Wrong Way Home*. His work profoundly affected my thinking and how I approached the world. More importantly, his work began to not only offer insight into human consciousness and cognition, it also shined the light on my self. Arthur's approach and teachings are much more than a set of theories or ways to help individuals in psychotherapy. His books and approach helped me know what I am and what I am here for, and they can do the same for you.

Nearly five decades later, his work is a map for our current times. To find healing and to rise to our best, we must see what wounds us and drives us apart. To be truly free, we must know what freedom is and what imprisons us that is of our own making. Deikman's books hold a contemporary relevance that is uncanny; in some ways, he was writing prophetically, knowing the issues of cult thinking vs. independent and the importance of genuinely free thought. Perhaps unpopular to frame it as such, but we live in a time when mass-cult thinking is so prevalent as to be a critical issue in the direction of politics and the fabric of society. The illusion of independence is frequently and fervently defended with the argument that we are "free" to think whatever we want, regardless of how unfounded, unscientific, or ultimately destructive it is. This kind of freedom is not free at all; it is bondage to egoistic insanity that has us barreling toward the proverbial cliff. This book will acquaint you with both the problems and the solution, but be forewarned, to fully grasp and implement its profound teaching requires us to step forward with unique honesty and grit.

This book is not political or spiritual in the usual sense. Still, it may be the most honest and insightful political writing you have ever read and the most impactful and insightful to the spiritual core of who you are. Amid our most significant challenges, we can become more compassionate beings, more aware of our power to free ourselves in ways we did not realize before. I enjoy stories that tell of meeting adversity in ways that require hard work to overcome. When I read Deikman's words, I am reminded that my freedom comes from my efforts to examine my thoughts and behavior to reach independence, different from what we see argued for in most world struggles. This sort of work is hard, plain and simple. It is also necessary if we want to individually and collectively wake from this delusion we have mistakenly called clear and independent thinking and freedom.

Over the decades, I have come to see Arthur Deikman as a pioneer in the art and science of showing us ourselves and how to rise to our highest human potential. His stories, examples, and direct teachings offer a profound structure to know our purpose, recognize our need for societal healing, and hope and motivation for peaceful global relations. In short, he teaches us to think and live sanely. He does not point a blaming finger; he teaches us how to work on ourselves to heal our fears, reduce greed, and see the results of vanity and ego-based actions. It is not easy to tap a person on the shoulder to point out how they act in ways that are irrational and blind, but Arthur Deikman's life work effectively does this and more.

How? By helping us answer the questions *"What is the purpose of living?"* and *"Why do I exist?"* Hardly a casual inquiry, but, as he points out, not addressing such questions has resulted in an "illness" that is best described as meaninglessness that has festered into deep unrest, division, and alienation. His work is ideal and comprehensive for our current times, for symptoms of the illness that include uncertainty resulting from a growing lack of purpose and lost principles grounded in who we are and what we are capable of achieving. Our leaders and healers, including myself, are not immune to the same illness. Healing through meaning and purpose also shifts our perception rather than narrowing it with logic entangled by overvaluing rationalism.

Deikman's approach helps us, quite literally, to see clearly, to move beyond all the concepts and constructs darting through our minds that result in ways of seeing others and ourselves that we believe are unquestionably real. Our mind and intellect are extraordinary in what they can create, but we can easily mistake the map for the territory. We develop theories and belief systems about most everything, but we tend to forget that we made them up. Arthur eloquently states a truth that is at first difficult to grasp: "...every thought we have is unreal, a selection, an abstraction. Inside the abstract rooms we cannot see the world. It is a perceptual problem."

In the early 1980s I was involved in the development of the emerging field of Peace Psychology and have since written books and taught courses on the subject. Though influenced by many over the years, Arthur's work in two areas fundamentally helped shape my approach: Understanding conflict via grasping the ingrained adversarial approach and his ground-breaking work on cult formation dynamics.

Look around. Listen to the news for five minutes. Lend an ear to someone in conflict with a family member. Listen to someone running for office. It does not take long to see that the adversarial approach is alive and well, cemented in our consciousness, arguing rightness while criticizing and disparaging others, or worse in the case of war. We learn in reading Deikman that perception is often more of a mirror than a fact, and information from our past we call true is never wholly accurate and always limited. As Arthur puts it, "Indeed, to some degree, everyone is in error."

Cult behavior is not easy to address because few think it applies to themselves. We like to think of ourselves as strong or at least capable of not blindly following someone who may be more interested in power than our well-being. Few people think they would ever fall prey to the psychologically manipulative and intimidating environments of the most dangerous cults. Deikman shows us irrefutably that behavior similar to cults unfolds in most people. Though we live in an open society where we may believe we are not coerced and have free access to information, we are well served to grasp that cult behavior is operating every day, mostly unnoticed, including within our consciousness. It is not easy to see and own within ourselves. The truth is that our psychological sophistication and technological advancements have not made us immune to cult behavior. To put it bluntly, most people lack the insight or recognition of dependency needs and how they covertly manifest within us and society. In reading Deikman, we see that though we may want to think that only the unsophisticated or weak-minded have vulnerability to cult behavior, we all do. Below is a checklist of everyday behaviors that are reflective of cult behavior [paraphrased from Deikman]:

1. Speaking of adversaries or outsiders (e.g., conservatives, liberals, rich, poor) as if they were all the same while characterizing them by negative traits only and attributing unflattering motives to them but not to oneself.
2. Lacking interest and information concerning the actual statements and actions of opponents or outsiders.
3. Failing to consider the possible validity of an adversary's point of view.
4. Not taking a critical look at one's own position.
5. Disapproving or rejecting a member of one's group for departing from the group position, devaluing the dissident, regarding him or her as an annoyance or a problem.
6. Feeling self-righteous.

Few of us can say we have never engaged in such behaviors, thus, the importance of this book.

We hear much about "fake news" and "alternative facts," almost always referring to practices of people with whom we disagree. Cult behavior has many prices, including deep division, diminished realism, and an inability to see essential common goals for happiness and planetary survival. Fortunately, Deikman offers a different path forward. A goal of this book, as I see it, is to increase awareness of the origins of cult behavior, adversarial relating, and implementing the power that comes with personal responsibility and finding meaning and purpose.

To frankly discuss this in light of our current challenges is essential. A hallmark of democracy is the right to dissent. However, we are increasingly divided so that we no longer listen or seek to understand and instead readily dismiss, attack, and defend. On a personal level, few are open or tolerant and are ready to reject another's view when it differs from their own. Increasingly, individuals and groups have little to no tolerance for opposing ideas and even less interest in examining if we may be in error. We have come to a place where we are prone to react to any person with an opposing view as an enemy or an idiot. Many people appear to have lost what little open-mindedness they may have had. As a society, we dig deeper into division and do not want to lift the hood of our own thinking to consider our prejudice, false righteousness, and reliance on the unquestioned tenets we believe to be fact. Common ground is not found through demonization but by seeing ways in which we think that imprison and divide us. It may sound overstated, but Deikman's work can help liberate us from our self-imposed limitations for peace, happiness, and joy. Reading this book will make you think, and you will likely become more realistic, responsible, thoughtful, and effective.

Please do not mistake my endorsement of Arthur's work for thinking he has all the answers. Paradoxically, in his authenticity and openness to self-reflection, I find the most solace:

"It is a matter of some chagrin to me that even in the process of writing this book I find it very difficult to practice what I preach; whenever my own opinions are challenged my first response is to put up my mental fists and fight back, defending my position. Only then do I catch myself and ask the dissenter: Why do you think that?" — *Lee Jampolsky, Ph.D.*

———————————

DR. LEE JAMPOLSKY has served on the medical staff and faculty of respected hospitals and graduate schools. A *New York Times* bestselling author, his eight books are published in more than a dozen languages. He has appeared in hundreds of publications, including *The Wall Street Journal, Business Week, The Los Angeles Times, Entrepreneur,* and *Women's World*. He is a retired psychologist and currently offers coaching, spiritual mentoring, and online courses.

Email: *Lee@Drleejampolsky.com*

THE WRONG WAY HOME

*Uncovering the Patterns
of Cult Behavior
in American Society*

INTRODUCTION

MUCH of my work as a psychiatrist consists of helping people become aware of the fantasies that influence what they do and how they feel. Interestingly, it is not fantasies of power and riches that cause the most trouble, but those of receiving protection, nurture, comfort, or praise; of someone keeping count, noting deeds, thoughts and efforts. It doesn't matter who a person is, no matter how outwardly independent, a child's wish for a powerful protective parent waits in the depths of the psyche and seeks expression. And express itself it does. The result is cult behavior even in people who do not belong to cults.

Usually, the word *cult* refers to a group led by a charismatic leader who has spiritual, therapeutic, or messianic pretensions, and indoctrinates the members with his or her idiosyncratic beliefs. Typically, members are dependent on the group for their emotional and financial needs and have broken off ties with those outside. The more complete the dependency and the more rigid the barriers separating members from non-believers, the more danger the cult will exploit and harm its members.

A number of books have been written about cults. Robert Lifton's landmark study of Chinese brainwashing, *Thought Reform and the Psychology of Totalism*, enabled us to understand the cognitive mechanisms operating in totalistic environments, where the author-Ities have complete control over people's lives and use any means to convert their subjects to their own rigid system of belief. Lifton's analysis is very applicable to extreme cults, one of which I will describe in Chapter Two. But our everyday society is not totalistic. We are not subject to the total control possible to the Chinese communists (who held their prisoners by force), or to the psycho-logically coercive environments of the worst cults. Nevertheless, I will argue that behavior qualitatively similar to that which takes place in extreme cults takes place in all of us, despite our living in an open society, uncoerced, free to select our sources of in-formation and our companions. We need to understand the cult behavior that operates unnoticed in everyday life.

Toward the end of his book, Lifton remarked that childhood helplessness and dependency produce "a capacity for totalism." I will focus in detail on the way in which the longing for parents persists into adulthood and results in cult behavior that pervades normal society. When I speak of a wish for parents I am not speak-ing of transference — the re-experiencing of a specific parental rela-tionship — but of a yearning for parents in the most general sense. This longing results in fantasies of wise, powerful guardians even in those who are themselves looked up to by others, the best edu-cated, the most cynical. Such fantasies exist in the borderlands of consciousness and may seldom be noticed, but they may be super-imposed on people who occupy real positions of authority, success, and power, or their images may be displaced to a heavenly realm. Only by recognizing the indwelling wish can we gain freedom from the childhood world of vertical relationships and gain an eye-level perspective.

Such recognition is not easy. Freud made us aware that child-hood experience may be expressed in the malfunctioning of the adult; this developmental understanding is now part of our worldview. But despite our sophistication in matters of individual pathology, we lack sufficient recognition of the dependency wishes that all of us express in covert form.

It is difficult to write convincingly about everyday cult behavior because some of the words I must use may sound like psychiatric jar-gon: dependency, unconscious fantasies, longings for security. Everyone exempts themselves from the description. The psycholo-gically sophisticated are likely to think they are beyond these things and others may think that only weaklings have such vulnerabilities. To try to circumvent this problem I will make extensive use of examples drawn from a number of sectors of society: government, large corporations, the media, psychiatry, and religion.

The price of cult behavior is diminished realism. We cannot afford that now, if we ever could. Fortunately, awareness is a potent antidote. Increasing that awareness is the goal of this book.

ONE

The Cult Mirror

A FEW years ago I took part in a research seminar on new religious movements, the religious and utopian groups which
sprang up in the 1960s and 70s and made the term *cult*
familiar to all newspaper readers. Like everyone else, we in the
seminar were impressed by the power of cult groups to dominate
their members. A most extreme example was the People's Temple of
San Francisco, whose mass suicide in 1978 was regarded as a piece
of insanity, a horror that could be condemned without hesitation,
in part because it appeared so alien to our lives. Other groups were
only slightly less notorious for such activities as mass sterilization
of their men or prostitution of their women; some cults engaged
in the breaking up of families and financially exploited devotees,
actions less newsworthy but nonetheless damaging.

In reading about cults, most of us in the seminar felt repulsion
and fear, but also fascination. Cults present us with images of surrender, violence, sex, and power. We respond to them with avid
interest because they speak to unconscious wishes. Moreover, we
can watch at a seemingly safe distance because the cults of which
we are aware usually have foreign trappings or unusual social structures that separate them from ordinary society and from ourselves.
Without such markings, however, cult behavior is not usually
recognized, especially when this behavior is our own.

Former cult members were interviewed by the seminar research
group. We talked first with a man and a woman who had escaped from
the People's Temple camp in Guyana on the morning of the mass suicide. These witnesses were not college graduates, nor were most

members of the People's Temple. At subsequent meetings we interviewed a married couple who had belonged to quite a different cult, one whose members were highly educated, possessing graduate degrees in psychology or related fields. (They had worked as psychotherapists and teachers, just as we in the seminar did.) After that, people spoke who had been members of a utopian rehabilitation group for ex-convicts and, still later, we heard from members and ex-members of several other new religions.

The variety of personalities involved, of differing racial, economic, religious, educational, and social backgrounds, was impressive. What was most striking was that no matter whom we interviewed, the stories of involvement in exploitative, harmful cults were similar. A distinct pattern of seduction, coercion, corruption and regression emerged, no matter what the outward trappings, no matter what dogma or purpose the group espoused. Basic human responses had been elicited by a process fundamentally the same.

THE CULT STORY

At the time they joined their particular cult, most of the people we interviewed had been dissatisfied, distressed, or at a transition point in their lives. Typically, they desired a more spiritual life, a community in which to live cooperatively; they wanted to become enlightened, to find meaning in serving others, or simply to belong. An encounter with an enthusiastic, attractive, friendly person served to introduce each of them to a group whose outer appearance was quite benign. At some point during that introductory phase an intense experience took place which was interpreted as validating the claim that the leader and the group were special, powerful, spiritual; that they could give the person what he or she wanted. This experience might have been an altered state of consciousness (induced by the leader or the group via meditation, chanting, or the laying on of hands), a powerful therapeutic experience, or just a wonderful feeling of being accepted and welcomed — "coming home."

Won over, the newcomer joined the group, embracing its doctrines and practices. Soon the cult's demands increased and the new member was asked to devote increasing amounts of time, money, and energy to the group's activities. These demands were justified as necessary to fulfill the group's goals; willingness to comply was always interpreted as a measure of the recruit's commitment and sincerity. In order to continue, most did comply, sacrificing much for the sake of the stated high purposes of the group (often put in terms of saving the world).

Relationships outside the group became difficult to maintain. The former life of the new member was given up; contact with outsiders was discouraged and the demands of the new life left little opportunity for extra-group activities. However, the sacrifices were compensated for by the convert's sense of belonging and purpose. The group and the leader gave praise and acceptance —at least initially.

Gradually, however, an iron fist was felt. Deviation from group dogma brought swift disapproval or outright rejection. The message to the convert became clear: what the group had given the group could take away. In time, he or she submitted to — and participated in — cruel, dishonest, and contradictory practices out of fear of the leader and the group, who by then had become the convert's sole source of self-esteem, comfort, and even financial support. Actions that conflicted with the convert's conscience were rationalized by various formulas provided by the leader. (For example, in one group lying to potential converts was explained as "divine deception" for the good of those deceived.) Critical evaluation of the leader and the group became almost impossible, not only because it was punished severely, but also because the view of reality presented by the cult had no challengers. Discordant information was excluded from the group's world.

Exploitation intensified and the recruit regressed into a fearful submission. Couples might be separated; members would inform on each other. Morals were corrupted and critical thinking suppressed.

Often the group's leader deteriorated as well, becoming increasingly grandiose, paranoid, or bizarre. In most cases, paranoid thinking tended to mark the entire cult and reinforced the group's isolation.

Our witnesses told of how, eventually, the demands became unbearable; a mother might be told to give up her child or her husband, or a spouse directed to take a different sexual partner. Although often the person would agree to the new requirement, sometimes he or she would not. In such cases, when the member finally refused to comply with the leader or the group's demands, he or she left precipitously, often assisted by a person outside with whom, some contact and trust had been maintained.

Leaving such a group was a flight because the group's reaction was known to be severe and punitive. Apostates were excommunicated. It was not uncommon for ex-converts to fear that they had been damned or had lost their souls as a consequence of leaving the group. (In some cases former members were convinced the group would hunt them down and kill them.) Many went through months of struggle to re-establish their lives, wrestling with the questions How could I have been involved in such a thing? How could I have done what I did to other members of the group? Were my spiritual longings all false? Who and what can I trust? At the same time, the closeness the group offered was often sorely missed, and until the ex-member's life was reconstituted, he or she wondered at times if leaving the group had been a mistake. This turmoil gradually diminished, but for many a sense of shame for having participated in the cult and a frustrated rage at having been betrayed lingered for a long time.

AFTER listening to many variants of this story, I began to see that cults form and thrive not because people are crazy, but because they have two kinds of wishes. They want a meaningful life, to serve God or humanity; and they want to be taken care of, to feel protected and secure, to find a home. The first motives may be laudable and constructive, but the latter exert a corrupting effect, enabling cult leaders to elicit behavior directly opposite to the idealistic vision with which members entered the group.

Usually, in psychiatry and psychology, the wish to be taken care of (to find a home, a parent) is called dependency and this is a rather damning label when applied to adults. Adults are not supposed to be dependent in that way, relying on another as a child would rely on a mother or father. We are supposed to be autonomous, self-sustaining, with the capacity to go it alone. We do recognize that adults need each other for emotional support, for giving and receiving affection, for validation; that is acceptable and sanctioned. But underlying such mature interdependency is the longing of the child, a yearning that is never completely outgrown. This covert dependency — the wish to have parents and the parallel wish to be loved, admired, and sheltered by one's group — continues throughout life in everyone. These wishes generate a hidden fantasy or dream that can transform a leader into a strong, wise, protective parent and a group into a close, accepting family. Within that dream we feel secure.

The dependency dream has great strength and tenacity. It should be recognized as a permanent part of the human psyche even though in adults it ceases to be as visible as it is in childhood. This dream is dangerous because in its most extreme form it generates cults and makes people vulnerable to exploitation, regression, and even violence. Even in the less intense, less obvious manifestations which occur in everyday society, the dependency dream may impair our ability to think realistically. If we recognize our dependent wishes for what they are we can make appropriate corrections in thought and behavior, but usually we do not. Rather, we engage in thinking and behavior more subtle than that of the People's Temple but qualitatively similar.

Eventually, we in the seminar were unable to maintain the belief that cults were something apart from normal society. The people telling us stories of violence, cruelty, and perversion of values were like ourselves. After listening and questioning we realized that we were not different from nor superior to the ex-cult members, that we were vulnerable to the same dependency wishes, capable of the same betrayals and cruelty in circumstances in which our sense of reality was manipulated.

As I studied the psychological mechanisms that made the cult experience possible, I began to recognize uncomfortably familiar processes. A little reflection provided many specific instances of my own compliance — conscious and unconscious — with the values and preferences of my peers, compliance that I had rationalized or ignored because I preferred to think of myself as very independent. Since no radical change or disruption of my life occurred and I was not acting at the behest of a charismatic leader or occult group, it had not occurred to me that I might be behaving like one who has been captured by a cult. Nevertheless, I now realize that the motivations and manipulations constituting cult behavior are present in varying degrees in my own life and that they play a role in the lives of most of us as they operate in our educational systems, the business world, religion, politics, and international relations. Just as many of the more notorious cults have proven to be costly and destructive, so ordinary cult behavior is damaging and harmful to some degree wherever it occurs, no matter how normal its outward appearance.

When the seminar began I viewed cults as pathological entities alien to my everyday life. By the time it ended, I realized that the dynamics of cult behavior and thinking are so pervasive in normal society that almost all of us might be seen as members of invisible cults. In fact, as I will argue, society can be viewed as an association of informal cults to which everyone belongs. Yet the groups most of us belong to do not appear strange, flamboyant, esoteric, or unnatural, nor do they defy society with lurid and violent behavior. Social infrastructures and behaviors that are similar to those of the People's Temple go unnoticed.

Surely, the reader may ask, while it is true that serious consequences result from membership in extreme cults, how can you say harm comes from the groups that make up normal society? I certainly don't recognize such effects in groups to which I belong. I am indeed talking about normal society, in which the damage resulting from cult-like behavior is not as obvious as that headlined in the newspapers. Our own cult story is much less pronounced, with no noticeable beginning and no end; our perceptions, beliefs, and critical judgments are affected nonetheless.

We Americans live in a constitutional democracy, priding ourselves on the freedoms we have achieved. We live, travel and work without internal passports; we have free choice of job or profession; we may hold any belief and, within wide limits, do anything, say anything, write anything, and protest anything. We choose our governing officials from a list we have ourselves determined.

Democracy is based on an "eye-level" world in which we look directly at each other; every citizen is a peer. Political power is delegated, not inherited, not taken, not given by divine right, but bestowed by each of us. However, I believe that a danger exists even in democracies that the omnipresent authoritarian impulse will manifest itself in disguised form, will lead us toward a world in which we are always looking up at those who must be obeyed or down at those who must obey us. This is so because authoritarianism draws its strength from the same source that supports cult behavior: dependency on groups and leaders.

I believe that we need to bring into awareness the unconscious motivations and excluded information that influence our behavior and thought at the personal, national, and international levels. This requires that we first understand the dynamics of obvious cults and then address similar processes in ourselves and in ordinary society. Such understanding can provide us with tools for detecting cult behavior — our own as well as that of others — and enable us to step outside the cult circle.

I will begin with the history of a group which evolved into an extreme cult. The story is told by two of the group's converts, a real couple who underwent the experiences chronicled, although all the names used in my account are fictional and other changes have been made in their story.

"Hugh and Clara Robinson" were members of the cult for nearly a decade. Their story is significant because what they began in joy ended in terror and pain, their own relationship almost destroyed. The progression from heaven to hell was gradual, the steps of the descent justified in the name of God and said to be required if the group were to save the world, as they came to believe they could. The Robinsons' history is also significant because they were an intelligent, well-educated, normal couple — yet they came to believe in evil forces and in a group soul that could hold their own souls captive. Prior to their departure from the cult they and other members were spending as many as sixteen hours a day conducting one another through rites of "cleansing," exorcism, and the warding-off of devils. It may be difficult for the reader to identify with the Robinsons in this final, bizarre phase, but their story is classic and their vulnerability is shared by everyone to a greater extent than we realize.

Hugh and Clara escaped; others have not. Although it is important that we know about cults to avoid being caught in them, it is even more important that we study such groups to become aware of the hidden cult thinking operating unnoticed in our daily lives. Cults are mirrors of ourselves.

TWO

Hugh and Clara: A Case History

T HE ROBINSONS first encountered "Life Force" psychology when they participated in a workshop led by a very dedicated couple, Alex and Barbara Monroe. During that weekend, Hugh and Clara were guided in individual fantasies that were like dream journeys, and for the Robinsons the results were uplifting beyond their expectations.

CLARA: I had the experience of feeling more loved and accepted than I'd ever felt in my whole life. It was a real downflow of energy within me, just amazing. I had the feeling that this was something that I'd always wanted, that I had been looking outside myself for — and there it was.

HUGH: I had a very deep personal experience, realizing that I wasn't alone, that there were other people who cared about the same things I did. So I felt a brotherhood among these people.

After this experience the Robinsons wanted to learn more. They took several courses of study with the Monroes, traveled abroad to study with Thomas Correll for a few months, and decided to devote themselves full-time to studying and teaching life force psychology.

At that time Clara Robinson was over thirty, married, the mother of a young child. She had a bachelor's degree in English literature and had completed additional graduate work as well. Clara's relationships with her parents, siblings, and peers had been good. A leader in both high school and college, she was superior in intelligence and socially adept.

Clara's involvement with the Life Force group was rooted in

her sense of a special beauty in the world, a transcendent quality. When she was a little girl she spent a lot of time alone in nature. The trees and birds were a special source of delight, as was her perception that light was very nearby, "a feeling of things being very beautiful, in a way that I never found too many people to share it with... I had that feeling when my child was born, too: the miracle of life."

Except for one teacher, the first person she met with whom she could share that reality was her husband, Hugh. She remembers thinking: *He knows the secret thing, too.* This shared sense of a greater reality was a central theme to their relationship. Clara wondered why more people didn't have that feeling of special beauty.

Later, life force psychology provided a way of understanding that experience. For the first time Clara could share her perception with others, could integrate this secret, precious part of herself into her life in a beneficial way. She found a way to express herself and to teach principles and techniques that she believed could help others as well.

The system answered other needs as well. After Clara and Hugh were married, they discovered the human potential movement and Clara joined a therapy group that unleashed a great deal of fear in her. Her anxiety became progressively worse, and psychotherapy did not help. At this point in her life Clara encountered the Monroes and had her initial "transformation session," a profound and exhilarating experience, convincing her that the transformation process — as taught by Alex and Barbara — would provide the help she was seeking.

The experience took place in a group setting. Clara had volunteered to work on her fear; "In those days I would do anything to get help." Alex Monroe asked, "What are you afraid of?"

CLARA: I'm afraid I will float away.

ALEX: Can you see what you are afraid you will float away from?

CLARA: No, but I know what it is — myself as a grown woman.

ALEX: Can you see her?

CLARA: And then I saw this really wonderful, grounded Earth Mother... like an enormous earthy woman... the opposite of my kind of thin, wispy, mystic identification. And I cried and cried and cried. It was just wonderful. And he [Alex] worked with that in dialog and imagery and then he said, "There's a wise old man in the sun" and so I went up toward the sun and there was this wise man and he said to me, "My child," and I climbed in his lap, like a child — he was very much like a father, as I retell it I realize that — I just felt like I was home. I felt a downflow of love and affection that I have never felt before or since... like being totally okay. This must be what I have always been looking for... "I'm really all right"... It was very important... like this big sigh in it... I could rest. It was that experience that made me feel that I needed to do more of whatever this system was.

Alex told her she could think of that wise person any time she wanted. Afterwards Clara did that and it helped calm her, as did visualizing the earth mother. This vivid experience of what I would interpret as the dependency dream was profoundly important to Clara. "It felt like unconditional love, being totally accepted." She felt it had spiritual connotations as well. Clara thought everyone must want and should have this acceptance.

Hugh was also over thirty when he joined Life Force. He had studied at Princeton and was working on a Ph.D. in psychology. Like Clara, he had good relationships with his family and was close to his father and mother whom he described as spiritual people although not formally religious; "They were just committed to making changes for a better world." His father and mother both worked for liberal causes.

Throughout his school years Hugh had been an outstanding student and leader, yet he felt isolated from his peers. There was an artistic, sensitive side to himself that he was unable to share. Hugh appeared strong, confident, and successful in studies and athletics. He was a musician, popular with women, and the leader of his class. Inside, however, he felt alone, missing the security of his home environment where the spiritual part of himself was shared and supported. He strongly associates this spiritual aspect of his life with his love of music; when asked about early mystical experiences he refers to his artistic side.

"I had this intense, private spiritual life which I had always experienced in terms of music... what I would call superconscious experiences... and then at age nineteen, in the Rockies in Colorado, I had a spontaneous experience of unity with everything. That never left, in a way. I think that was always a backdrop to my searching."

This sense of the spiritual Hugh felt unable to share with his friends. Looking back, he recognizes that his peers' jealousy of his accomplishments added to his sense of isolation, "so there was this mixture of not feeling really connected but yet being admired by them and being a leader."

In college Hugh had a few good friends but felt even more like a loner. He was disillusioned with the pretensions of academic life and ceased trying to achieve the top.

At the time he encountered Life Force, Hugh was ripe for something to believe in, "to put my energy into... I had a wife and child and I didn't feel too comfortable with what it meant to be in the world and make a living. I was anxious about my life and wasn't sure that it was going to work out. I'd had to leave thing after thing because somehow it didn't satisfy me."

During that first workshop with the Monroes, Alex conducted Hugh in a long fantasy in which he climbed a mountain. At one point Alex suggested that Hugh become a beautiful tree that had been created in the fantasy. He did so.

"There was this wonderful flow of energy, of roots and light... very powerful. I had never experienced anything like this before."

Alex then suggested that he leave the tree, continue on up the mountain, and then look at the sun.

"Out of the sun came this figure and he came down... Greek, with a Franciscan robe on... a marvelous black beard, sort of green eyes... very alive and powerful figure and he just looked at me and we embraced and there was this wonderful feeling between us. Then we threw our arms around each other and we said, 'Let's take on the world!' There was this sense that we were going to work together to help the rest of the world."

The guided fantasy went on for about an hour. At the end of it, Hugh opened his eyes. The original group of twenty-five had been reduced to four in addition to Alex and Barbara. It was midnight. Two of those who stayed had met Hugh previously, two had not.

"They were all men... this was overwhelming to me, it was as powerful as the daydream... these people had stayed to be with me during this thing. Here were people who were sticking by me and not abandoning me for not understanding. And then Barbara said to me, 'You don't have to be alone anymore.' I just wept and wept... that I didn't have to be alone anymore."

Hugh and Clara shared an intuitive sense of a larger reality that was very important to them. However, I believe that this perception was confused with unresolved dependency longings that led them to interpret the guided daydream as spiritual and to accept the Monroes as guides or agents in that domain. Their enthusiasm for the new system was also due to its affirmation of their perceptions of the numinous world, perceptions which had not been acceptable to their peers. Suddenly, they found meaning, purpose, and helpful work to do.

The procedures and theoretical system of life force psychology had been put together by Thomas Correll, who had taught the Monroes when they had visited him four years before. Alex and Barbara were Correll's chief disciples, seemingly modeled after him in gentleness and altruism and in the loving attention they paid to those who came to learn and be helped by the system. They were totally dedicated to bringing this wonderful new teaching to others, to the world they believed needed it so badly.

Over the next four years life force psychology became popular, numerous workshops were given, and training sessions were developed for mental health professionals. The Robinsons had many sessions with the Monroes and received personal instruction abroad from Correll, as did almost all those who joined the Life Force group at the initial stage. Soon Clara and Hugh began to lead workshops and training sessions, moving to be near the Monroes so they could be more involved in the work. They felt they had the life they had always wanted. The spiritual values formerly split off from their working lives were now directly expressed and shared with a group of peers to whom they felt connected, people who validated and gave support to each other.

Hugh could now put his leadership abilities to use for a cause he believed in. He was appointed to the executive committee of the Life Force Psychology Center and conducted workshops and training sessions all over the United States. The theory of life force psychology particularly appealed to him.

"I loved the ideas, I loved the system... It felt like the most comprehensive and humane way of looking at people I'd found. I could work with these ideas about human nature that fit with how [I felt] when I played music or studied literature or whatever... There was just a very deep personal connection. It was mental as well as emotional ... like being on a frontier. There was a tremendous amount of excitement and intellectual stimulation...."

For Clara also, life force psychology and Life Force (the group) fulfilled important needs and involved her deepest feelings.

"It really fit with what I valued, what I had always hoped for. I must always have been a closet mystic, I suppose... suddenly there was a form [for the spiritual] and there was someone teaching who said you can work with people this way. So I gradually got more involved in teaching, in designing workshops. I was doing work with women at that time and there was quite a lot of freedom in the beginning to do my own thing. The workshops were attended and they grew and my confidence in teaching grew."

The members of the Life Force Psychology Center supported and encouraged her teaching.

"What was exciting for me was that there was a place for my

spiritual experience within the psychological system and I could learn to work with people to evoke that, and have them trust that and tap into it... learning how to help people get in touch with more love and compassion and with their creativity. I think affirming is the best word I could use. It just felt like it was affirming the best in people."

Gradually, this sense of high purpose gave rise to feelings of specialness which later led to the devaluation of those outside the group and to the elevation of Alex.

CLARA: [During these early years] there was a growing sense that this group was special and that we were doing something special that nobody else was... and that Alex was special.

The Robinsons were happy with their teaching role in Life Force. Five satisfying years went by. They conducted therapy sessions, taught workshops and classes. They believed that what they were doing was making a unique contribution to the world. Hugh in particular felt this to be a time of growth and personal fulfillment. He was an executive of the Center and, at the same time, had good friends in other professional organizations devoted to humanistic and spiritual concerns. He helped plan conferences, gave major presentations, traveled widely, and interacted with Life Force groups in other countries. Thus, for a long time there was a balance between Hugh's involvement with the Life Force Psychology Center and the rest of the world of humanistic and transpersonal psychology.

Clara engaged in similar activities, although to a lesser extent. She divided her life between Center work and her family. While Life Force took up a large part of her time and energy, she felt a reasonable share remained for her son and Hugh. Clara and Hugh were both pleased with the way their lives were going, convinced that Life Force was making a unique and vital contribution to the world.

Then the Center moved to better offices in the city and expanded teaching activities in other parts of the country and to Europe. With that move, the Robinson's life and that of the others in the group became more and more conflicted, painful, and distorted. More time was demanded from each member. This demand was made by Alex Monroe at a meeting of the executive committee, which transmitted it to a larger meeting that included the other members of the group (such as Clara). Pressure for compliance with this and other demands was usually from the group as a whole although Alex would personally exert extra pressure, if needed, on a balky member.

Clara experienced most of her conflicts with the Life Force group over the issue of commitment to her family. There was a competition for time and energy between the group and her son.

"I dragged my heels [against an increased commitment to the group]... There was a meeting where we were all supposed to make a commitment to take the work of the Center further. I was the last to, as they put it, 'put my sword on the table.' I said, "I'm not sure I can do it. I'm not sure it's really right for me."

Finally Clara agreed. Such conflicts were continual, but she told herself that giving increasing time to the Center was right because it was needed.

"Everyone around me seems to think it's okay... all these reasons. Somehow I let it be all right, I told myself it was all right, even though I didn't feel good about it. There were lots of things like that. The first impulse would be: This isn't right. And then someone questions it... maybe it's me or maybe it's someone else... and they get really put down. Sometimes there would be an awful silence in the room, sometimes it could be twenty people all looking at you incredulously and someone saying, 'How could you worry about that? Don't you see that we really need to.... There wasn't any opening for a different point of view; there was no space for other opinions... I told myself it must be right, but I don't think I ever stopped hearing that voice, saying it was not right."

Thus the group enforced compliance and dissent was stifled. Over the next few years, questionable practices, introduced by Alex, gradually increased, requiring further suppression of the members' sense of what was right. One such incident concerned a publicity write-up for Clara's workshops.

"There was a real effort to puff up the write-ups [make them look more impressive]... I had taught several night courses at the university but they wanted to put down that I had taught at the university itself. I remember questioning it and when you would question, from all sides there would come, 'Why were you thinking that? This is an opportunity to get our work more known....' There would be a response that made me feel like I couldn't keep pushing for it. I backed down a lot... 'Clara! How could you suggest that!' was the message. Alex would say, 'Here we are doing such important work and you let that bother you? What a petty little thing to be concerned with.'"

A great deal of "psychotherapeutic processing" among Center members took place over the telephone. When the issue was taping phone conversations, Alex (as always) had many justifications.

CLARA: Incredible, elaborate reasons, sometimes reasons you just couldn't understand, they were so complicated. The idea was that if we have a record of phone calls between people if something goes wrong we can have a record and then look and see whose fault it was or what the problem was... [As far as outside phone calls were concerned,] Well, by then the outside world was the enemy and so we wanted to know exactly what happened.

Eventually, Alex asked them to tape everything.

CLARA: I really encountered my ability to rationalize. If I had paid attention to all those occasions when everything inside of me said, "No, this isn't right," I couldn't have stayed there. If I had really taken a stand, let's say on the taping, and said, "I will not go along with this," first of all, it would have taken a kind of strength that I don't know I had at the time because everyone in the room [would be saying] "Clara, you want to have dinner with your son? You're so selfish..." I would have had to be willing to stand there and have everyone in the room say "No."

Thus, the group enforced compliance by the use of rhetoric

that exploited Clara's idealism for the group's own purposes. Alex led the way. If he was opposed on grounds of principle, Alex attacked those principles by equating them with selfish desires. The members had doubts about Alex's reasoning, but they never really discussed the matter among themselves out of fear that Alex might learn of it. Sometimes, after a meeting, members would walk home together and say, "God, that was weird, wasn't it?"

CLARA: We would sneak those little things to each other. But you could never be sure that person wouldn't get home and call Alex and say, "Boy, Clara Robinson was really identifying with her desire nature. You should have heard what Clara said after the meeting."

This suspicion extended to close friends.

"I couldn't even be sure that Hugh wouldn't do that; I did that on him. There was no safe person to trust with that intuitive sense [of something being wrong]... You couldn't be sure... sometimes someone else would say, 'Yeah, I didn't like that, either,' but you didn't know if that would be kept in confidence. There was no one but yourself to corroborate. If someone coming home had said... if we had said together, 'It isn't right, what happened to so-and-so...' Any of that would have made a tremendous difference — there was none.

So dissent was silenced. Typically, Alex did not demand that members inform on each other; rather, they were asked to provide information that could be used to "help" the other person.

CLARA: It used to be a way of getting in with Alex. He was always glad for that information. I remember the first time I was asked to give [information]... Alex said, "I'm going to bring this thing up about Jerry and if you could share that piece in the meeting that would be very helpful." I remember [saying] "I'm not sure that is right," but then the rationale would be that it would really help Jerry and I'd say, "Oh, that's right, Jerry can learn from that if he can see that; that will really help him." A lot of things went under that reasoning — a lot of bad things. Then there were times when people would volunteer... getting Alex's favor was a pretty important thing, particularly toward the end, getting his approval... He definitely had real favorites and they'd change. It was never a very secure favoritism, you could lose it at any point.

Hugh's experience was similar. Like the others, he wished for Alex's approval, and fear of losing it led him to compromise his principles and avoid dissent.

HUGH: There were things that were beginning to happen there that I was uncomfortable about. But because my personal connection had been so deep, I kept saying, "It's worth it. This work is so good, it's so effective, that I'll overlook..." Alex lied. Just little things, like changing the date on a letter, but I hated that. And I would say, "Why do we have to do that?" and he would have some quick answer that would say why it was necessary, because someone would screw him if he didn't, basically. And so I said, O.K... And then it was lying to people about different situations [in order to control them]. The Executive Committee would get together and plan exactly what was going to go in the meeting, what was going to happen, so that there was no trust of the natural caring or power or whatever in people in the Center. But because the work was so "good," you know, I loved it, I turned a blind eye. Every year. I'd think, "Something's not right here. And yet, something is so right here." We pushed away a lot of stuff... that's what we realize, now, but we didn't at the time.

Alex's power derived from the assumption that he knew much more than the others about the teaching and thus was entitled to special authority. Indeed, it turned out that there had been a secret, mystical side to Thomas Correll that only some knew about, a deep involvement in an esoteric group devoted to occult writings. Correll had given occult books to Alex, who eventually began to teach his own version of the elaborate esoteric system to an inner circle at the Center, those people whom he felt to be most committed to the work.

HUGH: I thought Alex was smarter than me, more evolved, because he knew all this occult stuff... [he would] use chapter and verse to rationalize these things. It was like a priest using a Bible.

He read it much more than anyone else and no one could refute it.

Then Thomas Correll died. The Robinsons later recalled that Alex had begun making disparaging comments about Correll prior to the man's death, remarking that he was too vague, too lax, too generous with his time, too indiscriminate, not focused enough, something of a fuddy-duddy. After Correll's death, such comments were more frequent. Alex became the only source of the teaching, the one who determined whether others would or would not continue to receive its benefits. Barbara Monroe became more and more subordinate. As Alex gradually exerted more and more control over the group's other members, their dependence on him increased. While he claimed to work and share power with the executive committee, in fact he subtly retained all power and control in his own hands. The committee soon realized that their job was to discuss and debate until they reached the decision Alex wanted. Alex did not acknowledge what he was doing and maintained the facade of democracy for a long time after it had become perfectly obvious to the others that he was the sole authority.

Clara's request for enough time to be with her child was labeled a selfish desire by the group. She recalls that there had never been any respect for her role as a mother. There was constant pressure on her to comply with the group's demand for more and more time. First, it was all mornings and then it was mornings and two afternoons, then five, and then meetings on Saturday as well.

CLARA: "Clara, when you really get it that your family is the whole world then you'll understand that David is just one of the many children you are responsible for." When we were asked to take the Center another step, I dragged my heels. There was this noise in my head: "Should I do this? Shouldn't I do this? Maybe it will be wrong and then what?" I remember at one point saying, "I'll do it", and everything got quiet around me and the noise in my head stopped and I thought, "God, maybe that is right. What I am being asked to do is to make a fuller commitment to this good work… And inside me I thought the quiet or sense of rightness means I'm doing the right thing to get more involved.

After several months of commuting to the new Center, the Robinsons moved to the city. The pressure on group members to give totally of their time and energy became overwhelming.

HUGH: By that time we were working six or seven days a week... leaving at six o'clock in the morning and coming back whenever. We had two cars and sometimes we had to drive separately... what that did was to fragment our family life.

Hugh was having a harder and harder time maintaining balance in his professional life as well. His involvements outside the Center drew increasing fire from Alex and the inner circle. He had never been one of Alex's favorites. On the few occasions when Alex had tried to use him as a confidant to help deal with another member, Hugh had felt very uncomfortable and failed the task. On occasions when Hugh disagreed, Alex justified everything with arguments and by citing the occult books. Hugh's rebellions against Alex's control were always short-lived.

"I would kick up a fuss and then I would give in, that's the pattern. 'All for the good'... he would get me on the 'good.' 'Oh, I see, for that reason, because it's spiritually right.' There was always a host of reasons that would evoke my caring for the cause and then I'd go along with it rather than saying, 'Look! The cause is being violated right here!'"

When Hugh asserted the importance of his family's needs, Alex would say, "Hugh, if your family was starving and you had one pound of wheat, would you make bread for your family or would you plant it to feed the starving million?"

This appeal to higher purpose, to the greater good, was Alex's stock in trade, and was copied by the group when it needed to pressure uncooperative members.

HUGH: It didn't quite fit but I had to go along with it because intellectually it made sense. I would discount my strong feelings. Everything was to be sacrificed to the greater, the larger: bringing Life Force into people's lives... I never won a battle; it was just a matter of how long I could stand up to it before it became too painful and then I would let myself be persuaded and would give in. [But] then I would subvert the system by just going right out and doing what I was doing.

The executive committee attacked Hugh's outside activities.

"This allegation of evil began to come at me... that I was identified with my "elemental" [selfish nature] and so forth... More and more it would be that I had done something wrong and I had to fix it and I would try. Every time I would return from a committee meeting [of an outside organization] to the Executive Committee of the Center I was called on the carpet for doing power trips, for not telling them everything that happened, for not getting Alex on the [conference] program. So I felt increasingly at odds but I was confused and wanted to do the right thing... [I was] torn between my loyalties... torn to pieces."

Alex planned to establish a graduate school of life force psychology with branches in North and South America and in Europe. It was a very ambitious project and required even more time and effort from group members. The actual establishment of the first of these graduate schools in the city, after the group moved there, was a pivotal event, one which inspired a further intensification of the cult process. Anyone who questioned the direction of the group was seen as an enemy who needed to be controlled or pushed down, whether the questioner was a group member or an outsider. As a result, members became more and more isolated from colleagues in other human service organizations and their time and energy were even more tightly controlled.

Abruptly, Hugh was removed from his position on the executive committee. At a meeting of that body he was told he was not contributing to the "group mind," asked to leave the executive committee's circle and discontinue almost all activities at the graduate school, where he had been teaching. He was instead given the lowest, least important assignments and asked to teach beginning workshops. Much of his time was spent cataloging cassette tapes and xeroxing. Occasionally, when he was allowed to teach a course at the graduate school, his proposal would be severely criticized.

"I became increasingly filled with fear and self-doubt... fear of what the group could do to me, fear of hurt, of rejection; fear of somehow being alone again. I was very alone and had lost whatever fellowship I had in the earlier years that had drawn me toward the group... turned against by people within the Executive group that I cared about."

At the same time, Clara's loyalties were being drawn away from Hugh towards the group. Lewis, Hugh's close friend, was echoing the group's abuse. Hugh was afraid of being abandoned completely. The isolation he thought he had left behind by joining Life Force now had reappeared within it.

"I was afraid of being alone, afraid of being cast out of Eden... even though Eden had turned into Hell... afraid of being cast out even further. There was still, 'Well, we're doing the graduate school, Hugh, and you can't think, so you can do these other things and we'll still be nice to you and we won't tell other people that you are no longer an Executive.' In other words, there was still 'caring' for me and I was still grasping for any care I could get."

For Clara, also, Eden was turning into hell. Not only did she experience an increasingly painful struggle to meet her son's needs, but her relationship with Hugh came under attack. One evening, late at night, she was called to meet with several executive committee members with whom she had warm ties. They told her that Hugh was having trouble and that they were having trouble with him:

"Hugh has been asked not to be on the Executive and we just want you to know that we really value you... we want you to stay no matter what happens... we want you to know that we really trust what you do."

Lewis offered further reassurance: "Clara, if anything happens, you can come to my house and bring your kid."

CLARA: That always happened whenever anything was done

to a couple; the other member of the couple would get a lot of attention: "You're different... you're special," whatever... These men whom I cared about made a real effort to get me to stand with them in their condemnation of Hugh and to see him with their eyes. I betrayed our bond in that time... there was always truth [in the accusations], there were seeds of truth... there was stuff in me that both wanted to hear and also saw some of the things they were saying. And that part of me that was always dependent on Hugh was delighted to get that much attention from these men in the group, just delighted... and support for my teaching and all that came after that time... That was just one of those times that I betrayed Hugh and betrayed the bond we had from all those years together.

The meeting with these men had been carefully planned by Alex, and he had met with them earlier to lay out the strategy they were to use on Clara.

The splitting of couples was one of the most malignant and prominent features of Alex's tyranny, the foundation whereby he established and increased his control over the members of Life Force. The support and reality testing provided a given member by his or her trusted partner was subverted; ties and loyalty that supported his or her sense of self-worth were compromised. The guilt experienced may have provided substance to charges later on that the couple harbored evil forces, accusations hurled at them by Alex, the person orchestrating their mutual betrayal.

This direct attempt to split the Robinsons capitalized on the erosion that had already taken place in their relationship. Ever-increasing demands on their time left almost no opportunity for them to be together. "Circles of silence," the structure of secrecy that Alex established, further weakened their relationship. The executive committee did not share what happened at their meetings with the senior members, those at the next level down. They, in turn, withheld information from those below them, the members, who did not share with the students. Finally, in the year before the graduate school opened, Hugh and the other executive committee members were asked to take a formal vow of secrecy. Hugh was not to confide in Clara, as he had been doing. As he had done with similar matters in the past, Hugh protested, struggled, but then yielded to the pressure. When he was thrown off the executive committee he was not able to share what had happened with his wife, nor did she confide in him about what had been said to her.

A few months went by before Clara also found herself in trouble. She was said to have "bad energy." This time it was Hugh who was asked to cooperate with the group in dealing with her. When he went out of town to teach they persuaded him to leave Clara a note saying that he wouldn't have any contact with her during the ten days that he would be away. Soon after, they put Clara in "quarantine."

Quarantine was a procedure of restricting a member to his or her house or apartment, having contact with no one except Alex or one other executive that Alex might designate. Quarantined members were supposed to reflect upon their "bad energy" or "power trips" or their "elemental" (basic evil) — whatever fault had been detected by Alex. They waited until a phone call came, which might mean being "processed" for hours by Alex or an executive until they saw the error of their ways.

HUGH: I remember waiting fourteen hours for a phone call in panic, and it turned out the Executive Committee had decided not to call me and had gone to bed... and I was sitting there, waiting.

The period of quarantine was one of acute deprivation lasting days or months. To an outsider, there would seem to be no reason for a member to put up with it. To understand, one must recognize that despite the negative aspects of Life Force, there were also times when the members laughed together, when the entire group was close and caring, times when they shared food and felt a love for each other that seemed genuine and precious. In quarantine, all this was withdrawn.

HUGH: People who a day before you had been laughing with,

having fun with, working with, would just turn their eyes away; they wouldn't even make eye contact. If you have the experience of love and then you're cut off from it, there's a tremendous motivation to get back to it, tremendous desire to reconnect with that love... And you'll do anything to get back because it makes you feel good... makes you feel you're a good person.

The effort to split the Robinsons continued. When Clara fell from grace, Hugh was exhorted to stand up to her, to "be a man!" Hugh later recalled a particular moment when Alex said, "Hugh, we want you to own your power."

HUGH: For just a minute I had a perception of Hell... I saw a devil's face... red, everything. It was a perception that the totally opposite thing was happening than what he was saying. I saw that this was Hell... and then it [the perception] went again. I rationalized and said, "He wants me to own my power so I am going to go stand up to Clara." I couldn't. I came back from England — she'd been isolated ten days — she met me at the door... she was in tears. I came and sat with her and we had a good talk... [later] I told Alex and the others that we'd talked and I got lambasted for giving in, for being manipulated by her tears. [They said] that I should have been tough and told her to cut out the bullshit. Well, I didn't.

Following the establishment of the graduate school, Alex had placed more and more stress on "the elemental", which he defined as evil, selfishness, the opposite of spirituality, the anti-Christ. This concept came from the esoteric system the group had studied, but Alex magnified it until protecting the group from evil — from within and without — became the major focus of the group's activities. Members who opposed him were said to be yielding to their selfish side, identifying with it, harming the group and themselves through its influence. Although not directly stated, the implied message was that the only hope to free themselves from their own evil lay in Alex's guidance. As Clara recalled, the message was: If you don't watch out, if you don't look, if you don't see evil, if you don't listen to me, you will be caught in eternal hell.

The ultimate in devaluation was directed against anyone who left the group. They were declared to have completely given in to their elemental, their selfishness, their badness; and whatever had been good in them, their soul itself, was said to have been left behind in the group. Such people were shunned as contaminating forces, they were declared to have turned against their own souls.

CLARA: Once you left, they didn't speak to you again. They passed you on the street without speaking, even though you'd been with them for years... There was a feeling toward the end that you ought to be careful of who you got involved with, because you could lose anyone at any minute. Someone you really loved might just go or... get bad, so don't get too involved. Anyone you saw as good might flip [become bad] any day... your husband, your best friend... that's a strange feeling.

Alex was feared because he could judge someone to be bad and the rest of the group would go along. Dissent was invariably punished.

CLARA: When he would say, "Mary is selfish," we could usually pick out things that would support that. Your seeing would be affected by it: "Oh yeah! I remember when I had lunch with her last week..." And you'd take an incident that in another setting you might not notice, but you could pull them out... particularly if you wanted to get in with him at that moment, you would look for those times. You'd certainly not say, "I haven't seen that; that hasn't been my experience." Boy! If you disagreed with how Alex was seeing it you were in deep trouble. The times I did were invariably used against me, if not at the moment, then later.

Opposition of any kind would call forth processing so that the member could see that he or she had been giving in to their selfish nature. Such experiences could be devastating:

CLARA: I had two experiences of being in a large group where I was on the spot for supposedly not being a good person, with about eighteen people — my "friends" — bringing up information about why I wasn't a good person. I don't think I've ever been through anything so awful in my life, but I bought it... I think that in some funny way those meetings were usually triggered by a time when a person was seeing that something was wrong... being "difficult"... When Alex said, "We're going to have three campuses, continue the Journal of Life Force Psychology and start a training program to compete [with independent Life Force groups in other cities]... ," I said, "How can we possibly do this?" My question was met with stony silence from the whole group. Erica worked with me three or four hours the next day to let me see that that was my elemental that had asked that question — not just my common sense!

Coupled with the emphasis on evil was Alex Monroe's growing interest and belief in past lives, a theory of reincarnation at the group level. Alex told the executive committee that they had all been together in many past lives and he had them play out past-life scenarios. One of the first past lives was called the Persian Past Life. Alex was a priest in ancient Persia; Hugh was a king and there was a church-state conflict. Everyone had a part. Typically, Alex did not need to specify the others' roles. Patricia, another member (whom Hugh had been trying to protect from criticism by the executive committee) became his sister. The priest, Alex, burned Patricia at the stake; thus the group fantasy translated events happening within the group into terms of past lives.

Alex's control over the Life Force members' lives increased further. Each day they were supposed to fill out time sheets detailing every activity conducted throughout the day. Although most hated this, the procedure was rationalized as improving efficiency and it soon became an instrument of control. The sheets were often collected and looked over when a member was thought to be a problem; then there would be a meeting with one or more of the executive committee who would take the errant person to task. Meeting with people outside the group required the permission of the executive committee. Behind them, controlling everything, was Alex.

Supporting Alex's power, keeping the members committed to the organization, no matter how bizarre their lives became, was the shared belief that they were a special group, doing work of great importance to the world.

CLARA: I think in the end, [we believed that] we were the only people doing this... and I remember thinking, "Isn't this strange that [our little group] sitting around could be this special group." I think we had the feeling that Alex was an important articulator of the Christ or the coming of the Christ... I think he believed that more and more himself.

Hugh's behavior continued to be "bad" and he was placed under surveillance. When he went to Baltimore to conduct a workshop, Margaret, one of the executive committee, accompanied and supervised him. Hugh's mother and father lived in Baltimore, but he was not allowed to stay with them. Instead, he checked into a motel. When he did visit his parents, Margaret went with him.

Hugh's brother was involved in the Baltimore Life Force group and a few months after Hugh's visit there trouble developed.

HUGH: Alex used his power to split up the Baltimore group and my brother became the evil one there. Alex got three of the people to put him and a friend out in twenty-four hours... telling them they couldn't come to their office... a kind of strong arm job which was tremendously upsetting to my brother because his friends with whom he had built this thing turned against him. My mother got very upset, understandably, and called up one of her friends [in the Center] who she knew and said, "What is going on there?"

As far as Alex was concerned, this intervention by Hugh's mother made her a source of evil.

HUGH: I went to lunch with Alex and some of the other Executives and he said that evil energy was coming from my mother toward the group so I was going to have to cut off from her. I remember feeling this terror because I had seen this happen in other situations and I said, "Oh, my God, it's coming here." But again,

I was immobilized, filled with fear and self-doubt, afraid to resist. We did a long session that afternoon, I connected with the Christ... Alex used the thing of... Christ says, "You have to leave your father and your mother in order to follow me"... I bought it and although I again had this terribly ambivalent feeling of disorientation and confusion and being in over my head, yet, at the same time being too afraid to disagree and, so, I felt I had to go along with it.

Hugh wrote to his parents expressing anger at them for criticizing the organization, telling them that what happened in Baltimore had nothing to do with his group. His parents wrote back letters of apology which Alex read. Alex was momentarily moved by the letters and admitted that they were very beautiful. A half-hour later, he declared the letters were "too perfect." Hugh was ordered to "cut" from his mother as well as from his brother. This demand was made despite the fact that during that period, Hugh's brother was ill, diagnosed as having cancer. What had been oppressive control by the group and Alex was becoming horrific.

The horror can best be sensed by visualizing the procedure of "cutting," which was practiced more and more in the later phase of the group. Cutting was a process in which members separated themselves from whomever had been declared a source of evil energy — a friend, lover, parent, husband, or wife. They were to visualize cords stretching from their heart to the heart of the other person. Then they were instructed to cut the cords. Sometimes they would go a step further and "burn the image," visualizing the person being consumed by flames. Later, when Clara reflected on all that happened, the cutting she had done was one of the things that was still painful, about which she felt most ashamed.

"I feel I betrayed myself at these times, I let myself do that... on some level it didn't seem right, it felt wrong... We asked about it, 'Why was this necessary?' Alex would say, 'Well, it's not really them that you're burning, it's your projection of them.' I feel sad that I did that... that one feels really hard to live with."

Hugh discontinued all communication with his parents. His

brother became more and more ill, but phone calls from the brother went unanswered. During this time Clara was increasingly critical of Hugh, seeing him as identified with his elemental, accepting Alex's evaluation of him and believing, with the group, that his refusal to speak to his family was correct, although difficult. The rest of the group also supported his action and rewarded him with positive attention.

HUGH: I got a lot of reinforcement from it which reinforced my desire to get back into the group... here were these people approving of me cutting off my parents... But there was a lot of dread and not wanting to go on, [not knowing] how we could get out of this nightmare. But I didn't know how to get out short of leaving and that didn't cross my mind. I guess by that time I knew that if I left I would have lost Clara and David [their son].

Hugh's sister visited him and told him that their brother was worse and that his parents were desperately trying to get through to him, calling the Center repeatedly, but being put off. Hugh called Debbie, one of Alex's inner circle, and told her something must be done. It was agreed that Hugh would phone his brother but that the call would be taped and monitored by Alex and Debbie.

HUGH: Strangely enough, in the middle of all this chaos, my brother and I sort of reached through to this place of connection between the two of us... talking about his dying, how much we loved each other, how we cared... and I have this tape which I listen to every once in a while.

About a week later, Alex worked on Clara to convince her to tell Hugh to leave their house.

CLARA: Alex said Hugh's energy continued to be bad and I, too, felt that Hugh didn't seem good... and then, after a meeting, with about ten other people watching... Alex talked with me to the point of my deciding what was really best for Hugh was for me to ask him to leave the house... I cried and cried... it was very hard.

As soon as Clara agreed to tell Hugh to leave, something happened to her that seemed to validate the decision.

"When I made that choice, I had a lot of energy coming in, I mean literally... not only did everyone in the room say, 'Clara, you're so brave and I really support this and I see how hard it is,' but something happened in my head... I felt sort of strong and full... I saw this happen to Mary... when she chose to leave Bill, to stay in the group and let Bill quit... the same kind of downflow happened... it is like some letting go and you get more energy...

"I interpreted it inwardly, 'Oh, not only do they say it is all right but look what is happening to me!' I saw that again and again... for instance when Margaret announced she was leaving Fred, when Dick announced he was divorcing Connie and was never going to see Connie and his children again — that has got to be one of the worst stories in the whole group... all those times those people looked big and shiny... Margaret when she said, 'I'm not going to be with Fred,' looked as beautiful as I had ever seen her and inside of me I went, 'God, it must be right — look at her!'"

Probably, what Clara and other members in such situations experienced was the effect of a sudden release from the intense conflict that was tearing at them, coupled with a child-like surrender, a letting-go to the protection and power of the parent/family group. Later on, when he or she had finally left Life Force, the reality of what had been done became clear.

Clara experienced this letting-go phenomenon again when, a short time later, she was asked to break off communication with her own mother.

"I know this second hand. They said one night, 'Clara has got to leave her mother' — that came up around the dinner table — so they called me down... They worked on me and worked on me and I just wouldn't budge on it. And Alex said, 'Clara, I think you're asking Hugh to do something you're not willing to do.' That was heavy and I realized that was probably true... and then he had me go up [in imagery]... there was a star we used to see and he said, 'Ask the star what to do.' Then, somehow, the star said something about 'You need to let go of your mother and follow me'... or something like that. What happened was that again I got that really big hit of rightness... I cried and then, 'Oh, that's right, I do need to do that.' I remember at that moment Alex was saying, 'If you do that, He [Christ] can take care of her too, help her more.' And I said, 'Oh, that's right.' At that moment I thought I was loving her and that he [Alex] was, too."

Clara had her phone disconnected and changed her number so that her mother could no longer reach her. Her very perception of her mother was altered.

"When I was out of touch with my mother I would get letters from her. I would read them in the set [context] that she — or part of her — was trying to get me away from this work, trying to get me off my spiritual path. When you read a letter with that in your head it almost feels like there's [negative] energy in the letter. It's amazing because I've also seen those letters later, when it wasn't like that at all."

A week after Hugh made his last phone call to his dying brother, Clara told him to leave the house. He packed his bags and spent the night in a motel.

HUGH: It was the worst night of my life. I felt like I had lost everything. There was no Clara and David, no contact with group members, any family members. My only contact was with Alex and Debbie. I was totally surrounded in darkness. I did come through that night realizing two things: that light was important, spiritual light... and that giving was important.

A few weeks later, Hugh's brother died. His family had been sending telegrams as his condition worsened but Clara, having been told that Hugh did not want to see them, passed them on to the executive committee.

HUGH: By then, they had influenced her very much. I certainly felt betrayed by her, too. So my brother died and I didn't know when... that was one request I made to Alex and Debbie: that I would know the day he died. They wouldn't tell me because they said I was holding on to my brother. I found out that he had died a week or so after when my sister was threatening to come find me. So the Executive Committee had to do something, had to tell me. Otherwise, I don't think they would have.

Hugh continued in quarantine, having contact only with the executive committee. Several months after Clara asked him to leave the house, the group began pressing her to file for a divorce. She resisted, but eventually agreed and wrote to Hugh informing him of her decision. When she told her son David of the plan he became very upset, screamed, pounded on the floor and then ran out of the house. When he finally returned he phoned Alex's children, who were his friends. This created a disturbance in the Monroe household, with the result that Alex's wife Barbara had to be processed.

Alex had no sympathy for David's distress and interpreted his behavior as showing that David was elemental, that he was using his pain at his parents' separation to manipulate people. It was a theory of Alex's that when a child is born the mother sees the evil part of the baby but does not want to recognize it. He said that it was very important that the mother, in this case, Clara, be aware of the evil element in her child and teach him not to act on it. Alex told Clara to go to a special room at the Center where she could scream, pound pillows, and express rage at David, while he [Alex] guided the experience over the telephone. As standard procedure, a team of group members gathered in another location to support the processing by engaging in "subjective work," "cleaning up" Clara from contaminating influences.

CLARA: [They would be saying,] "Well, I see Clara connected with David, so let's cut Clara from David and let's burn David's image. Oh, and Clara is connected with Lewis, too, and Hugh. Let's clean her up (cut her from them).

Throughout the session, Alex kept insisting that Clara see the evil part in David.

CLARA: "I remember saying, "I don't want to see this, I don't want to see this." And Alex saying, tenderly, "Clara, it's all right, it's all right. He's just a boy trying to find his way." And I thought,

"Oh, that's right." And: "You can help him, you can help him with it [the evil part] if you let yourself see it." I believed it for a few days... and Alex would tell me that I really needed to discipline David... there was a lot of stuff about David's evil part... it really pushed me to my limit.

After Hugh received Clara's letter asking for a divorce, he wrote back that he still wanted responsibility for his son, whom he hadn't seen in four months. He gave the letter to the executive committee, who kept it and did not give it to Clara.

CLARA: We came to fear and distrust each other. Hugh was afraid I was this awful way, and I was afraid he was the way Alex was telling me.

HUGH: We were taught to see the other as evil. Everybody began to see everybody else as predominantly this evil part, the part that was selfish and wanted to control people, that was separative, and so forth.

At this stage, to leave the group was a fearsome step because it meant, literally, to be damned.

HUGH: Increasingly, one's spiritual fate became identified with the group. So we all thought our souls were members of this group soul and that if you got taken over by your evil part you would be cut off from your soul. "This is the way to salvation and if you deviate in any way, you're siding with your evil part, you're identifying with it, you're making it bigger." If you thought about leaving the group you had to face the fact that in that system you'd be spiritually damned.

Members came to believe that without the help of Alex Monroe and the Life Force group, a person would have no chance of avoiding "the left-hand path," their evil side would overcome them despite their best intentions.

CLARA: It was never really said, but that was the implication... to leave meant to be eternally lost or caught, trapped in the selfish, comfort-seeking part of you that didn't care about the larger world, about alleviating suffering. We began to talk about it more and more and people who left were seen that way, "Poor Jennie, she just went to her selfishness." When we finally left that was the fear we had to struggle with.

Nevertheless, Clara did manage to leave the group, just three days before she was to start divorce proceedings against Hugh. At the time, she had been in quarantine again.

"First when Hugh was in quarantine I was very much in favor and getting lots of attention... then I lost favor... I began to be seen as bad by Alex and a number of other people. One of them was Mary, a close friend. She turned me in to Alex and that was really the final straw...

"If Mary is going to see me this way, who else is there? I'm not with my husband; I'm out of contact with my parents; I'm making my son bad... and now Mary thinks I'm bad."

One morning Clara was told that the executive committee had some subjective work for her to do. For the first time, Clara refused. She was immediately told to cut from Lewis and Hal (who both had recently left the group) and two or three other members who were thought to be influencing her.

CLARA: I don't know if I even did it but I said that I need to take the day off... So I walked all day long and around where Hugh was living hoping I would run into him. I think that was the day that I began to consider going and to let that thought be a reality. The fact that Lewis and Hal had left already really influenced me. Leaving became an option in that universe, it suddenly became a possibility... something you could do... leaving exists... it was real... and it hadn't been up 'til then.

For Clara, the deciding issue was her son.

"I sometimes thought... [what enabled me to leave] was the mother lion energy in me. It was like... 'My husband, my parents and my friends, but not my baby... you just can't have him. I don't care if you're right about this. I'm not going to let you have him'... And that got me out of there as much as anything did. Alex was capturing every piece of my life, every relationship I had, every piece of my time... Oh, God!... capturing it and taking it into himself. I'm glad I had a child, that was the touchstone, although in the week before I left there was one moment when I considered I would give him up if Alex asked me to... I remember that thought coming into my head, 'Am I really committed here? Would I give up my son if I was asked to?' And I thought maybe I would... other people have given up their children, so it isn't something that might not have happened."

That night she told a representative of the group that she wanted to stay but that she wanted three things: to have dinner with her son each night; to go to bed at midnight and get up at 7:00 instead of 3:00 or 4:00 (members of the group had been averaging from four to six hours of sleep for over a year); and to have some time for herself to swim and garden. She was challenged: "Clara, if you had to let go of those things for the group, would you do it?" Clara replied angrily, "I don't know why I should! I don't know why it has to be that way!" The response was, "Well, you'd better think about it some more."

"That was the night, really. As soon as I hung up the phone I went upstairs and called a close friend who was outside the group. It happened very fast. She was someone who had been in a spiritual group. She had known Alex and something about Life Force, so I knew she'd be someone who would understand the spiritual commitment we had made; I didn't want to talk to someone who would be critical of all that...

"She was wonderful. She didn't just say, 'leave,' or anything. It was like a little crack opened. I said, 'Just talk, just keep talking.' So she said, 'I've made this commitment to my family and I'm committed to our work as a spiritual group, as well.' It was like the sky opened a little bit and I said, 'Just keep saying more things,' and she did. She said things that somehow made me know that I wasn't going to need to give up my spiritual commitment if I left... that there were many ways to free your soul... one could live a family life and that her caring for her children was part of her commitment to God and her commitment to her husband was part of that, too... and I would say, 'I hope I'll be able to help people,' and she said, 'Clara, you already are... you already have helped many people'... things like that... It was very, very important. And I hung up the phone and then I called her back ten minutes later and said, 'Say some more things,' and the crack got a little bigger."

Clara stayed up all night. Over and over, she played a tape of Mother Theresa talking about working with the poor, about kindness and Christ.

"It was sort of lovely to be close to that... to get some perspective. I could feel my response... wanting to heal and wanting to help. She was expressing my resonance with that, particularly the kindness... the kindness was all gone from the group by that time... just the gentle kindness I could feel, that I have and that somehow I had betrayed a lot during that time. So I listened to that tape... and then at one point I realized that the energy that I thought we were working with was in me, and that it would be in me even if I left the group... I really had that experience, it was not just mental but all the way through me. When I realized that, I knew I could leave. I decided that was what I needed to do. I wrote a note: 'I'm leaving the group. It is no longer a place that I want to be. I don't know what my service will be but I know that it needs to involve family and children more than this does.' The next morning I dropped it in Alex's box and then I ran into Hugh almost immediately afterwards."

Leaving was not joyful. Clara had joined Life Force because it made her feel loved and accepted, and it had been a way to help others. At this point she felt worthless, evil, and alone, and she doubted her ability to help anyone.

"For a week I didn't tell anyone that I had left except Hugh. I just sat upstairs in a chair... The first night I kept feeling that there was an enormous cloud of darkness just off my fingertips or on the edge of the room or certainly down in the direction of the Center. I had to keep it out, I had to protect myself from it... I made a circle on the floor of a book of Gandhi and the Mother Theresa tape and I had a picture by Kathe Kollwitz of Mary and Elizabeth embracing... like a protective circle, good friends who had made a spiritual commitment to the world. I wanted them near me. The great fear was that I was bad. The picture of my future was that I would do penance... redeem myself in some way. I volunteered at a nearby hospital on the cancer ward and I worked there three mornings a week for the next few months. I just wanted to give people water and hold their hand... I was still grappling with maybe I was really bad... I wrote and wrote and wrote about it in my journal. I kept wishing someone would tell me that I was good and I also knew that wouldn't do it. Eventually [in meditation] I was saying to something deep in myself, I really do want to help, and I heard a voice say, I know you do. And then it was all right... that was the turning point... then I knew that I was still good, that I was still the person who wanted to love and wanted to make my commitment to love. I didn't really wonder about it after that time. Working it through on my own was real important... something I had to figure out for myself that I don't think anyone else could have told me. I feel proud of that moment... of staying with that."

Clara had hoped that when she left the group, Hugh would also. But he did not, although he knew that as long as he stayed he would not see his child, since contact was not allowed between those in the group and those who had left.

HUGH: For some reason, I'd made a vow to stay a year, no matter what happened. I was going to go on and do great spiritual work.

Hugh was expected to have no contact with Clara, to give her no money, no support, just to wipe the slate clean. He was told that Clara had left the group because she had become identified with her evil part, that all the good qualities she had were left in the group.

HUGH: Luckily we had this wonderful friend... I wasn't about to abandon Clara so I sent money through her. There was contact with this woman friend from both of us. I would go there for dinner and we would talk a little bit about Clara and I would say, "Is Clara angry at me?" And she said, "Oh, Hugh, Clara loves you so much!" She would say the same thing to Clara... So, slowly, over those months there was an indirect healing or reconnection.

After several months Clara sent a letter to Hugh through their mutual friend, secretly, apologizing for what had happened and sharing her distress over the events. Hugh phoned Clara and over the next few weeks they had several clandestine contacts.

HUGH: There was the beginning of trust and love flowing again between us... and Clara asking me some wonderful questions... Not pushing me but saying. What do you see? Is this the kind of group that Christ would be near? Is this really the way people who love each other treat one another?

Hugh also contacted others who had left the group, setting up clandestine meetings at street corners or in cars.

Having gained in confidence from these contacts, Hugh then wrote to the executive committee stating that he needed to make an arrangement to take care of his son, to spend time with him, and that he also needed time for his music. Hugh was immediately put back into quarantine.

HUGH: It was the sixth or seventh time it happened — this was the first time I wasn't paralyzed with fear. I started cataloging my fears... I would sit there in quarantine in my room and write down all the different levels of fear I had. It was fascinating... fear of inadequacy, fear of damnation, fear of becoming just a vegetable. They were still giving me tapes of the meetings and I would listen to the tapes and I'd draw a line down the middle of the page and I'd write down on one side the world view that was being put out in the group that I could buy, and then I would write down on the other side what I could see actually happening... It was fascinating because the things that Alex was describing, what these subjective [evil] entities were supposedly doing "out there" to us were precisely the things that he was doing in relationship to the group, right there. You could hear it on the tapes. I was holding these two world views side by side. That was where I felt the most schizophrenic, the most stressed... I had this image of the back of an envelope with "I quit" on it, and I knew that if I began to crack that I would grab the nearest piece of paper, write "I quit" on it, stick it in Alex's mailbox and run out the door. But I wanted to find out as much as I could about what was going on before I left.

During the last year of Hugh's involvement, the group and Alex Monroe had deteriorated markedly. Paranoia pervaded the members' lives. Fantasies had acquired so much power that even sensate perception changed to accommodate the group's delusional world. Alex's focus on past lives had become more pervasive. His fantasies included a particularly malignant creature who was cruel, cunning, scheming, manipulative, and very smart, very beautiful, and an assortment of other characters, including devils with wings — a complete cosmos.

HUGH: People would begin to see them [the devils], and then call teams to protect them. We had all become very paranoid by then... I would spend hours... fourteen or fifteen hours in a row on the phone, protecting [group members] and fighting some subjective entity who was attacking somebody else. Barbara Monroe was one who seemed to be attacked a lot... she would call and say this particular entity, "Charlie," a big, black devil with wings, was attacking her... we would call in the forces of light and we would do a visualization. To fight the dark force you would bring in an angel of light, an archangel with a sword... light against dark in imagery. Barbara would get better, or she would get over her migraine headache or whatever... Each person had their kind of private devils. It would happen among the Executive Committee and then we'd hear about it and have to clean it up. Each of the Executive Committee had his or her own [devil]. One had a panther-like cat, another this disembodied head and another this dark archangel, and so forth.

Such so-called subjective work had come to occupy more and more of the group's time, particularly as a team of three or four members would be giving support to meetings or processing sessions by conducting a group visualization of their own. Subjective work was extended to cover phone calls, not only within the group, but to people outside the group as well. The members could not go to sleep until protective measures were taken for members of the inner circle and for anyone designated as having trouble.

CLARA: At the end of a day's work, there would be a team that would call you and say, "Before you go to bed tonight, would you 'clean up' Erica? Would you 'clean up' Debbie? 'Clean up' their clothes and shop and stuff?" There would be this protection we would put around the whole group before we could go to sleep and that would take forever... we'd be falling asleep.

HUGH: By the end of my time [in the group] we were doing it [subjective work] almost exclusively, fourteen, fifteen, sixteen hours a day. The Executive Committee was so paranoid and Alex was so paranoid he stayed in his room the whole time and everyone else was in apartments and the Executive Committee couldn't even meet in the same room together for fear that they would do numbers on each other, trips, power trips, seduction trips, so forth... There were always teams "cleaning up" the Executive Committee so the Executive Committee could meet. Alex, also, was having to work with all four of them, there were only four Executives left by then [all women]... the men were gone... Alex and his women were all that was left.

HUGH: I knew I was going to leave... the more I talked to Clara, the clearer that became. I waited ten days and then a phone call came in the afternoon... it was Alex and another Executive, supposedly to talk about my letter. So they started in... I was able to stand up to Alex for about an hour. I told him, "I'm in touch with my soul but I see the group over here in a corner. I'm no longer connected to the group." He was furious... he attacked... I stood up to it for a while and then I just went [under]... as we all did... The best you could do was pretend... just try and bear it and hope it would be over soon.

The processing proceeded — all by telephone. Alex portrayed Clara and Hugh's son, David, as interpenetrated by a devil. It was done through suggestions:

ALEX: Are you thinking of going back to Clara?
HUGH: Well, that would depend but I certainly want to have some contact with her around David.
ALEX: Close your eyes and see Clara.
Alex would then evoke from Hugh's memory all the negative things that Clara had done to him.
ALEX: How do you feel about that, Hugh?
HUGH: I feel angry.

Then Hugh was sent to the special catharsis room at the Center where he ventilated his anger at Clara for two hours.
HUGH: I knew there were two things going on. I was play-acting it to some degree because I knew this was the kind of thing I would go through and on the other hand, it was so powerful, it was real. And it did reinforce once again, the negative image of Clara. It was a kind of shared fantasy of paranoia in which Alex's view of how things were would be infiltrated into the person's head through strong emotional reinforcement because he could get this anger out... That night I got out a lot of rage at Clara which I am sure was connected with the fact that I felt she had betrayed me. Then he would feed the feeling of betrayal and anger with images and slanted questions, "Who do you see behind Clara?" knowing full well and my knowing full well that it was supposed to be one of Alex's imaginary characters. "And what's she doing?" And then, "What do they [Clara and David] want to do to your heart? They don't want to love it do they?" It was that kind of leading question. He'd never say, "They want to eat your heart, Hugh," he'd get you to say it and then he'd reinforce it. "Yes, yes, they want to eat your heart and it's wrong, Hugh; it's a sin. It's wrong to love them." Alex implied that Clara and David just wanted my money and were loving me in order to get my money and not for myself. "They don't

deserve your love. They can't use your love. The people who need your love are the students in the training program." It was that kind of thing.

Alex would give [you] a choice, he would say, "Well, you don't want to live your life that way [selfishly], do you?" And you'd say, "No, no, I know I don't." "Well then..." It was a kind of nod to psychological processing in terms of catharsis, making choices, intention, higher values, but it became increasingly Alex projecting whatever was in his mind into people.

The processing continued for eight hours. Although Hugh tried to fake compliance he was terrified of the strong images that had been summoned. He could not prevent Alex from affecting him.

"I don't understand this, but this happened for other people, too, at the end of these eight hours there was this experience of love for Alex, and his love for me, and a kind of intimacy that was very compelling. I apologized to him for making it hard for him, that he'd had to spend these eight hours with me... and then he wept on the phone and I wept, and he said, 'Oh, that helps so much,' and I said how much I loved him.

"I woke up the next morning and it was like I couldn't find my head. Everything that I had put together had been shattered. I had been really beat up... I had been under severe attack from people who thought they were saving me from the devil. Looking back it feels like a snake whispering in my ears for eight hours. This ear is still slightly deaf... the hearing has never totally come back on this side."

However, Hugh was prepared. He went back to the notes he had taken so carefully and reconstructed what had happened. The battle to leave was a struggle against intense fear.

"The point of highest tension for me was to figure out what reality system did I want to commit to. Alex was saying, 'You need to turn away from your child and Clara and never even think about them anymore. There should be no contact. Nothing. Just turn away.' I was so afraid... fear of damnation is what it finally became and Alex would reinforce it... images of outer darkness, gnashing of teeth, just total and utter damnation... I had to go against that, I had to pit against that the principle that a father does not leave his child. I couldn't believe that God wanted me to leave my child for anything. I said, 'Even if I'm damned forever, even if I'm going to be cast into outer darkness. I'm not going to turn against David.' That saved me, woke me up. I'm so glad. I'm so grateful."

Despite this resolve, there were times during that last week when the pull of Alex and the group would threaten to overwhelm him. At one point Hugh phoned Clara in a panic.

"I could feel a maelstrom, a vortex and I was going to lose my will and be sucked into the center of this thing... I could see in the center... this nice, cozy place, where all your needs were taken care of and it was loving. I remember writing down in big letters, 'I've got to get out of here!'"

In the last few weeks before leaving Life Force, Hugh was helped by talking with another group member, Jerry (although communication between them had been forbidden), about his perceptions of what Alex was doing.

"At last there was contact with someone inside the group who saw things the way I did. There was just an explosion of talk... clandestine... after the work was over we'd call each other up and talk."

Finally, a week after the processing session, Hugh wrote a letter of resignation. The next morning, very early, he placed a copy on each member's doorstep and then left the city.

"The word went out that I was the anti-Christ and that my resignation letter was to be picked up with tongs, put in another envelope, sealed and burned. Everything I'd ever given to anybody — loaned a bed or a book or whatever — were to be destroyed or turned in. The interesting thing was that the people who were there were feeling closer and closer to the Christ while all this was going on."

Hugh stayed in communication with Jerry, helping him to leave also.

Hugh: [Jerry would say] "I'm sitting here and my whole body is shaking and trembling with fear... it's rising off the bed... my heart is shaking... if I bought the system, I would say that you were the devil and you were seducing me away from the group."

And I would say, "O.K., what's true?" I'd just sit there. "What's true?" And then he would gradually [say] "I know that's not true..." We spent a long time on the phone where he would go through the same process that I'd gone through. It was just like a buffer zone of terror around the group that a person had to cross. It was almost necessary to have a person on the outside.

Jerry left the organization soon after. Hugh's leaving set off a chain of resignations; each person who departed helped others to leave. A packet of letters of resignation was circulated among the graduate students, most of whom then left. With so many of the staff gone, the graduate school closed. Shortly thereafter, Alex Monroe and the remaining group members went underground, moving to another city where they were said to be spending their entire time processing each other.

The story of Hugh and Clara Robinson illustrates what can happen when thought and perception come to be controlled by desire and fear. The psychological damage the Robinsons suffered in the cult process was extensive; their sense of self-worth, emotional stability, and relationships with those closest to them were badly battered. Indeed, many months after leaving the group, the Robinsons were still recovering from the trauma of the experience.

Readers may wonder how different Hugh and Clara were from themselves. After all, prior to joining Life Force, Clara had become very anxious; Hugh was discontented, uncomfortable with his life. Yet, to us in the seminar, the Robinsons did not seem very different from most people. After further interviews (which I conducted myself), I found no reason to change that assessment.

Although the world of Life Force may seem alien to most of us, in a number of important ways Hugh and Clara's experience was not qualitatively different from that which occurs in everyday society, although it was more radical, more intense, less subject to moderating influences and, consequently, more pathological.

Analysis of Hugh and Clara's experience and that of others involved with cults reveals four basic behaviors found in extreme form in cults: compliance with the group, dependence on a leader, devaluing the outsider, and avoiding dissent. These behaviors are not distinct and independent but interrelated. In my view, they arise in part from what I refer to as the dependency dream, the regressive wish for security that uses the family as a model, creating an authoritarian leadership structure (the parent) and a close-knit, exclusive group (the children). Since the leader-parent has many of the insecurities of the follower-child, reality must be distorted by both to maintain the child's illusion (or wish) that the parent can always provide protection, that he or she has no weaknesses. Dissent is stifled because it casts doubt on the perfection of the leader and the special status of the group. Group compliance preserves security by supporting the beliefs crucial to the fantasy of superiority, beliefs which also explain the powers and entitlement of the leader and can no more be challenged than he or she. Outsiders, non-believers, are excluded and devalued for they do not believe what the group believes; if the group and leader are superior, the outsider is inferior.

Because group boundaries are more permeable in everyday society, hidden ("normal") cult behavior is not as intense as in overt cults, and the relative importance of one or the other of these interlocking behaviors may vary considerably depending on the social organization being studied.

In the next chapters, I will describe how cult behaviors are manifested in everyday life in our society, using examples from large corporations, religion, psychiatry, the media, and government. I do not mean to imply that other levels of motivation are not active also, but they are conscious. The danger of cult dependency is that because it is usually unconscious, it can powerfully influence us in ways that are not recognized.

We recognize an overt threat from powerful authorities, be it loss of job, injury to self or loved ones, or imprisonment. Likewise, most people are very aware of the lure of money, fame, and power. However, we are not accustomed to recognizing the effect on us of the threats and rewards of childhood's world: the parental frown or the parental smile, the invitation to play or the exclusion from a game, the blissful comfort of being cared for.

The dependency dream acts as an unseen regressive force, shaping our behavior to accomplish the desires of childhood while we are pursuing the goals of adults. It produces unconscious submission to the beliefs and demands of authorities. It leads us to seek reassurance by repeating dogma, to attack outsiders, to ignore and devalue dissenting opinions. Unwillingness to disrupt the fantasy that we have a wise, strong parent in charge leads us to accept the limits of debate established by authorities and the beliefs upon which those authorities depend. Thus, the anxiety evoked by a cult situation is not often recognized for what it is. Even when fear of the leader is conscious, a person is not usually aware that it may be based on the persistence in adulthood of a child's desire and vulnerability, as much as on any realistic need or possibility of reprisal.

Although a deprived or traumatic childhood may result in greater vulnerability to cult manipulation or deceit, the experience of childhood itself renders us susceptible to the blissful promise of a safe, secure way to return home. A continuum of behavior exists, from the People's Temple to Life Force, to rigid religious groups, corporate cultures, professional societies, and ordinary us/them categories.

What I wish to stress is not that every group is a cult, but that cult thinking is the effect of psychological forces endemic to the human mind, and that these forces operate in the everyday life of each of us; they distort perception, bias thinking, and inculcate belief. Our own behavior brings us closer to the experience of Hugh and Clara than we would like to believe.

THREE

Compliance with the Group

H UMAN beings are social beings. Mother, father, siblings, grandparents, and other relatives form our first social group. The family into which we are born has enormous influence upon us, not only because a long and complex learning process takes place before adulthood and self-sufficiency are attained, but also because the family becomes the paradigm for other social groups. In fact, most social groups share characteristics of family groups with members who occupy dominant (parent) and subordinate (child) roles. By considering the characteristics that social groups share with families, we can understand why individuals who are considered independent and adult outside the group may become dependent and childlike within it.

Of course, the family's adults — who transmit social attitudes, fears, and hopes to the child — are themselves subject to the influence of larger social units toward which they may have many of the same dependency feelings that their child has toward them. These overlapping reference groups are composed of friends, colleagues, and/or people of similar religious and political persuasions. Reference groups influence our behavior greatly, although we may not be conscious of how and when this occurs.

Conformity to characteristic views, dress, and conduct differentiate social groupings, marking the most outwardly rebellious as well as the most conventional. An amusing example comes from my own field of psychiatry. Janet Malcolm relates the experience of an analyst of the New York Psychoanalytic Institute who, shortly after he graduated, purchased a black and white herringbone tweed jacket which enormously pleased him. Two years later he met a fellow analyst wearing an almost identical jacket. "My colleague laughed and said, 'But, you know, everyone at the New York Psychoanalytic wears this kind of jacket.' So then I understood why I had felt so great about my jacket. I began to look around the Institute and, sure enough, the jacket was all over the place."

Imitation of our peers is basic to learning and development and the reference group is an important influence throughout life. Social psychologist Albert Bandura and his colleagues were able to cure children of nursery school age of fear of dogs by the simple procedure of having them watch another child playing happily with a dog. Even when films were used instead of actual demonstrations, the procedure worked. Even more striking was the research of psychologist Robert O'Connor on socially withdrawn school children who typically stayed on the fringes of peer group activities. Believing that their behavior predicted a pattern of lifelong isolation and social unease, and trying to change that pattern, O'Connor put together a film composed of eleven different nursery school scenes. Each scene showed a different solitary child observing a social activity and then joining in, to everyone's pleasure. O'Connor tried the film on a group of the most severely withdrawn children from four nursery schools. The results were impressive.

After watching the film, the isolates immediately began to interact with their peers at a level equal to that of the normal children in the schools. Even more astonishing was that O'Connor found when he returned to the schools six weeks later to observe. While the withdrawn children who had not seen O'Connor's film remained as isolated as ever, those who had viewed it were now leading their schools in amount of social activity. It seems that this 23-minute movie, viewed just once, was enough to reverse a potential pattern of lifelong maladaptive behavior.

Yet, as we know, the power of group influence has its negative side and not only in cults. For example, research indicates that the reason a group of bystanders may not come to the aid of a victim is not that they are indifferent, heartless or "numbed by urban living," but because in uncertain situations each person looks to others for cues as to how to interpret and react to what is happening. Each person's passivity reinforces that of others. In contrast, when researchers enacted an "emergency" in the presence of a single by-stander, that person invariably responded helpfully, whether in a city or not. Clearly, reliance on social cues, not empathy, is the issue.

Robert Cialdini, an experimental social psychologist, explains the group's influence on our behavior as being utilitarian.

"The tendency to see an action as more appropriate when others are doing it works quite well normally. As a rule, we will make fewer mistakes by acting in accord with social evidence than contrary to it. Usually, when a lot of people are doing something, it is the right thing to do."

But every society provides numerous examples of group influence which turned out to be injurious to the group itself, as well as unfair and harmful to others. How and why do groups affect their members so strongly?

THE remarkable influence of groups upon their members has been of interest to psychologists and psychiatrists for a long time. Gustave Le Bon was one of the first to study the behavior of people in crowds and mobs. Writing in 1895 about such situations, he described "the disappearance of the conscious personality, the pre-dominance of the unconscious personality, the turning by means of suggestion and contagion of feelings and ideas in an identical direction, the tendency to immediately transform the suggested ideas into acts."

Freud believed that these characteristics could be explained as a regression to a primitive mental activity, that of the primal horde. "The primitive form of human society was that of a horde ruled over despotically by a powerful male... Just as primitive man survives potentially in every individual, so the primal horde may arise once more out of any random collection."

Freud went on to emphasize "the contrivance by means of which an artificial group is held together and the constitution of the primal horde. We have seen that with an army and a Church this contrivance is the illusion that the leader loves all of the individuals equally and justly. But this is simply an idealistic remodeling of the state of affairs in the primal horde, where all of the sons knew that they were equally persecuted by the primal father, and feared him equally."

Freud's analysis — its exclusively male focus aside — would seem to have applicability in the case of the Life Force group, where the initial feeling of the members of being loved by Alex gave way to fear of him.

Since Freud, the theory of group psychology has been expanded. British psychoanalyst Wilfred Bion, drawing on Melanie Klein's ideas about primitive psychological defenses in the infant and young child, studied small-group phenomena and concluded that groups tend to adopt, unconsciously, one of three primitive emotional states — dependency, pairing, or fight-flight. Bion called these states basic assumptions, and thought of them as expressive of disowned impulses. Fie saw any group as likely to exhibit irrational behavior, indicating that one of the three assumptions is operating. What Bion designates as the dependency-assumption group is a very good description of the state of mind prevailing in cults.

"The essential aim [of the dependency-assumption group]... is to attain security through and have its members protected by one individual. It assumes that this is why the group has met. The members act as if they know nothing, as if they are inadequate and immature creatures. Their behavior implies that the leader, by contrast, is omnipotent and omniscient."

Object relations theorist D. W. Winnicott has suggested that the group may represent a transitional object for its members, who express regressive themes appropriate to that stage of development. Going further, Jungian analyst Arthur Colman, drawing on the work of Margaret Mahler, has proposed that group consciousness is a developmental phase prior to full individuation.

All these theorists endeavor to explain the powerful effect of groups from the point of view of the psychology of the individuals that compose them. However, from a sociobiological point of view, there is another basis for understanding why the group should be so influential: human survival has been enhanced by the tendency for families to combine in bands or tribes for mutual protection and support. As banishment from the larger group could endanger an individual's survival, an acute sensitivity to the group's wishes and requirements probably carried an evolutionary advantage. Socially aware, adept individuals would eventually dominate the genetic pool through the process of natural selection. Perhaps in this way the human race has developed a high awareness of the wishes, fears, and requirements of the groups on which each person depends. Such an evolutionary process may explain why certain basic group reactions and fantasies (such as those described by Bion) seem to take place regardless of the member's actual family experience.

Certainly, whatever theoretical model or models one might prefer, the desire for group approval and the fear of disapproval remain with us as very powerful controlling forces. In the Robinsons' case, Hugh's testimony makes clear how much his need for the group's approval influenced him, especially when he was in quarantine, and Clara recalled how seductive it was for the group to praise her while criticizing Hugh. Furthermore, numerous experiments show how a group can change the perceptions of its members, can even foster and maintain a bizarre, paranoid world view such as that which developed within the Life Force executive group.

We can feel secure in the protection provided by a group but that protection has its price. Compliance with the group often extends further than acceptance of the group's views to include participation in the attack on deviants by subtle (or not so subtle) disapproval, punishment, or rejection of any member who voices criticism of the consensus or disagrees with the leader. Dissident is criticized as disloyal, lacking commitment, interfering with the important work of the group.

As a psychotherapist, I frequently work with people oppressed by a punitive, controlling internal figure who lashes them with guilt and mocks with disapproval. Exploring the reason for this oppression, we often find that its purpose is to insure conformity to the group upon whose approval they depend and whose rejection they fear.

Although most social groups encourage dependency and compliance in civilized ways, the basic pattern can usually be discerned.

PRESSURES encouraging dependency, present in most groups, are intensified in a cult. As we saw in the case of Hugh and Clara, extreme dependence on the cult is fostered by isolating the member from other sources of self-esteem, financial support, and emotional closeness. Consequently, the cult's ability to reward or punish is markedly enhanced. With this in mind it is not surprising that a particularly pernicious feature of cults — and often an index of their power over their members — is the attack on couples and families. In the case of Life Force, not a single couple who began with the group survived intact, even the marriage of Alex and Barbara Monroe failed. This destructive effect is characteristic of the stronger cults; the power of the leader and the sense of security of the group are diminished by any strong social bonds which set up conflicting loyalties. (Hugh and Clara's enduring bonds to their child and to each other eventually provided the motivation to break from the group.) Thus, powerful cult groups often attack the couple through arranged marriages, the breaking of love relationships by order of the leader or the group, pressure toward group marriage or chastity, sexual relationships with the leader, and/or interfere with the bonds between parents and children.

In her study of communes and utopian communities, sociologist Rosabeth Kanter described how 19th century groups coped with the threat to cohesiveness posed by two-person intimacy.

"Successful 19th century groups often discouraged couples in one of two extreme and experientially opposite ways — either through free love, including group marriage, in which every member was expected to have intimate sexual relations with all others, or through celibacy, in which no member could have sexual relations with any other."

She cites the Oneida community, which had been notorious for its practice of free love.

"Every member had sexual access to every other with his or her consent, while fidelity was negatively sanctioned; preference of one member for another was quickly discouraged. When two members of the community showed a marked preference of one member for one another, they were asked to mate with two others."

In such communities, ties between parents and children were minimized by varying degrees of communal childcare and by restricted contact between mother and child. In the Life Force group this was accomplished by making inordinate demands on Clara's time and devaluing her contribution as a mother, even labelling it selfish.

The weakening of family structures is not only an issue of loyalty. The role of parent and the roles of husband and wife are adult roles, whereas in a cult the leader and the group together constitute a parent-child structure in which adult autonomy has no place. For this reason it is in the cult's interest to foster the regression of its members to a pre-adult phase of psychosexual development, and such a regression is usually easy to observe. A family unit resists this push.

The attack on couples and families is usually restricted to tightly controlled groups that set themselves off from the surrounding society. Seldom is it a significant factor in ordinary society. However, the weakening of ties to others so as to strengthen dependency on the group and leader can be observed in strongly authoritarian political systems such as that which prevailed in Germany's Third Reich. The Hitler Youth were encouraged to regard parents as potential enemies of the glorious new Germany, to inform on them and to turn them in to the Gestapo for comments critical of the Nazi regime. Many did so. Parents came to fear and distrust their children, while the children scorned their parents as being weak, obstructionist or traitors. Mao Tse-tung encouraged a similar split between the generations of China.

COMPLIANCE and dependency can be strongly enhanced by the group's eliciting a powerful emotional experience. Lowell Streiker, a researcher who interviewed converts to revivalism, gives a composite description of a conversion experience as it typically occurs in a small revivalist group or church.

"The prospect is directly confronted with his sins. His physical and psychic space are invaded by these self-confident strangers. He is discomforted and thrown off balance. He becomes anxious. The group tells him that his feelings are caused by his sinfulness. He is overcome with guilt and sadness. He realizes that his life is not working. Eagerly he confesses his shortcomings — sexual lapses, lies, petty thievery, drug abuse, and so forth. Guided by the group, he prays that God will forgive him and receive him as His child. He is urged, 'Ask Jesus to come into your heart.' He does, and the inner turmoil subsides. The recruit senses an inner release and relief. The hugs and congratulations of the group tell him that he belongs, that he has identity, that he is accepted. Many ecstatic converts report, 'It was as though a great weight had been lifted from my shoulders.'"

Streiker suggests that such groups create an unbearable tension in the person on whom they are focusing, and that sudden release from that tension — "accepting the Lord into your heart" or "surrender to Jesus" — is interpreted as a spiritual experience, being "born again." He comments, "When Jesus told Nicodemus of the need to be 'born again' he did not badger his hearer until he underwent a group-coerced, programmed, stereotyped purgation."

To be born again doesn't require a Christian context. Listen again to Clara Robinson:

"So I went up towards the sun and there was this wise man and he said to me, 'My child,' and I climbed in his lap, like a child — he was very much like a father — as I retell it I realize that... I just felt like I was home... I felt a downflow of love and affection that I have never felt before or since.... It was that experience that made me feel that I needed to do more of whatever this system was."

Groups may enhance compliance and dependency by producing a variety of altered states of consciousness that are easily misinterpreted to conform with the beliefs and interests of the group. Hugh and Clara Robinson always had an intuitive sense of a larger reality that was very important to them. That perception was confused with unresolved dependency longings, leading them to interpret the initial guided daydream as being spiritual and to accept the Monroes as guides or agents in that domain. A variety of techniques — chanting, singing, dancing, sleep deprivation, meditation — can produce a state of consciousness quite impressive to the participant. The event may then be offered as proof of the group's value or the leader's spiritual power — the convert's wish to believe does the rest.

Demonstrations of psychic ability are especially potent in this respect, and Yogic disciplines, in particular, seem to have a technology for producing phenomena unexplainable by current scientific knowledge. Some years ago, while investigating a popular Eastern cult, I underwent an initiation in which a Yogi placed his hand on my head and I then experienced a spot of intense white light blazing briefly in the center of my mind — or so it seemed. This was interpreted (by the cult) as contact with the divine and proof that the guru was a new messiah. I still don't understand how the man did it, but the spot of light was just that — a spot of light — and no more a demonstration of the divine than turning on the faucet would be to someone who knows nothing about plumbing. Indeed, the mystical literature warns repeatedly that such experiences are distractions and should be ignored.(Nevertheless, this particular group's converts eagerly practiced the prescribed meditations hoping to repeat the experience and rushed to take part in any further initiations that were made available to them.)

Unfortunately, legitimate but subtle intimations of the spiritual that may have led a convert to search for a group and teacher may be displaced by such dramatic alterations of consciousness, which can then become a further basis for control. Just as the group's emotional support and validation can be provided or withdrawn, so can the dramatic pseudo-spiritual experiences. Before long, the positive force of idealism and service that may have been foremost in a convert's mind when joining a cult becomes corrupted by fear of deprivation and abandonment. As we saw in Life Force, idealistic concepts are then subverted when they are used to rationalize behavior a convert would have condemned before joining the group.

A MAJOR way a group exerts power is through threat of censure and expulsion, classifying the deviant as bad. I had occasion to learn about this firsthand a few years ago when I became involved in the anti-nuclear movement. (At that time I would not have believed that liberals such as myself could behave like cult members, although I was certain that right-wingers did.) The story is worth telling because it may connect with the reader's own prejudices and provide an experience of the very dynamic I am discussing.

In 1980 I attended a weekend conference given by Physicians for Social Responsibility, entitled "The Medical Consequences of Nuclear Weapons and Nuclear War." The presentations were intended to impress the audience with the ghastly consequences of nuclear war. That goal was certainly achieved; we were left in a state of great alarm and dread. I responded by becoming active in spreading the word about the enormous danger and the immediate steps that should be taken. (This was not a new role for me; I had been active in the 1960s in the effort to stop the atmospheric testing of nuclear weapons. Now the menace was worse and the catastrophic aspects more overwhelming.) I raised questions with other PSR members about what action people might take to increase their chances of survival if a nuclear war did occur. I was told that there was nothing that could be done; shelters were described as useless and prevention of nuclear war as the only answer. Some speakers declared that anyone who undertook civil defense planning was immoral, engaged in "a highly unethical act."

These summary judgments were not convincing to me, and I began reading outside the peace movement literature, encountering other points of view and other facts. Eventually, I came to the judgment that regional food stockpiles would save millions of lives if a war did occur and that establishing such stockpiles would not accelerate the arms race or give people a false sense of security, but would be a logical and appropriate response to a very real danger. Furthermore, I believed that people should be told the less alarming facts about radiation danger and about what protection a shelter could and could not offer.

When I mentioned these ideas to my friends in the peace movement, they would draw back slightly, their eyes would narrow, and I could see them mentally remove my name from the file of "good guys" and transfer it to the one marked "bad guys." (Perhaps you, the reader, have been having a similar reaction.)

I promoted a lecture about protection against a variety of radiation hazards including nuclear explosions. Almost no one came, except some protesters from the peace movement. With the radiologist who gave the lecture, I later appeared on a radio talk show. It was clear the host found it hard to grasp that although I was in favor of stockpiling food, a civil defense measure, I was opposed to the MX missiles and favored a nuclear freeze. He had assumed, as did others, that I must be a hawk. A cult-like propensity for a black-and-white division of the world was all too obvious.

This publicity, along with an interview published in a local newspaper, generated a response whose character and vehemence caught me by surprise. I was roundly attacked. No one from the peace movement asked me why I thought what I did. They weren't curious at all; they had simply decided I had become a hardliner, an immoral survivalist. The arguments advanced against my views seemed simplistic and illogical, much like the recitations of dogma I was familiar with from my study of religious cults.

In addition to seeing cult processes at work in others, I became aware that I was influenced by them. I began to avoid mentioning my views to acquaintances and even some friends, for fear of being cast out. Educational as the experience proved, being regarded as a bad guy within my own group was quite unpleasant. At one public hearing where I testified, I was attacked by a peace movement contingent who used the same rhetoric that I had used in the past as part of that same group. It was startling to be on the receiving end, to be the object of the glaring hostile eyes and the impassioned appeals to humanity. Ruefully, I realized that in the past I had been similarly self-indulgent in obtaining the emotional satisfaction that springs from being righteous in a good cause. I would not have known that I was to some degree a member of a cult had I not challenged my group's dogma.

COMPLIANCE with a group increases with one's psychological and economic dependence on it. This can be seen in many social institutions, including the corporations that dominate modern economic life.

Sociologist Diane Margolis studied the managers at a large corporation and found that the one effect of frequent transfers was to decrease a husband and wife's involvement in local politics and community life and to increase their dependence on the friends and activities of their particular corporate world. Moreover, they learned to buy their homes with a view to resale and this tended to place them in housing areas occupied by other corporation managers. Economic and social segregation played an important role in the corporation's becoming, for many managers, the chief source of self-esteem, companionship, and personal expression. For the managers of many corporations, "needs usually fulfilled by human relationships become increasingly difficult to satisfy because almost all relationships outside their nuclear families are distant and fleeting. So like half-starved people who in the absence of proteins will fatten but not nourish themselves on starches, managers and their families hunger for goods money cannot buy, but reach for those it can. Each year salary increases put these within easier reach, and the manager's family finds that every purchase just whets the appetite for the next.... He knew he was in a game he could never win, but he played on. For him it was the only game in town."

To leave the company would mean all that sacrifice has been in vain; security must be given up. Wishful thinking tends to replace critical assessment just as it did with the Robinsons who also had to face giving up a "warm cocoon." With few connections to the outside world that world can easily appear less desirable — and the corporation more valuable — than it is.

ALTHOUGH corporations do not attack the family directly in the manner of cults such as Life Force, most of them do require the subordination of the manager's family's needs to those of the corporation. This sacrifice is demanded as the price of career advancement.

A common practice is to promote managers by transferring them every year or two to positions in other parts of the country. Then their positions are filled by others who are moved in; a game of musical chairs takes place.

Certainly, it is in the corporation's interest to give managers wide experience and also to test their commitment to the company; however, the interests of the manager's children are served poorly. (Although corporations have begun paying more attention to this problem, the transfer is still a standard feature of corporate life.) Indeed, in my psychotherapy practice I often encounter people who have been socially impaired by frequent family moves that made them perpetually new kids on the block; just when friendships were established, their families would move again. Such children learn to limit their friendships to avoid the pain of loss and tend to interpret other children's reserve toward them when they arrive in a new town as indicating that they are not likable. For many wives the process is almost as painful.

Frequent transfers are also ruinous to a spouse's career ambitions. The wife of a Schlumberger manager in Cairo summed it up:

"Sometimes you really feel lost... The man has a job to do. You have nothing to do. So you have babies to keep you busy. Or you join a club. If you say, "I want to have a career of my own," and say you don't want to go where your husband goes, then you're headed for the divorce courts."

Commitment to the corporation is also measured by a manager's willingness to take work home at night and on weekends and to be absent from his family on frequent business trips. In the competition for a manager's time, energy, and attention the corporation is out to win. Conflicts that arise between family needs and corporate needs — which may have the look of accidental occurrences — are sometimes deliberate tests of the person's commitment, the outcomes of which are carefully noted. The manager who chooses family over the corporation fails the test, as does the family.

Furthermore, wives may become unpaid company employees as they fall in line to support the careers of their husbands.

Within the corporate culture of many companies, it is assumed that the corporate goals and the husband's career should have first priority in much the same way that Life Force and other cults regard their own activities as primary and the competing demands of marriage and family as distinctly secondary. As Harold Geneen, former chief executive officer of ITT put it: "The first requirement of a senior executive is instant availability. He must put his firm above his family; he must be prepared to go anywhere at any time, or simply to wait around in case he is needed."

Just as the commitment and spiritual worth of the Robinsons were judged by the extent to which they sacrificed their marriage relationship and their child's needs to the purposes of their group, the loyalty of the corporate manager is usually measured by the acceptance of corporation priorities over anything else in life.

Of course, corporations vary in their demands, and some managers sacrifice their family's interests over and above what the corporation requires. Personal ambition can take a toll without any pressure at all from corporate authority.

STUDIES of corporations generally recognized as continuously innovative, with long-term records of growth and profitability, indicate that a strong corporate culture is a key ingredient in their success. By corporate culture we mean a set of values or principles that permeate a company and form the guidelines for decision making at all levels. The inculcation of those values constitutes a process of corporate socialization that seems to be responsible for the survival from generation to generation of many large business organizations, providing stability and dependable responses.

For example, IBM teaches all employees three "Basic Beliefs": 1) respect for the individual, 2) best possible service to our customers, 3) every task performed in a superior manner. Delta Airlines "Family Feeling" and AT&T's "Universal Service" are other examples of core values taught to all employees and taken seriously. Although the phrases sound like platitudes, within the corporation they are very meaningful.

These "significant meanings," "shared values," or "spiritual fabric" have been described as superordinate goals guiding the entire organization. They play a very practical role because employees must often make decisions on their own; as long as they are guided by the corporate shared values, decisions are likely to fit in with company policy.

Achieving a strong corporate culture requires a process of indoctrination to convert a recruit to the corporation's point of view. Richard Pascale lists a number of steps in the process of "socialization," including "humility-inducing experiences."

"Humility inducing experiences in the first months on the job precipitate self-questioning of prior behavior, beliefs and values. A lowering of individual self-comfort and self-complacency promotes openness toward accepting the organization's norms and values.

"Most strong culture companies get the new hire's attention by pouring on more work than can possibly get done. IBM and Morgan Guaranty socialize extensively through training where "you work every night until 2:00 a.m. on your own material and then help others."

The use of overwork is also a feature of extreme cults, as in the case of Life Force. An ex-convert from the Unification Church described what it was like there:

"Sleep especially was viewed as an indulgence since God never slept in His efforts to save mankind. Sleep, more than food, thus came to represent the most sought-after 'privilege' of a future life in the Kingdom of Heaven. The staff averaged three hours a night; newer Family would average six. Recognized but unspoken was a state of constant exhaustion in all righteous children of God."

Overwork is part of many initiations. Army recruits rise early and are put through long forced marches. Doctors during internship may get only one night's sleep every two days. Overwork facilitates submission through a kind of anesthesia produced by exhaustion; rebellion takes energy. Immersion in the newly joined world to the exclusion of other influences is also important in initiations. Consider this description of how Schlumberger, until recently one of the most successful corporations of our time, initiates its engineers:

"Like military recruits who go through basic training together, they became a clan. They worked sometimes seven days a week for two straight months. They lived, ate, drank, showered, watched video cassettes, and vacationed together. They swapped stories about their work. For months at a time, the only people they had contact with worked for Schlumberger or for an oil company."

The resemblance of such initiations to the procedures of religious cults is striking. That the resulting corporate attitude evokes from observers the phrase "religious fervor" is not surprising. Indeed, some executives are quite explicit about the parallel with religion:

"People need to believe in something larger than themselves. To be successful... a corporation must learn from the Japanese that 'we have the responsibility that religion used to have.' A good company must not be just a slave to profits; it must strive to perform a service and to beat its competitors. But more... it must measure itself against a higher standard, seeking perfection."

Terrance Deal and Allen Kennedy, who studied the cultures of eighty corporations, also spoke of the corporate religion they had observed. "The Catholic church has something in common with IBM, Mary Kay, McDonald's, the Polaris project, the U.S. Forest Service, and countless numbers of other successful organizations — all of them capture some of the same religious tone."

At the same time, as in the case of Life Force, high purposes may be subverted, with destructive results. Thomas Peters and Robert Waterman, authors of *In Search of Excellence*, warn that the more worrisome part of a strong culture is the ever present possibility of abuse. One of the needs filled by the strong excellent company cultures is the need most of us have for security. We will surrender a great deal to institutions that give us a sense of meaning and, through it, a sense of security.

Richard Pascale and Anthony Athos, who wrote *The Art of Japanese Management*, sound an even stronger cautionary note.

"Having made the case for the importance of superordinate goals in motivating employees and sustaining an organization over time, we must note that a skillful grasp of the use of all of our seven variables can be directed toward truly tragic outcomes. The staggering horror of the Third Reich and the mass suicides in Guyana come to mind. It is not hard to imagine an indoctrination of people into some kind of corporate Hitler Youth Corps."

In the case of cults, moral principles are often violated to further the cult's success. The leader and the members justify immoral actions as being necessary for the greater good that the cult will achieve: To make an omelet one must break eggs. Implied in this attitude is an assumption that the leader's aims are sublimely important, as is the welfare of the special group instrumental in accomplishing these great goals. Also implied is a lowering of the importance of any individual's welfare and a lowering still further of the worth of the outsider. Part of the attraction of believing the leader's views and actions to be of paramount importance is that the follower's own sense of importance is heightened. One might sense such a dynamic behind the arrogance and self-righteousness displayed by Oliver North at the Iran-Contra hearings in 1987. (In 1989, with Reagan out of office, North took a different role, that of victim and scapegoat.)

Making the welfare of the corporation more important than anything else is the qualitative equivalent to a cult's belief in its divine mission. Charles Wilson, former CEO of General Motors, put it succinctly in his famous assertion, "What's good for General Motors is good for the United States."

An appreciation of the power of cult dynamics may help us understand immoral corporate actions by people who outside the corporation conduct themselves differently. For example, according to Paul Brodeur (a New Yorker writer), the board of directors of the Johns Mansville company deliberately withheld from their workers evidence that asbestos was dangerous to their health, asserting that there was no threat when they knew there was a very serious problem. Another writer, Morton Mintz, has described the actions of the A. H. Robbins Company in not withdrawing the Daikon shield (a birth control device) from the marketplace after they had evidence of its serious side effects. One reads of the failure of numerous nuclear power plants to correct safety problems. The list is long. I suggest that "the Corporation" evokes a fantasy of "the Big Parent" in the minds of the board of directors as well as in middle management. They identify with it and are reassured by it; the corporation is the protector and must be protected. Just as saving the world was used as a justification for the Life Force group's cruelty to its members or saving souls is used to justify unethical and illegal actions by religious zealots, so the economic well-being of the corporation may come to be considered important enough to justify actions that would otherwise be abhorred.

PSYCHOLOGIST Margaret Rioch has led many group meetings based on the Tavistock Group Relations Conference in which participants experience at first hand the power of authority-dependency relationships. She describes the participants' uncanny feeling as they realize how many of their own actions have been performed at the behest of the group's unconscious intentions:

"The sense of having a will of one's own, of being free to make one's own choice, disappears, and the individual experiences himself as a marionette pulled by the strings of the group or as being a channel through which the group pours its energy and expresses itself... The converse of the marionette phenomenon also occurs, especially in large groups, when an individual experiences himself as able to do anything with the group that he likes, sometimes so much so that he believes he is the group. This is often accompanied by a pseudo-religious fervor which carries the individual away into a grandiose sense of power. And this, too, is uncanny... These two experiences, the sense of being all-powerful and the feeling of being a marionette, although they appear to be opposite, are essentially two sides of the same coin."

Anyone who observes their own behavior will find many instances of compliance with one group or another. Furthermore, compliance becomes easier when we associate only with those who share our point of view. Then, hardly noticed, our window on reality may become so narrow that we cannot see the world, though we think we do.

FOUR

Dependence on a Leader

IT IS customary to think of cult leaders as powerful personalities who inspire, even hypnotize their audiences. Charismatic leaders from Mahatma Gandhi to Adolf Hitler have been described this way. But a cult leader need not be that impressive. Alex Monroe was cerebral, his discourses boring; he was intelligent but not inspiring. He developed power by distorting his followers' idealism, dividing their loyalties, using flattery, threats, and spurious logic to defeat objections and rationalize his demands. However, one particular characteristic links Alex with other cult leaders of greater charisma — he was authoritarian.

Authoritarians emphasize obedience, loyalty and the suppression of criticism. In the groups they lead, hierarchies of rank are emphasized and autonomy discouraged. (Sometimes such a leader takes a benign, "loving", tolerant position, but allows his or her lieutenants to enforce an authoritarian regime.)

Authoritarian leaders, especially, draw power from the dependency fantasy, from the individual's wish for an idealized parent. If we are sophisticated, we may reject, criticize, or look down on any public leader, but the wish remains, engendering seldom-noticed fantasies of someone (or something) who observes our behavior and rewards or punishes. It is not surprising that under certain conditions skepticism may be overthrown and conversion occur — as in the case of a prominent 60's radical who one day called a meeting and dismayed his admirers by announcing that he had become a follower of an Indian guru.

IN OUR society, the tendency to look up to others while feeling small oneself is expressed in the enormous number of celebrities that clutter our minds. Statesmen, movie stars, sports figures, socialites, and the super-rich are given larger-than-life status by television and movies, by newspapers and magazines, all of which cater to this fantasy. (Sports are instructive to me, personally, in demonstrating how much I have embraced those images. Having watched football mainly on television, I have been shocked to go to a stadium and see how small the actual football field is and how mundane, ordinary and un-godlike the players are when not projected on a TV screen.)

Our predilection for inequality has even more prosaic expressions. Friends and patients alike remark that they do not feel now as they imagined their parents felt and as they still imagine "adults" feel. This misperception tends to isolate the aged. One evening, waiting for a table at a restaurant, I sat in the anteroom surrounded by grey-haired men and women, also waiting. I was struck by a sudden realization that these "oldsters" looked out at the world with the same youthful consciousness that I had. With that perception, the sense of separation from them that I had been feeling disappeared. I believe that "ageism" is not just fear of growing old, but also reveals the hidden wish to maintain a child's parental world.

WE CAN trace our susceptibility to authoritarian leaders to the family structure, but in doing so we should not forget that the authoritarian character of the family is both functional and appropriate. Within the family parents and other elders are in fact superior in knowledge, experience, and strength to the children who depend on them for protection and satisfaction of needs. That parents command and children obey is realistic because of the large discrepancy in their respective capacities.

In a healthy family, as children mature and become more responsible and capable, the hierarchical, authoritarian structure becomes more democratic. Children are delegated appropriate responsibility and choice, which acts to reward competence and stimulate further growth. Eventually, the child's relationship to the parent reaches eye level psychologically as well as physically. This eye-level perspective is the hallmark of the mature adult. Such a perspective does not imply a denial of another's superior ability and knowledge; rather, feelings of appreciation and respect replace fear, awe, and dependency.

Just as the mature parent welcomes the child's ascent to equality and supports his or her maturation, the mature leader can and should exercise a similar function, according subordinates increasing responsibility, choice, and authority as they become capable. If this does not take place, subordinates remain in the position of children while the leader plays out the role of omnipotent parent. Thus, the key issue is not the strength of the leader, but the development or suppression of autonomy.

From this point of view, a hierarchical structure is not inherently bad; it can contribute to learning and is necessary when real differences in capacity exist. Furthermore, groups usually require a hierarchy for efficient performance of tasks. But a truly authoritarian leader is repressive and regressive.

The structure of cults is basically authoritarian; obedience and hierarchical power tend to take precedence over truth and conscience when they conflict, which they often do. Unfortunately, certain psychological benefits can make authoritarian groups very attractive — they provide the opportunity to feel protected and cared for. As noted earlier, the wish for parents does not disappear, but just goes underground when we become adults.

Mainstream politics provides many examples. Often, the key to a politician's popularity is the capacity to present the image of a strong, good parent, to convey an optimistic, sincere self-confidence, to communicate belief in a golden future. Apparent self-confidence and freedom from doubt are characteristics of all successful cult leaders because these postures resonate so strongly with the universal fantasy of a powerful, benign father or mother who will remove all difficulties and reassure the frightened child. As was widely remarked during Ronald Reagan's presidency, the capacity to evoke this image provides a leader with a "Teflon coating"; unpleasant, discordant facts about the leader's actions do not stick, are not held against him or her, but are pushed aside to preserve the good feelings he or she can arouse.

As adults most of us leave the conduct of public affairs to others whom we prefer to believe are superior in some way because to do so is less anxiety-producing. The reality may be quite different.

A poignant comment on this situation comes from an enterprising journalist, Craig Karpel, who gained access to the 1980 Bilderberg Meeting, held at Aachen, Germany. This exclusive, little-publicized summit conference of the West's power elite gathers every year to deal with whatever urgent problems face the United States and Western Europe. As Karpel points out, if the world were secretly run by someone or something, it would be the Bilderberg group. This particular meeting included David Rockefeller, Henry Kissinger, McGeorge Bundy, Helmut Kohl, Helmut Schmidt, Lord Home and a host of others comprising one hundred influential leaders in the fields of government, banking, publications, and industry from the various countries of the Western Alliance. The 1980 meeting took place at the beginning of a deep rift in European-American relations occasioned by Jimmy Carter's requests for sanctions against Iran and retaliation against the Soviet Union for the invasion of Afghanistan. There was also the matter of 16,000 Warsaw Pact tanks poised at the border of West Germany. The agenda for the meeting was entitled "America and Europe — Past, Present, and Future." Expecting that the men who ran things would plan a stealthy strategy of manipulation and control, dictating the future, Karpel was disappointed:

"One might imagine that the goal of Bilderberg must secretly be to attempt to shape future events and seek to profit from them. But in practice the purpose of the meetings is to assess what has already happened and to figure out how best to respond to it, with a view to hanging on to past gains."

Karpel concluded that the participants were not leaders, but managers devoted to stability and self-preservation. He concluded:

"It is not inherently sinister to convene an assembly of wise men, led by those whom the wise believe to be the wisest. But one feels a certain queasiness when, like Dorothy's little dog, Toto, one pulls aside the curtain and discovers that wizards haven't the slightest idea what to do. To insinuate oneself into such company, and to return then to the realm of roller disco and headphone radios, is like slipping up the spiral stairway of a transoceanic 747 and into the cockpit only to discover that there is no one there. The night is dark. A howling storm lies ahead. You descend to the main cabin. The dinner service has been concluded. A number of passengers are noisily airing petty complaints. The lights dim. The movie is about to begin…

"And so the secret, the hideous grisly secret of Bilderberg is revealed. There's nobody at the controls, folks. We're flying blind. Let's hope there's foam on the runway, friends and neighbors, 'cause we're coming in on a wing and a prayer. The driver's seat is empty, the parents have gone. But who wants to know?"

LOOKING up to a leader may be the result of a need to maintain a fantasy of the leader's superiority. Ronald Reagan was particularly attuned to fantasy's attractiveness to the public. James Barber, professor of political science at Duke University, commented in the *New York Times*:

"President Reagan's indifference to reality is hardly news. His criterion of validity is drama, not empiricism. As David Stockman, Director of the Office of Management and Budget, once summed up the White House system: 'Every time one fantasy doesn't work they try another one.' Mr. Reagan, told by a reporter that one of his favorite, endlessly repeated anecdotes — how a black hero at Pearl Harbor ended segregation in the armed forces — was total fiction, replied: 'I remember the scene…. It was very powerful.' What matters to him is the grace and theatrical force of a performance; as a life-long practitioner of illusion, he is in no way embarrassed by its vic-tory over the facts."

As Barber goes on to note, the contradictions ignored by the public are striking indeed. Advocating law and order at home, Reagan violated international law and order by mining Nicaragua's waters. He blithely hailed dictators as "friends of democracy" and compared the Nicaraguan contras to the founding fathers of the United States. He secretly sold arms to a terrorist nation and lied about it when the story first broke. In the "Baby Jane Doe" case, the Reagan administration tried to force hospitals to care for hopelessly defective infants while cutting the federal funds hospitals would need to provide such special services. Similarly, Reagan opposed abortion and at the same time endeavored to slash the budgets of agencies that would provide care for unwanted infants. It didn't seem to matter. People regarded President Reagan as a nice guy, warm-hearted, sincere. He survived the Iran-Contra debacle.

While Reagan's supporters ignored many of these contradictions to preserve the fantasy, his opponents erred in making Reagan a "bad father." Assigning him an evil capacity and intent, they often didn't consider that in believing his own fictions, willfully ignoring facts, rationalizing, accepting the reassurances of the friends who surrounded him, and preferring agreeable fantasies to disagreeable facts, Reagan behaved much like the rest of us. He didn't fool the public, he was the public, as other popular presidents before him have been. Those who hated him and those who loved him saw Reagan magnified, larger than themselves, and resisted an eye-level view.

Although Reagan provided a particularly startling case of wishes dominating facts, the same process takes place in America with every president. And woe to him who falls from grace. It is interesting that the principal charge against Jimmy Carter was that he failed to provide leadership; yet he led brilliantly at Camp David. However, Carter did not appear decisive, confident, protective, optimistic; he was not, as one young woman put it about Ronald

Reagan, "the father I always wanted." Jimmy Carter proved ordinary, like us, and I believe this was a major reason why voters felt he had to be replaced.

A leader's role is more complex than it might appear. As powerful as he or she might seem, a leader is also the captive of the group and may not fail the group's expectation or waver on the pedestal. If a leader does, the group may annihilate him. And so the eminence initially sought by the leader can become a prison; the tyrant is tyrannized. Leader and follower alike to some degree enact a dependency fantasy that requires an all-powerful parent who protects and rewards and a group of children who have no responsibilities other than obedience. The leader, as much as the group members, wishes to believe that an omnipotent, perfect parent is possible. And when a person assumes the mantle, he or she participates in the fantasy as faithfully as does the follower. Yet it is still a fantasy.

Margaret Rioch comments that "we do indeed long for a shepherd who will guide us into green and safe pastures. The trouble with this simile, when applied to human beings, is that the shepherd is another sheep. He may be dressed up in a long cloak and accompanied by a tall staff with a crook on the end of it or by other formidable symbols of high office. But underneath the cloak is one of the sheep, and not, alas, a member of a more intelligent and more far-seeing species. But the wish, and sometimes, the need, for a leader is so strong that it is almost always possible for one of the sheep to play the role of shepherd of the flock."

MOST people realize the danger a leader can pose; they have read of Jonestown and know of the crimes of Stalin, Hitler, Mao Tse-tung, Pol Pot. The danger of the leader role for the leader is not so well known, although it is illustrated by the face of many who have headed New Age religious and utopian groups.

For Alex Monroe, leader of the Life Force movement, the need to maintain the status of a superior, omnipotent being was a key factor. Carried away by grandiose wishes, Alex expanded his activities, publishing an ambitious magazine and establishing multiple training centers. At the same time, he was unwilling to share his power; he had to supervise and decide everything. Alex could not manage all these tasks, and he dealt with his failure by projecting blame on everyone; as a consequence, his paranoid thinking accelerated. It should be noted that his followers supported this process because they chose to overlook the contradictions between the mystical teachings he espoused and the dishonest cruel behavior he — and they — engaged in. For his followers, to recognize what was actually taking place would have been to cease to believe in Alex as a powerful, wise parent and themselves as his disciples/children pursuing an ennobling, special path. Neither Alex nor the group wished to give up the fantasy.

A study of history reveals numerous leaders overreaching themselves, becoming inflated with an omnipotent dream they share with their followers. Perhaps because of the behavior of their em-perors, the ancient Romans had an awareness of the problem of grandiosity. As a victorious general on his day of triumph rode past the cheering crowds, leading a long procession of soldiers, captured slaves, and booty, a man would stand behind him in the chariot continually whispering, "Remember, you are mortal."

It is hard for a leader to remember that he or she is mortal when followers wish for a divinity, when they attribute to the leader the qualities of a superparent. In addition, the leader finds that he or she can wield enormous influence over group members through the gratification he or she can provide or withhold. That gratification is seen in its most intense form as "bliss," which in this context can be interpreted as the joy that springs up when an adult becomes a child once again. How wonderful to relinquish all choice and decision, to be secure in the belief that the superparent will take care of everything. When, at the same time, this regression is said to be for the good of the human race, to help bring about the salvation of the world, then the bliss is complete because it seems noble as well.

OF COURSE, it takes some doing to maintain the fantasy of riding in the back seat of the car while an imagined parent manages the steering wheel. Frequently, I find that a patient has refused to exercise his or her full strength, fearing the loss of a feeling of protection, of being watched over by a parental force (even a cruel one) that stands between him or her and an imagined chaos. This tendency is widespread.

When a leader's actions conflict with the group's principles, standards, or values, followers may twist words and meanings to reduce cognitive dissonance and maintain the fantasy. According to published accounts, one well-known Eastern guru with a propensity for drunkenness became angered at a visiting couple who had withdrawn from a wild party (held during a retreat) and secluded themselves in their room, refusing his commands to appear. He ordered his guards to bring them by force — which they did, breaking down the door and engaging the man in a fight during which he wielded broken glass as a weapon, wounding one of the guards. The couple was finally brought to stand before the guru, who then ordered that they be stripped naked. The woman and man were thrown to the floor and their clothes torn off. The woman called for help but only one onlooker came to their defense (and he was struck). The nude couple were then brought to stand before the guru. Shortly thereafter, everyone at the party stripped. The guru's actions were later justified by a follower: "...vajrayana teachings are ruthless; compassion takes many forms."

Calling the drunken guru's behavior compassion is an example of what George Orwell, in 1984, called double-speak, manipulating the abstractions of language to suggest a meaning and value opposite to the real situation. This is one way discrepancies between group fantasies and actual behavior can be painted over.

The power of the dependency fantasy is underscored in the case cited above by the fact that the abused couple chose to stay on for the conclusion of the retreat. The man explained, "We'd come to study the whole course; we'd taken it (as he [the guru] knew) seriously; we wanted to finish what we'd begun, and not be scared off. The last lap, about to begin, was the famous Tantric teachings."

In such extreme cases, the individual's perception has to be narrowed and critical thinking suppressed. Groups have effective means of doing this. As in Clara Robinson's case, if a group member voices objections or criticism, he or she may be attacked as ignorant, unworthy, selfish, elitist — whatever term is used to define badness. Groups, as well as leaders, may punish dissent or deviation when maintenance of the superparent fantasy requires that no imperfections be revealed lest the whole structure be put in jeopardy. Seldom does anyone stand behind the leader to whisper: *Remember, you are mortal.*

In a cult the leader is accepted as having special powers and/ or semi-divine status which places him or her outside the behavior norms of the ordinary person. As we have seen, similar exemption from the rules and the accompanying claim to infallibility enables many a leader to perform unethical acts that would otherwise not be countenanced. In ordinary life traces of this dynamic can be seen, although the situation is seldom as stark as in extreme cults.

When facts become impossible to ignore, the leader is dethroned; but all too often the dependency fantasy continues; a new "parent" is found.

We find examples of the abuses of the role of leader in recent political history. Richard Nixon's handling of the Watergate break-in suggests that being president had eroded his judgment, encouraged grandiosity, and blinded him with the righteousness which arises easily in powerful leaders when they are criticized and challenged. For absolute rulers the danger is even worse; witness the career of Idi Amin, who ended up rivaling Caligula in the bloody, paranoid expressions of his vanity and fear.

WE HAVE seen how the idealism of Hugh and Clara was used as a lever to break their ties with family members and to justify unethical, harmful actions. Idealism can be exploited as a source of a leader's power; he or she need only inspire and mobilize the readiness for self-sacrifice which exists within many people.

In the business world, the importance of generating fervor was noted by Thomas Peters and Robert Waterman, Jr., in their studies of "excellent" companies. They found that "transforming leadership" played a crucial role in the history of outstanding corporations; charismatic leaders stirred the emotions of their employees so as to instill a sense of elevated purpose, fulfilling the crucial human need for meaning and purpose.

Sometimes the meaning may not seem very profound to an outside observer. Charles Edward Wilson, president of General Electric from 1940 to 1950, created a strong impression on Reginald Jones (who himself later became president of the company):

"I still remember Charlie Wilson, the very epitome of the inspirational leader. He told us, in the Town Hall, how Westinghouse planned to surpass us in sales and earnings. 'They should live so long!' he roared. 'Their grandchildren should live so long.' And then he got us out behind the marching band, and they led us out to the flagpole playing 'Onward Christian Soldiers.' At that moment, I would have followed him anywhere on earth — and beyond if necessary."

Even if the summons is for political or economic goals rather than religious ones, the energies mobilized will be the same and the final result is declared to be for the greater good, creating paradise on earth, saving the world. What matters is that people's deepest desires for the Good be mobilized. That is why the most effective leaders inspire rather than overpower. This was the conclusion of a study of audience reactions to a charismatic leader:

"They were apparently strengthened and uplifted by the experience; they felt more powerful, rather than less powerful or submissive. This suggests that the traditional way of explaining the influence of a leader on his followers has not been entirely correct. He does not force them to submit and follow him by the sheer

overwhelming magic of his personality and persuasive powers...
he is influential by strengthening and inspiriting his audience."

Anyone who has watched films of Hitler's speeches and the
crowds' reactions would agree. Hitler, transformed by his own
fantasies, brought his audience's fantasies and wishes to life, made
them seem possible. He whipped his listeners to intoxicating heights
of emotion, restoring significance to their lives, asking for sacrifices.

Most of us need to feel that our lives have meaning and purpose,
that we are special and are living in a way that is consonant with
our ideals. And it is not only the young that long to live ideal-
istically, older people who have led practical lives and have accepted the necessity of compromising their ideals may respond
with great commitment if offered the opportunity to sacrifice for
a good cause. This appeal to the perception of a larger reality, to
unsatisfied idealism and the wish for meaning can be very powerful,
and it can be put to good or bad use.

AUTHORITARIAN leadership tends to become established in large
corporations where power has become overly centralized. Harold
Geneen, who ran ITT like a potentate, knows whereof he speaks:
"The authority vested in the chief executive of a large company is
so great, so complete, and the demands made upon his time are so
consuming, that most chief executives slip into authoritarian roles
without realizing that the process is going on."

John De Lorean, former General Motors executive, describes
the increase in authoritarianism at GM in the years following the
departure of Alfred Sloan, who had been chairman of the board:

"I watched GM's operations slowly become centralized. The
divisions gradually were stripped of their decision-making power...
The guiding corporate precept of centralized policy making and de-
centralized decision making was totally and purposefully ignored...
There was no system of checks and balances. The divisions reported
to The Fourteenth Floor. But The Fourteenth Floor reported only
to itself."

The authoritarian attitude results in an emphasis on punishment and the manifestation of power by saying no. The veto is safer and more impressive than granting permission. Although innovation and creativity may be given lip service, even insignificant mistakes are usually punished despite their being the inevitable price of developing a new approach or a new product." Peters and Waterman, in reviewing the problem, came to the conclusion that this behavior reflects the same superior/inferior perspective that Erich Fromm emphasized in his study of authoritarian political behavior: "Central to the whole notion... is the superior/subordinate relationship, the idea of manager as 'boss,' and the corollary that orders will be issued and followed. The threat of punishment is the principle implied power that underlies it all."

The hierarchical emphasis is underlined by corporate class distinctions. The executive washroom, the special dining room for upper management, superior furnishings and more space are all indicators of a higher position. Indeed, the top executives usually will be found on the highest floor. This institutionalization of the upward gaze is accepted almost everywhere and seldom questioned any more than is the assumption of parents having the largest bedroom in the home, a separate bathroom, and other prerogatives.

Even when the chief executive officer wishes to make the organization less authoritarian, the task is not easy. Comelle Maier, former CEO for Kaiser Aluminum recalls a lesson he learned when his corporation began to decentralize decision making:

"As we started giving more authority to our operating divisions an interesting thing happened... all of the managers working for me felt that they should have a lot more authority in their decision-making: capital spending, personnel moves — what have you. That wasn't a surprise. What was a surprise was that nearly all of them felt that the people working for them shouldn't have more authority!... They wanted a lot more authority but they didn't want to give that authority away."

Nor did they wish to give up the symbols of elevated status they had acquired as part of the superior/inferior authoritarian world.

THE chief executive officer of a large corporation does not usually claim divine attributes. However, the CEO's power to hire, fire, reward, and punish is very great and in the hands of an authoritarian personality this power can result in a suppression of critical thinking within the corporation and a mindless conformity and fawning support for whatever the CEO believes and decides to do. Sometimes this behavior extends to a slavish copying of the style of dress and behavior of the boss. In his book *The Fanciest Dive,* Christopher Byron gives an amusing description of the antics that took place at Time, Inc. when a new boss, Richard Munro, entered the scene:

"No sooner did word spread that the company's new president ate breakfast early most mornings at the Dorset Hotel on West Fifty-fourth Street than numerous subordinates began doing the same. It was there, one hot September morning in 1982 that Munro, having breakfast, stood up and removed his suit jacket to be more comfortable; all around the room Time Inc. executives promptly rose and did the same... And when Munro took to carrying a red bandana with a corner flapping loosely from his hip pocket, the corridors of the Big House were soon ablaze with red bandanas waving jauntily from the hip pockets of hopeful executives."

Like similar leaders everywhere, authoritarian executives can easily end up valuing the conformity, loyalty, obedience, and subservience of subordinates more than actual performance. A boss wants to trust his or her subordinates, to count on their loyalty, to know they fit in and will not cause trouble. Subordinates who conform to the boss's own style of dress and behavior evoke in him a sense of support and comfort. The boss feels he knows where his subordinates stand and can rely on them to perform as he would in unsupervised situations. In turn, the employees know that salaries, promotion, and assignments within the company lie in the hands of their boss. When obedience, loyalty, and conformity matter more than performance, cult-like behavior takes place all along the hierarchy. Secrecy about salaries, competition for the boss's favor, and fear of being left behind can create an atmosphere reminiscent of that which occurred in Life Force.

WHAT is a god if not a supreme authority? In religions the world over, the devout acknowledge their god's divine wisdom, mercy and awesome power; they pray for protection, forgiveness, and benefits. Even in Buddhism, whose founder declared that notions of gods and heavens were illusions, most believers bow to a Buddha idol with all the expectations found in theistic religions.

Few people take seriously the injunctions of mystics against seeking to understand the Ultimate via familiar images. Typical of such an injunction is the statement of Saint John of the Cross:

"That inward wisdom is so simple, so general and so spiritual that it has not entered into the understanding enwrapped or clad in any form or image subject to sense, it follows that sense and imagination (as it has not entered through them nor has taken their form and color) cannot account for it or imagine, so as to say anything concerning it, although the soul be clearly aware that it is experiencing and partaking of that rare and delectable wisdom."

Saint John maintained that knowledge of God cannot be expressed in terms of this world, cannot be articulated by using the images and concepts of everyday life; family, mother, father, children, reward, punishment, etc. Similar statements about the unknowability of the Godhead have been made by mystics of widely differing cultures throughout history. They are very consistent. Nevertheless, formal religions tend to use the familiar relationship of parent and child as the model for a human being's relationship to the divine. This model inevitably creates cult dynamics in religious organizations. In part, the problem arises because the founding mystics of the theistic religions, in their attempts to communicate the ineffable, made use of the concept of God the Father, the supreme parent, although only as a metaphor. However, their listeners took the meaning literally. Thus, religions end up teaching, *Be good* (obey God's wishes) *and you will be rewarded* (enter heaven or nirvana); *if you are bad* (disobey God) *you will be punished* (with hell or reincarnation).

The dependency wish usually requires tangible authority figures and they are seldom in short supply. Mohammed abolished the priesthood but equivalent ecclesiastical officials, the mullahs, arose after his death and in some areas, such as Iran (now a theocracy), the chief mullah rules with more authority than the present-day Pope. Another example is provided by Hinduism. Although the Upanishads preach the oneness of all being, the Brahmin priests whose function it is to transmit Hindu teaching have maintained the caste system and their superior status within it. It took all the power of Gandhi to begin to crack the caste barriers enclosing the untouchables of India.

Theistic religions, such as Christianity, Judaism, or Islam, are intrinsically authoritarian, expressing the belief in God as a Supreme Being who transcends the material world, is infinitely superior to human beings, and to whom we owe obedience. God's absolute superiority in power, goodness, and knowledge may be used by religious leaders to justify their own authority and to legitimize their demands for submission. For the most part, theistic religions teach that compliance with God's will, coupled with an appropriately humble attitude, will be rewarded by protection and help for the supplicant: that pride (putting oneself at eye level with God) is a sin and submission a virtue. The greater the emphasis on the supreme god (the superparent) versus the inferior follower (the child), the more the stage is set for cult behavior in any religion, orthodox or not.

Thus, as in any authoritarian system, the basic perspective of most religious groups is one of superior/inferior relationships; as obedience is the prime virtue in all authoritarian systems, so obedience to God's commandments is a prime virtue in theistic religions. This is espoused most rigidly by fundamentalists, those who believe in the literal, inerrant truth of the Bible, the Koran, or any other religious text. Rev. Jerry Falwell puts the matter most unequivocally: "We must be obedient to the Word of God. Obedient. Whatsoever He sayeth unto you, do it! That's all there is to it! Find out what God is saying to you and obey Him. Obey the Lord. Obedience!"

Of course, the critical issue is not obedience, per se, but why we are obedient and to what or whom. Blind obedience leads to totalitarianism, refusal to obey anything leads to chaos. Free will (as distinguished from impulsivity) combines obedience with choice; it is "the experience of being the author of the law you obey." Being the author means to choose the values expressed in the law, to freely assent to them based on one's judgment, experience, and sense of the Good.

The best religious leaders teach that a truly spiritual choice is an expression of one's self and not an expression of fear (of punishment), or greed (for reward), or vanity (being one of the chosen few). A story from the Sufic tradition, here told by Idries Shah, addresses this issue:

> THERE was once a powerful conqueror who had become emperor of a vast territory peopled by representatives of several beliefs.
>
> His counselors said, "Great king, a deputation of thinkers and priests from each persuasion, is awaiting audience. Each hopes to convert you to the way of thinking of his school. We are in a quandary, because we cannot advise you to accept the ideology of one part, since it would alienate the goodwill of all the rest."
>
> The king, for his part, said, "Neither is it fitting that a king should adopt beliefs for political reasons, and without thought for his own higher dignity and well-being."
>
> The discussions continued for several hours, until a wise dervish, who had attached himself to the king's reti-

nue many months before and had been silent ever since, stepped forward.

"Majesty," he said, "I am prepared to advise a course in which the interests of all parties will be safeguarded. The applicants will be abashed, the courtiers will be relieved of their anxiety to find a solution, the king will be able to retain his reputation for wisdom, and nobody will be able to say that he holds sway over the king's thoughts."

The dervish whispered his formula into the royal ear, and the king called the deputation to enter the throne-room.

Receiving the clerics and thinkers with all courtesy, the king said to them:

"I shall hear first of all the arguments of those among you who do not say 'Believe or you are in peril'; or 'Believe because it will give you happiness', or 'Adopt my beliefs because you are a great king.'"

The applicants dispersed in confusion.

ALTHOUGH a person may be drawn to a religion through the wish to find meaning and purpose, to serve God and humanity, religious organizations all too often fail to avoid stimulating fear, greed, or flattery in recruiting members. Consequently, the obedience commanded tends to evoke the attitude of the child toward its parent. Obedience is certainly necessary for certain kinds of learning and development, and has a definite function in religious instruction, but great religious teachers agree that the highest obedience is to the religion's essence.

Obedience to the literal scriptures, to the form rather than the essence, opens the door to cult process. This problem of form taking precedence over content is one that plagues all religions and is defined as idolatry. Anything can be idolized, including rules and rituals, and the resulting behavior may contradict the values that the religion espouses. A Benedictine prioress reflected on the reversal of priorities that marked religious life during her early years with the order:

"Formalism and legalism had completely replaced either spiritual direction or blessing. Every day life got smaller. Religious life had become the celebration of the trivial. While McCarthyism raged, I was told to guard myself from spiritual distraction by not listening to the news. While Martin Luther King began black sit-ins of white lunch counters in a country that routinely lynched blacks, I believed it when they said that had nothing to do with religious life and concentrated on darning my socks, a real sign of poverty, I was told."

When a religion's texts are regarded as literally true and infallible, a likely next step is that the leader's interpretation becomes what is true and sacred. Then a member's obedience is transferred to the priest, rabbi, mullah, or minister; this is the lowest level of obedience, most likely to lead to overt cult behavior. Rev. R. G. Puckett, the Baptist evangelist who heads Americans United, warned of this development taking place in American Christian fundamentalist churches:

"The church is centered in the pastor. He is the authority, the ruling force. Falwell, Robison, Robertson, all the rest — these are personality cults. People follow the person, the pastor, not Jesus Christ. He may say he is not telling anyone how to vote or how to live, but the very climate and mentality of the whole church says: what the pastor wants is what we do."

Such preachers do not claim divinity, only that God speaks to them, inspires them, guides them. That claim may be quite enough to demand complete obedience and to brand disagreement with their views and wishes as a sign that the defiant member is lost to salvation.

Religious leaders may be as attracted to the security of certainty and surrender as are their followers. Many really believe they are commanded by God, that they have become instruments of his will, and that their pronouncements are beyond error. Others with less exalted views of themselves evertheless succumb to the lure of certainty and rightness. From a priest who has faced the shortcomings of his church we have an eloquent testimony to that attraction:

"I do not [now] live without worry or responsible concern. In fact, I have never felt so responsible since I discovered that the Church cannot absorb my conscience, nor replace my mind. Life was easier when I knew where everything fit, when I could lose myself in the structure of a massive organization. There heaven and hell were governed by careful laws. There God's friendship was certain and manageable, and I was satisfied when I kept the Church's rules."

Liz Harris, writing in the *New Yorker*, contrasted her own state of uncertainty with the security of the Hasidic world.

"I envied them their sureness and the sheer weight it gave them. I had, of course, my family, my friends, my work, and the various pleasures that came my way, but spiritually I felt as if I floated weightlessly in the universe. The Hasidim had a world without time, eternal life, and the extraordinary sense that everything they did counted."

SURRENDER is a basic feature of the spiritual life. As an acceptance of selfless goals in place of self-centeredness, it is something most recognize as inherently desirable. Yet the call to surrender can become a tool for manipulation and control when critical judgment is set aside. As we have seen earlier, Clara Robinson was exhorted to give up her concern for her child and surrender to Life Force's greater spiritual task as set forth by Alex Monroe. Her reluctance to do so was defined as selfishness. Barbara Underwood, a former Moonie, described similar coercion in the Unification Church, and total surrender is called for by fundamentalist preachers and organizations such as the Campus Crusade. Bill Bright, writing in *Jesus and the Intellectual* makes it quite explicit: "The secret is surrender. Commitment to Christ involves the surrender of the intellect, the emotions and the will — the total person."

There is no place in such groups for independent judgment; no free will, no responsible choice, only literal adherence to sacred text as selected and interpreted by the church leader or organization. With surrender, the authority of the leader is maximized, the follower feels relieved of uncertainty and can then experience the "bliss" of someone who has "returned home."

SINCE most of the examples I have cited are from the fundamentalist and conservative wings of established religions, some readers may feel my conclusions do not apply to them because they are involved in less doctrinaire, more moderate, more sophisticated beliefs and practices. I would respond that it is a matter of degree and that each person needs to assess the extent to which cult behavior and the dependency fantasy are operative in his or her religious life. I believe that such awareness is of particular importance because the goal of religion should be to facilitate the direct experience of the spiritual dimension. Although human beings carry within them the potential for regressive dependency they also contain the potential for the intuition of the spiritual — that perception, however dim, of something that transcends the reality accessible to the senses and ordinary thought. This intuition is universal and can be very powerful.

Indeed, mystics claim that spiritual development consists of strengthening that intuitive capacity, permitting one to "know" the larger reality called Truth, God, Original Mind, Brahma — whatever name may be invoked. Assuming the existence of that perceptual capacity, latent in everyone, the question arises of the effect of cult-like behavior on one's capacity to experience the spiritual.

Study of the mystical literature of many religions reveals all these traditions to be in agreement that to develop the ability to perceive God or Truth, one must shift from a self-centered orientation to serving the underlying reality. This service must be without concern for personal gain; basic intentions must change. There can be no cheating on this one because motivation determines the form of consciousness. You cannot grasp the spiritual world as you can the material since a "grasping" mind is necessarily focused on discrete objects and cannot encompass a world of connectedness, of unity. It is for this reason — a functional, not a moral reason — that mystics assert that no matter what you may say or do, no matter how you may appear, if your underlying intention is self-centered, perception of Truth or God is impossible. The necessary shift in motivation takes time, effort, and skillful guidance. To "repent and believe" is not enough.

An organization that enhances selfish intentions is at cross purposes with spiritual development; it is anti-spiritual. To stimulate fear of punishment, greed for reward, or vanity at being among the saved versus the damned, is to stimulate a self-centered orientation. These powerful motivations are not in the service of spiritual development. This is why one saint declared:

> O Lord!
> If I worship you from fear of hell, cast me into hell.
> If I worship you from desire for paradise, deny me paradise.

Dependence on a leader/parent can be doubly destructive in the sphere of religion. Not only does it impair ordinary judgment and create a regressive pull on members and converts of religious groups, it prevents them from progressing beyond a self-centered orientation. This blocks the perception of the spiritual force that is the vital element within religions, a force that might otherwise enhance and guide their lives.

I do not mean to say that a religion's members may not devote themselves to actions benefiting others. To the contrary, great charity and service have been inspired by religious beliefs and administered by religious institutions throughout the centuries. Cult behavior is largely an interior problem in which form (doctrine and authority) dominates content (the experience of the Real), producing idolatry. Understanding the nature of the problem facilitates an attitude vitally different from the authoritarian. A School Sister of Notre Dame comments:

"Although as a woman religious I am identified with church

institutions, in the final analysis, God, not any institution, is paramount. To associate with and to preserve any structure at the expense of serving God and humankind is idolatry. To follow God's call rather than an institutional call, if the two are in conflict, is a moral imperative. I pray always for the grace and the insight to discern God's call."

Certainly, if a religious group provides us with security and identity, we will not see its cult features very readily. One's own group is thought to be above such behavior; a cult is seen as something that you yourself don't belong to. But perhaps in some ways you do. It just isn't obvious when measured against Jonestown or the Life Force Institute.

My own profession of psychiatry is not immune from cult behavior. To begin with, the psychotherapeutic situation itself encourages the emergence of a dependency relationship. In psychoanalysis and analytically oriented psychotherapy, the therapist reveals almost nothing while the patient is expected to reveal all.

Since the therapist is calm, reticent, and an authority while the patient is distressed and seeking help, a parent/child feeling quickly develops. With time, the unique character of the patient's early relationship to his or her parent or parents tends to be transferred to the therapist. In fact Freud emphasized the transference in helping the patient, seeing the intensification of the parent/child fantasy as a desired effect of the psychotherapeutic situation.

Nevertheless, it should be recognized that Freud intended that the patient reclaim the power he or she bestowed on the therapist. He hoped that analysis of the transference would give to the patient an eye-level perspective toward the analyst, as well as toward others. I know of no other profession or institution that has established a goal of relinquishing authority and built in comprehensive techniques for its accomplishment. Even though the return of power takes place imperfectly (and in some cases not at all), dedication to an eye-level relationship is a direct counter to cult-like behavior and offers hope for a more mature society.

Regrettably, the ideal may be preached but not always practiced. Psychotherapists may exploit their position in the same fashion as do cult leaders. This can take place in several ways, from automatically interpreting a patient's criticism as neurotic, dismissing any questioning as projection or acting out of the transference, to outright sexual seduction. I remember a cartoon about psychiatry with the punch line "This is the only business where the customer is always wrong."

The patient is not always wrong in his or her perceptions of the therapist. It is crucial that the therapist be able to see in what ways the patient is correct, acknowledge and support the patient's perception and go on to investigate what the therapist's error or limitation means to the patient. Competent therapists do this, but only an ideal therapist is completely free from defensiveness and denial.

Therapists, like other leaders, often are flattered and idealized by their patients, who wish them to be omnipotent, omniscient, surrogate parents. Resisting this seduction is particularly hard for a psychotherapist because he or she is likely to have entered the profession with the very fantasy of being an ideal parent, one who "saves" grateful patients. (In this context, the patient may represent the therapist as a child or the therapist's parent, whoever needed saving.) Having become a therapist, one may fall in with the patient's wish when it supports the savior fantasy. While the patient is not officially a follower, nor is the therapist a cult leader, the dependency needs of the former and the omnipotent fantasies of the latter can create cult-like behavior.

Actual cults may develop in therapeutic situations. Although this is rare, there have been instances of therapists who develop relationships with their patients in which they occupy the roles of colleagues, teachers, lovers, friends, and employers simultaneously. Such a violation of professional ethics and psychiatric principles is not necessarily due to substandard psychiatric training. In one study of five such "therapeutic cults," two of the leaders were psychoanalysts, members of the prestigious American Psychoanalytic Association, yet these therapeutic cults functioned almost like religious cults." Although actual cult formation by psychiatrists is unusual, there are two areas where covert cult-like behavior is significant.

IN THE 1950s and 1960s, psychoanalysis was in its heyday of acceptance and power. The heads of departments of psychiatry in medical schools were usually psychoanalysts; it was assumed that the best psychiatry residents would become psychoanalysts — the second-best would have to settle for something inferior. Indeed, as a psychiatric resident, I was told that only psychoanalysis offered a patient real change, real treatment; psychotherapy was a patch-up job. (How powerfully such a consensus prevailed and affected judgment is hard to convey, even though there were abundant cases of unresolved neurotic problems among former analysands and among the training analysts themselves, and although one heard anecdotes of psychotherapy results that rivaled the best of psychoanalysis.) This assumption pervades much of the psychoanalytic literature today and I think it has had a debilitating effect on psychoanalytic thinking.

Psychoanalytic institutes, where psychoanalysis is taught, are not cults, but cult behavior does take place in them. Cult features have been so prominent that noted analysts have remarked on the similarity between psychoanalytic institutes and religious organizations. Otto Kernberg, training analyst at the Columbia University Center for Psychoanalytic Training and Research, points to features of psychoanalytic education that justify its designation as a system of religious beliefs:

"The religious assertion of faith in the existence of the deity and the essentially irrational nature of such a faith are not unlike the sense of conviction about the truth of psychoanalytic theory particularly about the unconscious. This sense of conviction is usually traced to an emotional experience connected with the discovery of the unconscious in oneself and the experience of psychological change following this discovery. In both instances a highly subjective personal experience, an emotional encounter with the unknown rather than rational analysis, constitutes the anchoring pillar of the educational program."

This could be a description of Hugh and Clara Robinson's conversion to faith in life force psychology, or of the experiences of converts to the numerous new religions of the sixties and seventies. Kernberg goes on to point out further similarities:

"In addition, this deeply transforming emotional experience is carried out in the context of an intense relation to another person, idealized and experienced as a spiritual guide... complemented by other mentors who focus on the limitations, shortcomings, mistakes, and inadequacies of the student's performance, while sustaining the assumption that they are working at a higher level, which the student must reach through ongoing self-exploration as well as learning about the formulations of the masters, in the end, the original master of the school, Freud."

The analogy to religion is seconded by Jacob Arlow, a past president of the American Psychoanalytic Association, who pointed out that psychoanalytic education is unique among learned disciplines in that most of its basic texts are fifty years old. He observes that this can't be wholly explained as the debt of psychoanalysis to Freud because of a characteristic clinging to the past that marks the educational emphasis. Freud's earlier writings receives greater attention than either his later writings or the contributions of recent analysts. Arlow further notes that psychoanalytic training is experienced as a prolonged initiation rite:

"During a long course of tests which the initiates undergo (personal analysis, admission to courses, first case, second case, etc., graduation), the training analysts serve the double function characteristic of all initiators. Some intimidate the candidates; others act as sponsors and guides... anxiety propels the candidate into effecting an identification with the aggressor; the initiate re-models himself after the image the community holds up as the ideal."

The situation of the candidates is not unlike that of members of Life Force who were dependent on the good opinion of leader/therapist Alex for their graduation to the inner circle of the Center. Depending on the candidate, the effects could easily be similar in kind.

IN 1961 John F. Kennedy made the disastrous decision to go ahead with a covert invasion of Cuba by anti-Castro exiles, an operation commonly referred to afterwards as the Bay of Pigs. It was a spectacular failure. About a year later, when it was discovered that Russian nuclear missiles were being installed in Cuba, Kennedy was successful in bringing about their withdrawal, an operation usually called the Cuban Missile Crisis. Because the Bay of Pigs and the Cuban Missile Crisis were historic events whose decision-making processes are exceptionally well documented, I will use them to illustrate both cult behavior and the possibility of more realistic behavior at the government level.

Irving Janis, a psychologist who studied the effect of group process on presidential advisory groups, pointed to the important role of shared illusions in disasters such as the attempted invasion of Cuba. One was "the illusion of invulnerability." People believe that if their leader and everyone else thinks a proposal will succeed, then it will, even if it is risky and requires luck.

An air of omniscience is fostered by political leaders, in part because the public demands leaders who are forceful and confident; unwavering optimism is preferred to doubts and uncertainty. The fantasy of invulnerability is identical in cults, where it may lead to disaster. For example, an epochal celebration, brainchild of a young Indian guru, was held some years ago in Houston, Texas. With the guru's approval, his followers hired the Astrodome, expecting to fill it with thousands of people who would be drawn there to hear his message. Confidence was unbounded, no doubts were heard, as the guru was presumed infallible. Publicity and preparations were extensive and lavish, media coverage nationwide. The celestial appearance of the comet Kahoutek was interpreted as a cosmic herald of the grand event. What actually took place was a grand fiasco; although droves of the guru's followers arrived at the stadium, very few others availed themselves of the opportunity to adulate him and share in the momentous event. The monetary and public relations losses were staggering; the organization went into decline.

From the blissful, blind optimism of this guru and his followers to the arrogant overconfidence of top U.S. government officials in the Bay of Pigs advisory group was not such a large step. Robert Kennedy recalled, "It seemed that, with John Kennedy leading us and with all the talent he had assembled, nothing could stop us."

Arthur Schlesinger felt the same.

"One further factor no doubt influenced him [John F. Kennedy]: the enormous confidence in his own luck. Everything had broken right for him since 1956. He had won the nomination and the election against all the odds in the book. Everyone around him thought he had the Midas touch and could not lose. Despite himself, even this dispassionate and skeptical man may have been affected by the soaring euphoria of the new day."

One cannot understand the phenomenon of authoritarian behavior in democratic presidents without appreciating the attraction for both leaders and followers of a parent/child perspective.

I have a vivid memory of an incident that occurred during a Tavistock Group Relations Conference. Participants were divided into several large groups and each group was asked to relate to the other groups by appointing suitably empowered representatives. No group leaders were designated, no goals or structure provided. In the absence of authority and direction, anxiety built up rapidly. Everyone talked at once. I tried to reduce the chaos by establishing leadership. "Make me leader!" I pleaded. The group would not appoint any one to that power position. The disorganization and tension increased. Finally, I stood up; shouted, "I'm taking command!" and began appointing people to assume the functions of door-keeper, ambassador, and so forth. The same people who would not voluntarily delegate authority now obeyed with alacrity. The conference conditions had intensified our primitive impulses and we behaved like a group of sibling children, no one willing to take the adult action of delegating power. When my discomfort drove me to take the role of dictator/parent the others readily submitted, for they were then freed of responsibility.

A parallel need — to structure a situation in terms of a child rebelling against a bad parent — was illustrated, for me, when I had to hospitalize an adolescent against his will. A state trooper arrived at my office to take him away. It was clear that the officer wanted to be compassionate and helpful. My patient would have none of this. He resisted, struggled, taunted, and provoked the trooper until the man became angry and, finally, cuffed him on the head with his open hand. Immediately, the young man became docile and accompanied him readily. It was clear to me that my patient had succeeded in his aim of making the policeman a "bad parent." Later, a teacher at the boy's school denounced this "police brutality" and was indignant when I replied that I thought the state trooper was the one who had been brutalized.

In each of these incidents, those involved refused or were unable to go beyond the child/parent relationship and insisted on an authoritarian structure. I see the compliance of the first instance and the rebelliousness of the second as two aspects of looking up at authority.

LIKE most cults and formal religions, governments cite a higher principle or authority to justify their actions. (This is probably what Samuel Johnson mocked when he said, "Patriotism is the last refuge of the scoundrel.") As Alex Monroe's lies were justified as being necessary to advance the work of saving the world, other cult leaders, tyrants, and terrorists invariably defend immoral and violent actions as serving God or truth or country or freedom.

Psychologist Stanley Milgram's research demonstrated the effectiveness of this reference to a higher authority. People from all walks of life participated as subjects in his studies. An experimenter in a grey lab coat told the subjects that the purpose of the experiment was to advance science, and then instructed them to give increasing electric shocks to a "learner" strapped into an electric chair. (Unbeknownst to the subjects, the learner was a confederate of the researchers and actually received no shocks at all.) The subjects were told that although the shocks could be extremely painful to the learner, they caused no permanent damage.

As the experiment proceeded, the learner became increasingly vocal, agitated, and desperate, and eventually screamed each time the subject shocked him. He demanded and begged to be released, expressing concern for his heart. Most subjects showed evidence of considerable stress as they were ordered to continue despite the anguished cries of pain, which they could hear from the other room. (In further experiments in which the learner was in the same room with them, the subjects could also see his tortured appearance.)

Contrary to predictions, most subjects continued to administer the electric shock right up to the supposed limit of 450 volts, labeled "Danger: Severe Shock." When the learner was in the same room 40 percent of the subjects continued to the end of the scale and even when the subject was required to force the learner's hand down onto the shock plate and hold it there against his struggles, 30 percent applied the most severe shocks possible. To appreciate these results it is important to understand that the acting of the learner was convincing; follow-up studies confirmed that almost all the subjects believed that shocks were actually being administered and that the man was suffering severe pain.

Many of the subjects showed evidence of great stress as they complied with the experimenter's instructions. What direct pressure made the subjects continue despite their own distress at what they were doing? It consisted of the following statements, said firmly but politely by the experimenter, using as many of them as might be needed to overcome the subject's protests and concerns: "Please continue, [or] please go on," "The experiment requires that you continue," "It is absolutely essential that you continue," "You have no other choice, you must go on." There were no threats, no physical coercion, no other inducements.

Milgram came to the conclusion that in such situations people enter into what he terms an agentic state, one in which they see themselves as agents for carrying out another person's wishes. This shift from autonomous functioning to submission to a hierarchy of command is considered by Milgram to be an evolutionary development that has enabled human beings to take advantage of the benefits of being in large groups. Unfortunately, it may also lead one to administer suffering on others if it is justified by authority:

"The human element behind the agencies and institutions is denied. Thus, when the experimenter says, "The experiment requires that you continue," the subject feels this to be an imperative that goes beyond any merely human command. He does not ask the seemingly obvious question, "Whose experiment? Why should the designer be served while the victim suffers?" The wishes of a man — the designer of the experiment — have become part of a schema which exerts on the subject's mind a force that transcends the personal."

It is easy to see how this type of justification has led to nations' transgressing human values. In our own country after the Japanese bombed Pearl Harbor, blameless American citizens were dispossessed and forcibly moved into internment camps for the duration of the war because they were of Japanese descent. In the name of national security the fundamental values and principles of our democracy were thrust aside and great injustice done. Similarly, as a nation (and despite internal dissent), we justified our actions in Vietnam by the concept of "fighting Communist aggression" as we attempted to defoliate the forests with Agent Orange and napalmed civilians. The American government has supported

— and still supports — governments whose murderous savagery and sickening use of torture equals, if not surpasses, Stalin's and, with the possible exception of genocide, rivals that of the Nazis. We are likely to be told that the national interest requires our support. Just as the experiment in Milgram's study assumed an impersonal, overriding authority, even more so does the national interest. As Noam Chomsky noted in a symposium on human rights:

"The concept of 'national interest' [is] a mystification that serves to conceal the ways in which state policy is formed and executed... Within a particular nation-state, some groups are sufficiently powerful to exert a major, perhaps dominant, influence over state policy and the ideological systems. Their special interests then become, in effect, 'the national interest.' To take again the case of Guatemala: in 1954 the United Fruit Company had an interest in blocking land reform: I did not... What was 'the national interest'? In practice, it was the special interest of those with the power to influence and execute state policy and to shape the basic structure of the ideological system, including the flow of information."

We can understand the power of "the experiment," "the state," and "the national interest" if we recognize these abstractions as representing Higher Authority: the parent of the dependency fantasy who protects, rewards, and punishes.

Appreciation of the power and ubiquitous nature of the dependency fantasy helps us to understand how, at every level of government and society, people set aside any doubts by assuming that "they" must know what they are doing. Even national leaders can react like small children ready to believe that the driver of the car must be wise. But the "shepherds" are not different from the "sheep."

FIVE

Devaluing the Outsider

THE security of a cult is bound up with the idea of being special, better than those outside the group. Indeed, outsiders are likely to be seen as threatening since they do not share the cult's belief in the leader and in the special entitlement of its members. This threat is met by devaluing the non-believers. In part, this devaluation is an expression of the child's wish that his or her parents be the most powerful, that they know everything and can obtain for their children good things which others do not have. Furthermore, feeling blessed and favored confers a sense of protection, calming anxieties about the world outside.

Devaluing the outsider is probably the most common cult-like behavior in everyday society, where it takes the form of regarding one's opponents as if they were a homogeneous group with only negative traits. Bad motives are attributed to the other, but not to oneself. This devaluation is usually done by designating the adversary as, for example, "stupid," "rigid," "lazy," "reactionary," "bleeding heart," "cold." When one devalues another no real proof is offered. There is seldom any inquiry into the actual statements and actions of members of the "bad" group, or any serious consideration of the adversary's point of view and its possible validity, and critical analysis of one's own "good" view, discriminating between assumptions and facts, rarely takes place.

Examples of this everyday cult behavior can be found on radio talk shows. One major program I have encountered has a host who is perpetually exclaiming at the stupidity of whatever political or bureaucratic figure is the target for the day. He and the caller-in indulge in a festival of indignation and self-congratulation, shaking their collective heads over the "ridiculous" actions that have so astonished them, seldom seeking to understand how the action under attack might be reasonable from a different point of view or even being genuinely curious about it. Instead, the host and the caller engage in cult behavior. By designating someone else as bad or stupid, they are reassured that they themselves are good, their views commendable.

PERHAPS the most important thing to understand about devaluing the outsider is that it is a necessary preliminary to harming others, to doing violence. Whether the conflict is between nations or individuals, the attacker devalues the victim prior to the violent act. Sociologist Jack Katz studied street gangs and juvenile delinquents and noted the special function of cursing in propelling an attack:

"Cursing... is a direct and effective way of doing just what it appears to do: symbolically transforming the offending party into an ontologically lower status... If the other is a shit, attacking him becomes a community service — a form of moral garbage collection performed on behalf of all decent people... Cursing at once makes the accursed repulsive and conjures up an altruistic overlay for an attack on him or her."

The person you devalue becomes easier to kill. But when you look at him, be sure you do not see who he really is, for if you do, you cannot believe he is inferior to you. A man who had been a medical corpsman in Vietnam remembers the time when he was asked to guard an old Viet Cong. His prisoner looked right into his eyes, and the corpsman looked back. Then the old man was dragged to death behind a truck.

"I will never forget the man's face, and I will never forget his eyes, and I will never forget holding the rifle at his face... I'll never forget how old he was. There was something about the internal solidity of this human being that I will never forget... Something went on that changed my life."

Devaluation relies heavily on projection, a defense mechanism, operating unconsciously, in which what is emotionally unacceptable in the self is unconsciously rejected and attributed (projected) to others. Projection occurs when we attribute to others those aspects of ourselves that we wish to deny. By identifying the bad impulse or trait as being outside ourselves, we can feel more secure. Thus, projection offers protection from the anxiety of being bad and the punishment of being abandoned. In addition, by making other people bad in our own mind, we can legitimize behavior that would otherwise be morally unacceptable, even to the point of sanctioning cruel and vicious actions.

I saw a vivid demonstration of projection at the conclusion of a five-day group relations conference when I joined a small group that was discussing what had been learned. Opposite me was a stocky, muscular young man with a hostile demeanor. I felt that he would physically attack me if I gave him the slightest excuse. I was afraid of him. My feelings were similar to what I had felt toward school bullies when I was growing up. Because during the conference we had dealt with projection, I tried questioning myself to see if I had any aggressive impulses toward the man whom I was afraid of. Immediately, I became aware of a desire to attack, to punch him to the ground. The violence in me was unmistakable. I looked again at the young man and could not believe the transformation that had taken place. He now appeared mild, non-threatening, a perfectly nice person. This reversal of perception had happened in that instant of recognition of my own hostile feelings. The experience was vivid, probably because the conference had been designed to intensify projective defenses, but I am sure that similar distortions of perception take place under more normal conditions and that these perceptions can also be reversed.

The effect of projection is often a perception of the other person as being fundamentally different, a morally inferior species, undeserving of empathy. Perhaps the most common form of projection is to condemn others without noting good qualities that may lessen our sense of distance between them and us. In fact, noting an enemy's less admirable similarities to us can provoke strong feelings. Many people were distressed when Hannah Arendt's study of Adolph Eichmann, the Nazi war criminal, led her to conclude that he was not diabolical, but banal, a poor thinker, common. Although the research of Stanley Milgram and Philip Zimbardo suggests strongly that the potential for cruelty and the carrying out of heinous orders is common to all human beings, it is hard for us to acknowledge that we may be less unlike the Nazis than we would wish. Projection protects us all from what we fear.

The more authoritarian the human social system, the more likely a separatist world view will arise because any anger or resentment stimulated in the follower by his or her submission to the leader requires displacement onto other persons — the outsider, the infidel, the non-believer. Feelings of rebellion toward the leader, which are defined by the group as evil, make the cult member anxious, even ready to believe in satanic possession, an apt metaphor to describe the sensation of being invaded by unwanted feelings and images. Projection and a division of humanity into the saved and the damned are called into play with increasing intensity. As a result, the more rigid the system the more powerful is the belief in the Devil or Evil — and the more violent the feelings toward the outsider.

Because projection requires the establishment of separation, of discontinuity, of fundamental differences, the person or group onto whom the badness is projected must be a "not-me"; otherwise one's condemnation would rebound onto oneself. For this reason we project most often onto other nations, other racial and religious groups, opposing political parties, and economic and social classes different from our own. However, projection may also be used in ordinary social relationships when the need to feel superior rather than inferior arises often.

Thus, we increase our moral security by seeing others as evil, stupid, backward, or arrogant. When we do this we create and maintain cult consciousness in a fashion similar to the fanatic who perceives outsiders as damned, degenerate, and suitable for killing. When average, non-fanatic citizens devalue others they rarely murder them as a consequence, but they may well acquiesce in a political order that does.

Upon reflection you can probably identify your own focus of projection, your "not-me": Republicans, Democrats, rich, poor, black, white, Christian, Jew, Muslim, Northerner, Southerner, dove, hawk, old, young, men, women. Projection is so much a part of our thinking we seldom notice it, except when someone else does it. Again, I heard a radio talk show provide a fine example when a caller made the following comment about a political candidate: "I wouldn't vote for him; he's a Southerner. They're all prejudiced."

ONE OF the symptoms of projection is an attitude of righteousness coloring persons' statements of their beliefs and views of others. As we have seen, through projection we reassure ourselves that we are good (as in the child's world) by pointing out that someone else is bad. The covert "I am good" is signalled by self-righteousness, which requires the devaluation of someone else.

Self-righteousness is the dominant attitude of cult members, although it may be masked by false humility and public confessions of unworthiness. Righteousness has a special vocabulary that establishes two species of human beings. Jerry Falwell put it clearly: "The war is not between fundamentalists and liberals but between those who love Jesus Christ and those who hate him."'

Of course, the vocabulary of righteousness is seldom as stark outside of the religious or political arenas, but may include such terms as "unscientific," "neurotic," and "infantile," as opposed to "mature," "realistic," and "rigorous." Being thus negatively labeled amounts to rejection. Understandably, we are usually very sensitive to our own group's criteria for inclusion or casting-out.

Righteousness protects against self-doubt and at the same time provides a rationale for actions that would otherwise place us in the bad category. By intensifying righteousness a person can retain the feeling of being good while performing shameful acts; cruelty is justified, may even become a duty. The breaking of Clara's ties with her child, the splitting of couples, and the alienation of Hugh from his dying brother were all supposedly done for the highest spiritual reasons, as sacrifices for the high purposes of the group.

The following example of righteousness running amok is from a speech by the late Ayatollah Khomeini, who established a theocracy in Iran:

"If one permits an infidel to continue in his role as a corrupter of the earth, his moral suffering will be all the worse. If one kills the infidel, and thus stops him from perpetrating his misdeeds, his death will be a blessing to him. For if he remains alive, he will become more and more corrupt. This is a surgical operation commanded by God the all-powerful.

"...Those who have knowledge of the suffering in the life to come realize that cutting off the hand of someone for a crime he has committed is of benefit to him. In the Beyond he will thank those who, on earth, executed the will of God."

There is no cruelty like the cruelty of the righteous. Righteousness can be seen in many one would assume were not susceptible to cult thinking, scientists, for example. Proponents of theories which challenge accepted views are sometimes vilified with a zeal that combines righteousness and arrogance. One example from the history of medicine is that of the nineteenth-century Hungarian physician, I. P. Semmelweis. Semmelweis came to the conclusion that the high incidence of puerperal fever (which killed many in childbirth) among women who delivered their babies in hospitals was due to contamination by attending physicians who, at that time, routinely went from the autopsy room to the delivery room without cleansing their hands. His theory and his recommendation that physicians wash was received with such ridicule and followed by such professional persecution that he eventually went mad.

A more current example of the effects of scientific righteous-ness and the arrogance it fosters is provided by the development of the atomic bomb. Although the research was initially justified by the fear that the Nazis would attain the bomb first, the work did not stop when that concern was eliminated by the Allied in-vasion of Europe. Only one scientist left the enterprise; the rest continued what they had begun. Recently we have begun to re-cognize the responsibility borne by scientists for the nuclear threat that now hangs over the world. Following a reunion at Los Alamos of many who had worked on the atomic bomb, Isador Rabi, the Nobel prize-winning physicist, was asked if he thought it likely that there would ever again be such a collection of scientists working with the same dedication and idealism. "Rabi's response was unhesitating. 'I hope not,' he said. 'We had no doubts about what we were doing.'"

RELIGIONS are particularly prone to devaluing outsiders because to accord outsiders equal status is to give respectability to their different versions of God and lessen the certainty of faith. Doubt may arise.

Even if the outsider is not specifically devalued, scorned, or hated, theistic religions tend to reward followers with special status; the Jews are the chosen, good Christians are saved from hell, true Muslims go to paradise. The non-believer, in many instances, is a damned infidel. Within religions different sects or denomina-tions vary in the absoluteness of this judgment, but the basic attitude is often the same — else why profess that faith over some other? *Because my faith is true!* a devout believer may exclaim.

But it is not the search for truth which leads a person to mas-sacre or torture, to ostracize and expel, to scorn and to hate; nor is it a search for bliss or other, spiritual, states. In subtle or not so sub-tle ways, most religions utilize devaluation despite their best inten-tions. If you think not, listen closely to the next sermon you hear.

The consequences for the outsider can be significant indeed.

Because religions deal in absolutes, the devaluation of the outsider can be absolute also, justifying behavior toward the innocent and helpless which the religion's founder would have condemned and which by any humane standard is barbaric. The Crusades were often a license for the murder, rape, and devastation of "infidel" peoples, those with different religious beliefs. Within Christianity, the religious passions of Catholics and Protestants fueled the Thirty Years' War which almost totally destroyed Germany in the seventeenth century. More recently, Hindus and Moslems created the nightmare of fighting in Bangladesh, featuring indiscriminate slaughter and numerous examples of gang rape all under the banner of their respective religions.

Less violent forms of devaluation are almost universal. Members of most religions can be hostile, or at best uneasy, at the prospect of their children marrying outside the faith, even outside the particular sect to which they belong. When a son or daughter of Orthodox Jewish parents marries a non-Jew the parents sometimes conduct services for the dead, psychologically burying their errant child. Until 1984, a non-Catholic who married a Catholic had to sign a promise to raise their children as Catholics if the couple were to be married by a priest.

This exclusivity is not hard to understand. All groups exist by virtue of membership boundaries; the more lax those boundaries the weaker is group cohesion and group strength. As a consequence, group boundaries are defended vigorously. Since intermarriage poses the greatest danger to religious boundaries, it is punished in overt or subtle ways; natural family ties may be subordinated to the larger religious group. As in extreme cults, family bonds may be seen as secondary to preserving the exclusiveness of the religion, the superior status of the followers and the inferior status of those outside.

Fundamentalist religions, in particular, tend to devalue the outsider to preserve the certainty of their scriptures and their leader's connection with God. In recent years, a conservative American Christian fundamentalism has experienced a resurgence and now claims many millions of members. (Since many of these fundamentalists are also members of mainline churches, it is hard to know exactly how large the group is, but informed estimates suggest they number well over twenty million.) Over recent years this movement has established powerful radio and television broadcasting networks, made extensive use of direct mail for fundraising and recruitment, and sponsored a vast increase in fundamentalist parochial schools where authoritarian, separatist, and sectarian views are taught. Many teach that only "true" Christians — those "born again" — will be saved; the rest will go to hell. The Jim Bakker and Jimmy Swaggart scandals did not appreciably change the popularity of these religious movements.

An assortment of devils came to dominate the consciousness of Alex Monroe and the Life Force group. Satan and evil spirits dominate the world of many fundamentalist religious sects, whether Christian, Islamic or of any other denomination.

EVEN in psychiatry, the readiness to classify as alien those who do not belong to one's group may result in a devaluation similar in kind to that which what takes place in cults. This is not usually identified as cult behavior because there is no specific cult of psychiatry nor, with few exceptions, are there hospital cult leaders. Nevertheless, the use of projection may occur and the result is a distortion of reality and adverse effects on the "outsider."

To identify with a person who is crying because his or her spouse has left is not difficult for a psychiatrist. To identify with one who is screaming, smearing feces, psychotically suicidal, assaultive, or self-mutilating is quite another matter. Although the impulses represented by extreme, psychotic behaviors are present to some degree in every person, including the psychiatrist, they constitute precisely those impulses most strenuously suppressed and rigidly controlled. The deepest infantile wishes are represented in the overt and seemingly guilt-free regression of psychotic patients, who abandon the status of the adult for the humiliation and gratifications of the infant. Such passive, infantile wishes are more taboo in our culture than neurotic sexual behavior. I believe the difference in treatment usually given people exhibiting psychotic symptoms versus the treatment provided for those whose symptoms are closer to the therapist's cannot be understood only as the result of a belief in biochemical causation of psychosis. Rather, I think we need to recognize a therapist's unconscious wish to see as alien the person whose behavior represents the bad qualities that threaten rejection in one's own group.

I believe this separation and devaluation lies behind the striking difference one can observe between the way psychiatric treatment is conducted in outpatient departments and the way treatment is provided to inpatients, even in university-affiliated hospitals. Inpatients receive drug therapy with neuroleptic drugs such as Thorazine or Haldol, plus a smattering of psychological treatment under the euphemism of supportive therapy. If psychiatric residents are being trained on the ward, patients may also have individual psychotherapy, but neither patient nor novice therapist expect it to be effective (and under these conditions psychotherapy seldom is). In contrast, most outpatients receive analytically oriented psychotherapy, psychological treatment based on psychodynamic principles, unless the outpatient is a transfer from the hospital; in that case, therapy is often focused on medication, dealing with drug side effects, and managing the living situation. (Such patients are often seen for less than the fifty-minute hour usual for outpatient therapy.)

The division of patients into two classes, the psychotherapy-outpatient group and the medication-inpatient group, seldom receives critical comment, nor does the fact that inpatient procedures frequently violate the psychodynamic principles assumed to be operative for outpatients. For example, at one medical school where I taught, nursing students were assigned young, first-time schizophrenic patients with whom they were expected to establish rapport and a therapeutic relationship. After six weeks the nursing students left for other duties; psychiatric residents stayed for six months, then they too left. These practices were standard despite the knowledge that the loss of a parent, spouse, or lover was often the precipitating event for the psychosis from which the patient was suffering. The departures of the nursing students and the residents could only intensify feelings of loss. One had to conclude that psychodynamic considerations received short shrift on the hospital ward.

Another indicator of the separate status of inpatients at this hospital was that although medication was supposed to be individually prescribed, almost everyone admitted to the unit with a diagnosis of schizophrenia arrived from the emergency room heavily dosed with neuroleptic drugs, and on the ward, the neuroleptics were continued. As a result, no drug-free period of observation and treatment planning occurred. If behavior did not improve, the drug dosage was increased.

When we studied the exact sequence of events that preceded a decision by ward staff to increase a patient's medication, we found that in almost every case the patient had shifted from inactivity, depression, or apathy to being noisy, "crazy," threatening, or messy. The possibility that this shift might signify progress in the patient, a beginning attempt to communicate feelings, was not considered. Where exploration, uncovering, and communication were highly valued in outpatient services, in the inpatient world management and suppression of behavior had priority.

The dividing line between neurotic (outpatient) and psychotic (inpatient) problems is not completely clear; it appears to be only if one compares the most healthy neurotic patients and the most psychotic. So many people suffer from intermediate conditions that the diagnosis of "borderline" has had to be employed as a bridging category. Even the diagnosis of schizophrenia encompasses such a wide variety of conditions that numerous subtypes are employed and the diagnostic criteria are non-specific and constantly revised. If one grants that both psychological and biochemical factors influence human behavior, the sharp split in psychiatric practice cannot be defended on rational grounds.

The split occurs, I believe, partly because the seriously disturbed patient is devalued as an outsider by the psychiatrist. This became clear when a colleague and I changed a drug-oriented psychiatric ward into an intensive psychological treatment unit, one that focused on the relation between early life experience and the patient's behavior on the ward." Drugs were not used unless psychological treatment proved ineffective. As a result of this change in orientation, staff paid much more attention to the ward dynamics and the role of both patients and staff in intensifying or diminishing psychotic behavior. There was much to learn.

One day "Jerry," a weird-looking adolescent sitting crouched in a wheelchair and diagnosed as paranoid and retarded, was admitted (by mistake) to our ward instead of being shipped off to the state hospital for what I would call warehousing. Jerry seemed like an idiot, would occasionally drool, liked to wheel rapidly around the ward with a crazy look on his face, and replied to questions and orders only in the most halting manner. The nurses were afraid of him, but we had to keep him for a few days until a transfer could be arranged. During this time one of the nurses remarked that she didn't think Jerry was as retarded as he seemed; she thought he knew what he was doing. So we confronted him, saying, "Jerry, what's this big act you've got, trying to scare everyone? You're not that crazy, you're not that dumb."

A big smile spread slowly over his face and the crazy look went away. We never did send him to the state hospital. He wasn't an idiot. He was paranoid, but not severely, and much of his behavior related to family dynamics which then became the focus of treatment. Jerry was more like us than different, doing what he thought necessary to meet his needs and protect himself. He had made use of people's readiness to see him as alien, to devalue him, in order to gain power for himself, the power of frightening others and of being able to hide.

Juanita, a very depressed Mexican-Indian woman in late middle age who had almost no formal education and spoke very little English showed us how outsider status can be conveyed by cultural differences as well as by psychiatric symptoms. Juanita gave all the appearance of a backward peasant who could not comprehend much of what was going on around her. We gave her a suitable therapeutic task for someone as limited as she seemed to be — cleaning tables. Before long, Juanita was causing considerable turmoil on the ward, covertly expressing her anger at the staff and other patients. We were forced to recognize that underneath, Juanita was a strategic planner like the rest of us. When we were able to see who Juanita was, we took her off the cleaning job and treated her as a conscious, equal member of the patient group. Her depression decreased and the disturbance on the ward disappeared.

MEDIA owners, editors, and reporters, like other people, are motivated by ideals, not just money or power. Most believe (some passionately) that reporting the society's imperfections and providing the public with a diversity of views and information is their special function and responsibility, that which gives meaning to their work. (I am speaking here of societies which value a free press.) The problem is that discharging that responsibility may conflict with support for the status quo. One way in which this dilemma can be solved is by being careful to report that dissent exists while devaluing it at the same time. This can be done covertly, even unconsciously, by means of the selected image.

Most newsmagazines and newspapers maintain a file of photos of prominent people and it is easy to select one in which a politician or other celebrity looks ridiculous, sinister, or ugly. Additionally, the photo can be juxtaposed with one that flatters whomever the editor wishes to promote. If you look for this device you will see it used frequently, especially at election time. Technically, it is fair, all sides are receiving publicity.

The selected image is used most powerfully by television, which presents, after all, a series of discrete scenes while attempting to convey a reality much larger than what can be framed. What the commentator or editor selects tells a part of the story, not the whole story. The power of the selected image resides in the fact that we respond to news photos and television as if they are showing us objective facts devoid of interpretation. The image seems to validate itself. Sociologist Todd Gitlin experienced this aspect of the media as a leader of Students for a Democratic Society (SDS). Later, he analyzed the media's use of the image and found that "news photos operate under a hidden sign marked, 'this really happened, see for yourself.' Of course, the choice of this moment of an event as against that, of this person rather than that, of this angle rather than any other, indeed, the selection of this photographed incident to represent a whole complex chain of events and meanings, is a highly ideological procedure. But, by appearing literally to reproduce the event as it really happened, news photos suppress their selective / interpretive / ideological function. They seek a warrant in that ever pre-given, neutral structure, which is beyond question, beyond interpretation: the 'real world.'"

Television makes optimum use of this see-for-yourself power. Consequently, in many parts of the world, the nightly news shows probably shape people's perception of events more vividly and more effectively than any other source of information. Considering this power, it is worth noting that what appears on the ABC, CBS, and NBC nightly newscasts is a selection and interpretation largely created by six people, the executive producers and anchor-persons of each of the three networks.

Words also can be used very effectively to devalue opposition. I remember how the media in the early sixties characterized the members of SANE (myself being one of them) who opposed the atmospheric testing of nuclear weapons. While dutifully reporting our campaign, the media tended to dismiss us as having no significance; one columnist called us "small dogs barking at an express train." Being consigned to ineffective canine status was a frustrating and depressing experience. The media preferred the image of President Kennedy, who dramatically drank a glass of milk at a convention of dairy farmers to express his disdain for charges by SANE that nuclear testing was contaminating milk products with strontium 90. Fortunately, the media were wrong. After Kennedy eventually signed a treaty banning atmospheric testing, SANE acquired respect.

The same devaluing, followed eventually by acceptance, has taken place with regard to anti-nuclear power activists. The accidents at Three Mile Island and, later, Chernobyl resulted in the anti-nuclear movement being legitimized; groups that had been ridiculed now receive more serious treatment than in the past. However, those who challenge nuclear weapons development by committing civil disobedience at Lawrence Livermore Laboratories or at submarine bases and missile sites are still labeled radical. Their arrest by police is reported, but their critique of weapons policy rarely is.

Reality may be distorted simply by screening out dissenting views without the outright censorship seen in totalitarian countries; reality may be distorted by giving great prominence and validity to the established view while devaluing dissenters and making them marginal. Gay rights activists, anti-nuclear groups, and others outside the establishment evoke clear contemporary examples of devaluation. The treatment of student dissidents in the mainstream media during the 1960s offers good examples of the use of negative adjectives and selective photos combined with the ignoring or minimizing of the issues raised. As Gitlin pointed out with regard to American politics of the sixties, an official typically was given the voice of calm rationality; dissidents were often portrayed as unreasonable, naive, impulsive, ridiculous, violent and extreme. Some may have been, to be sure, but those who were not were seldom given a forum:

"Most of the time the taken-for-granted code of 'objectivity' and 'balance' presses reporters to seek out scruffy-looking, chanting,

'Viet Cong' flag-waving demonstrators and to counterpose them to reasonable-sounding, fact-brandishing authorities... Hotheads carry on, the message connotes, while wiser heads, officials and reporters both, with superb self-control, watch the unenlightened ones make trouble."

Writing about the same era, Daniel Hallin found a similar devaluation in the media, in which protest was equated with violence, authority with competence and order.

"Cronkite began one report on college antiwar protests by saying, 'The Cambodia development set off a new round of anti-war demonstrations on U.S. campuses, and not all of them were peaceful.' The film report, not surprisingly, was about one that was not peaceful, and dealt mainly with the professionalism shown by the authorities who restored order."

In contrast, when the protest occurs in a communist country, American news media are likely to handle it differently. During the June 1989 demonstrations in Tiananmen Square, in China's capital, the students were presented in a sympathetic light; their point of view and statements by their representatives were carried by all the American media.

Of course, devaluation also takes place in the American media's coverage of international affairs. Consider the view of the Soviet Union that was maintained by our mainstream media until very recently. Princeton University professor Stephen Cohen describes "a pattern of media coverage that systematically highlights the negative aspects of the Soviet domestic system while obscuring the positive ones. Soviet crop failures and abuses of political liberties have been the regular focus of American news stories since the early 1970s, but expanded welfare programs and the rising living standard have gone largely unreported...

"Much American commentary on Soviet affairs employs special political terms that are inherently biased and laden with double standards... The United States has a government, security organizations and allies. The Soviet Union, however, has a regime, secret police and satellites. Our leaders are consummate politicians; theirs are wily, cunning or worse. We give the world information and seek influence; they disseminate propaganda and disinformation while seeking expansion and domination.

Following Gorbachev's announcement of the policy of glasnost and his visit to the United States, a marked change has taken place in media coverage of the Soviet Union. For the first time that I can remember, television has shown me Russians in surroundings much like mine, enjoying themselves, voicing concerns for country, children, peace — Russians like us. According to my TV set, Russia has undergone a chromatic revolution, as well. Where before it had been grey, now it is in color. The weather has also changed. Sunshine has occurred in Russian cities for the first time in 40 years."

There is an implicit devaluation of others in nationalism. I consider myself to be internationally minded, free of jingoism. However, not long ago, curious to hear what other countries were saying about world events, I bought a shortwave radio. As I dialed from one foreign station to another, I was surprised to find that the United States was not the center of the world. In Brazil, South American affairs and not those of the United States were being discussed; in England, the focus was local politics and reactions to a proposed tunnel to France. The effect was a little eerie; my own country seemed to have disappeared. I knew that nationalism was a pervasive phenomenon, but my own parochialism — revealed by my surprise — had been unrecognized.

DEVALUATION of other nations seen as enemies is a pervasive problem for governments. An example from the era of the cold war of our own negative stereotyping is the general surprise and consternation that occurred when the USSR launched Sputnik, the first satellite. Soviets, who were regarded as backward, primitive totalitarians, weren't supposed to be able to do this. Truman is said to have expressed his own surprise that "those Asiatics" could do something like that. Similar surprise greeted the first test of a hydrogen bomb by the USSR.

Misperception of the enemy (basically a devaluing of the foreigner), seeing its people as less advanced, less principled, less admirable, and more deserving of punishment and harsh treatment than ourselves, has affected international relations throughout history, contributing to conflict and to spirals of increased armaments. The arms race is not a new phenomenon and the view that the enemy must be "dealt with firmly" has had adherents. Political scientist Robert Jervis, in discussing the way misper-ception takes place in international relations, cites two statesmen of the nineteenth century, whose devaluing statements mirror each other:

"[James Polk:]... if Congress faultered [sic] or hesitated in their course, John Bull would immediately become arrogant and more grasping in his demands; & that such had been the history of the Brittish [sic] Nation in all their contests with other Powers for the last two hundred years.

"[Lord Palmerston:] A quarrel with the United States is... undesirable... [but] in dealing with Vulgar minded Bullies, and such unfortunately the people of the United States are, nothing is gained by submission to Insult & wrong; on the contrary the submission to an Outrage only encourages the commission of another and a greater one — such people are always trying how far they can venture to go; and they generally pull up when they find they can go no further without encountering resistance of a formidable Character."

Polk was ready to see Britain as responding only to "firmness," meaning force, while Palmerston had the same view of the United States. Each was the outsider to the other and, accordingly, was devalued to maintain the righteousness and purity of the home nation's position, as in the following (one of countless modern examples of reciprocal devaluation):

"[John Foster Dulles:] Khrushchev does not need to be convinced of our good intentions. He knows we are not aggressors and do not threaten the security of the Soviet Union."

"[Khrushchev:] It is quite well known that if one tries to appease a bandit by first giving him one's purse, then one's coat, and so forth, he is not going to be more charitable because of this, he is not going to stop exercising his banditry. On the contrary, he will become ever more insolent."

The righteous indignation of contemporary leaders echoes statesmen throughout history who have believed that the armaments of others demonstrate aggressive intentions but did not apply that reasoning to arms build-ups of their own. Estimation of the significance of another country's military budget is especially vulnerable to this error. Intra-service rivalries and parochial political maneuvering are at least as important in promoting the current arms race as any grand, organized strategy, but neither the USSR nor the United States appear to give these factors much weight in evaluating the armaments decisions of the other side, certainly not as far as public pronouncements are concerned. The psychological problem is that recognizing these internal concerns would soften the distinction between good and evil governments and suggest areas of uncomfortable similarity.

Devaluation of the enemy played a role in the Bay of Pigs disaster. Journalist Peter H. Wyden believes it was a pivotal factor.

"The final arrogance, the failure to inform themselves about Castro's strength and his people's spirit or even to inform their own infiltration teams, I attribute to the gook syndrome. American policy makers suffer from it chronically. They tend to underestimate grossly the capabilities and determination of people who committed the sin of not having been born Americans, especially "gooks" whose skins are less than white."

The same devaluation, leading to far more tragic blunders, took place later in Southeast Asia. Shad Meshad, who had been a psychology officer in Vietnam, recalls his attitude:

"I was from the southeastern part of the United States, and spent my entire life there... I knew nothing about Asians. The only thing I did know about them were the names we gave them, both four-letter words, gook and dink. And our attitude was that the only good dink is a dead dink. This was my introduction to the culture of Asia."

Devaluing the outsider is made manifest in righteousness, in blindness to the implications of one's own behavior, in the refusal to acknowledge similar intentions on both sides, in the identification of the other as bad in contrast to oneself as good. All these are hallmarks of cult behavior. While examples of this abound on both sides of the iron curtain, Ronald Reagan provided a prime specimen in his "evil empire" speech.

"Let us be aware that while they [the Soviet Union] preach the supremacy of the state, declare its omnipotence over individual man, and predict its eventual domination of all peoples on the Earth — they are the focus of evil in the modern world... I urge you to beware the temptation of pride — the temptation of blithely declaring yourselves above it all and label both sides equally at fault, to ignore the facts of history and the aggressive impulses of an evil empire, to simply call the arms race a giant misunderstanding and thereby remove yourself from the struggle between right and wrong and good and evil."

Certainly when one considers Stalin's starvation of the kulaks, the monstrous gulag prison system, or the barbarities the Soviets have committed in Afghanistan, there is justification for the use of the term *evil*. Reagan's speech, however, showed no awareness of moral lapses of our own which, although markedly different in degree, are not so totally different in kind as to justify the self-righteousness of his pronouncement.

Unwillingness to acknowledge one's own evil is characteristic of all government leaders. It is precisely that need for purity of self-image, for displacement of all badness onto the enemy, that is "the temptation of pride" of which Reagan spoke, but did not apply to himself. In that same speech, in complete innocence of the image's applicability to himself, he cited C. S. Lewis:

"The greatest evil is not done now in those sordid 'dens of crime' that Dickens loved to paint. It is not even done in concentration camps and labor camps. In those we see its final result. But it is conceived and ordered (moved, seconded, carried, and minuted) in clean, carpeted, warmed, and well-lighted offices, by quiet men with white collars and cut fingernails and smooth-shaven cheeks who do not need to raise their voice."

IN EVERY person's life, given a psychologically threatening situation, devaluation can extend to friends with the consequence that slights and insults may be perceived when none are intended. I remember hearing Abraham Maslow, the psychologist who helped create humanistic psychology, as he reminisced about his life and spoke of his sense that his own death was near. Shortly before, he had made a pilgrimage across the United States to visit all the people with whom he had once been friends but had fallen out. He wanted to understand what had happened. What he learned was sad, ironic, and hopeful at the same time. In each case he and the friend had an interaction whose meaning was ambiguous; Maslow might have ignored an invitation or the other person might have behaved coldly toward him. Of all the possible explanations that he or his friend considered at the time — he's worried about his job, he forgot, he is ill, he's angry at me, he dislikes me — each placed at the top of the list the explanation that was least flattering to himself. And in every case they were wrong.

I call this the Maslow principle and frequently tell the story to my patients, since the problem comes up so often. Even in daily life, it is often hard to realize that the other person is just like us, to see him or her at eye level. Almost everyone tends to give a negative interpretation to another person's behavior in ambiguous situations. When we do this, it seems logical; when someone else does it, we find it paranoid and hard to believe.

Governments, composed of people, behave no differently. As Jervis points out, they usually view the actions of other governments

as deliberate and give scant consideration to the possibility that confusion, chaos, accidents, and coincidence may be responsible; that
the consequences of the other's actions may have been unintended.

Everyday paranoia can extend to the business world, where
the battle is economic; cultural differences may be ignored in favor
of explanations assuming craftiness or conspiracy. For example,
discussions over the joint production of the Concorde almost broke
down and aborted the project when the French preference for
Cartesian precision ran up against British preference for cautious
empiricism.

One British aircraft executive involved [in conversations with
the French over the Concorde] was reported as having complained
that: "The French always think we're being Machiavellian, when in
fact we're just muddling through."

RECENTLY we have had a devastating illustration of the price of
devaluing the outsider — the failure of our society to respond
adequately to the AIDS epidemic. Randy Shilts, in his book *And
The Band Played On*, chronicled the lost opportunities to control
the disease, the needless deaths of thousands of people, and the
even greater losses to come in future years as a consequence of
this neglect.

"The reason for our failure is clear. From early on, when its effects first appeared as a high incidence of Kaposi's sarcoma, AIDS
was regarded as a disease of homosexuals. To many in mainstream
American society, homosexuals are outsiders, ridiculed, feared and
often despised as alien. Because it was homosexuals who were dying,
few people outside that group cared. Extreme fundamentalists
regarded AIDS as God's punishment, and others felt it served
'them' right.

"In contrast, Legionnaires' disease had evoked an instant, fully
mobilized response by health agencies, the government, and the
media, even though it was a less deadly, less horrible killer than
AIDS. In the first twelve months of the AIDS epidemic, the Center

for Disease Control had spent $1 million compared to $9 million spent on Legionnaires' disease.

"Newspapers paid little notice to the growing AIDS disaster until intravenous drug users were afflicted. Drug addicts, too, are outcasts, but they are heterosexual. The first coverage of the epidemic by the Wall Street Journal came in 1982 under the headline, 'New, Often-Fatal Illness in Homosexuals Turns Up in Women, Heterosexual Males.'"

Shilts's chronology of the disease is a chilling portrayal of the effects that devaluing the outsider can have upon the outcast group and, eventually, upon those who cast them out as well. After four years, AIDS cases in the United States totaled 9,000 and of these 4,300 people had died. No massive response by the government or the media had yet taken place.

To appreciate the magnitude of these figures it should be recalled that Legionnaires' disease had claimed 29 lives, the poisoned Tylenol capsules had caused 7 deaths. Both of these crises elicited mobilization of all the resources the nation could muster and front-page, extensive coverage by the news media.

Not until the middle of the 1980s, when it became clear that AIDS could strike anyone, did the media give AIDS the full treatment and the government follow suit. Unfortunately, by then there were 12,000 cases, 6,000 people had died, and a virus whose latency can run eight years or more was lodged in tens of thousands who would yet fall ill.

Shilts describes how in Washington, Arthur Bennet, an AIDS sufferer, stood in the rain with other protesters and gestured toward the White House, saying, "I think in the beginning of this whole syndrome, that they, over there, and a lot of other people said, 'Let the faggots die. They're expendable.' I wonder if it would have been 1,500 Boy Scouts, what would have been done."

SIX

Avoiding Dissent

ALTHOUGH we all need dissent as a corrective, cults tend to punish it, to inhibit and stifle disagreement and criticism, and to restrict access to information that would challenge group beliefs.

Cults employ a variety of means to exclude dissent. Mail may be monitored or withheld, only certain literature allowed, and discordant views may be labeled bad or satanic. In addition, members' attention is confined to a narrow field; if free time is spent studying and reciting dogma there is less danger that subversive information will be encountered or, if it is, that it will be thought about and its implications understood. Dogma itself may be simplified into slogans, rendering members' thinking even more primitive and further hampering critical thought. These means are enhanced by the punishments meted out for challenging authority.

Such coercive forces create conflicts. The cult member wishes to continue riding in the back seat of the car, but at the same time his or her self-respect is threatened by compliance with censorship and subjection to rewards and punishments. So the inhibition of dissent may be pushed out of awareness, become unconscious. Conscious and unconscious suppression and restriction of dissent is perhaps the most characteristic feature of cult life; the more severe the restriction, the more control exercised by the group and the leader.

Cults further restrict dissent through decreased contact with non-members. Outsiders are likely to raise critical questions about the leader and the group's activities, thus weakening the group fantasy. In addition, as discussed earlier, outsiders are a threat because they may be sources of support, self-esteem, and comfort, offsetting the need for the group. Research suggests that the fewer social ties a cult convert had before joining, the more likely it was that he or she would remain in the organization. When Hugh and Clara Robinson finally made their escape from Life Force, their contact with outsiders was crucial.

AVOIDANCE of dissent is a prominent feature of normal society. We assume that in the United States our free press (including radio and television) voices all the dissent we would need. There is no government censorship; the First Amendment shields the media from interference. However, although America's mainstream media pride themselves on being independent, balanced, objective, in practice those characteristics are more limited than most, including media personnel, realize. Dissent is exercised within certain unspoken boundaries; beyond those limits it is avoided, downplayed, or ignored. Because the mass media are the major source of many kinds of information for the public at large, media behavior has far-reaching effects. The media can create by what it presents.

Ben Bagdikian, dean of the Graduate School of Journalism at the University of California, Berkeley (and former reporter, journalist, and *Washington Post* editor), comments on two key findings of his research on the mass media:

"What the public learns is heavily weighted by what serves the economic and political interests of the corporations that own the media.... The naïveté of working journalists about the influence of owners on the news they publish is more widespread than even my thirty years as a reporter and editor had led me to believe."

Although our media enjoy great freedom, they are in a dependent relationship to three types of authority: the corporate world that owns them, the advertisers that provide their revenues, and the government figures upon whom they rely for information. These dependency relationships involve both conscious and unconscious pressures that result in an inhibition of dissent not usually noticed by the public or by reporters and journalists themselves.

WITHIN the corporate world, the more authoritarian the leadership structure, the less dissent is appreciated, and the more emphasis is given to loyalty to prevailing corporate views. Former General Motors executive John De Lorean describes how this loyalty was manifested:

"If your appearance, style and personality were consistent with the corporate stereotype, you were well on your way to being a "loyal" employee. But loyalty demanded more. It often demanded personal fealty, actual subservience to the boss.... Lower executives, eager to please the boss and rise up the corporate ladder, worked hard to learn what he wanted or how he thought on a particular subject. They then either fed the boss exactly what he wanted to know, or they modified their own proposals to suit his preferences."

The devaluation and suppression of dissent can lead to financially disastrous corporate decisions or to violations of moral principles. The history of the Corvair is a case in point. As originally designed, the car had a tendency to flip over when making turns at high speed. According to John De Lorean, the problem was well known to the GM engineers, a number of whom fought to modify the car's suspension or keep it out of production. They were overruled by the general manager and finally told to stop objecting and "get on the team." The Corvair was produced and sold. De Lorean commented, "I don't think any one car before or since produced as gruesome a record on the highway as the Corvair."

The costliest failure in the history of magazine publishing occurred when top executives of Time, Inc. pushed ahead with a project to publish a weekly broadcast and cable television listings magazine, TV-Cable Week, without market testing recommended by their own researchers and without first solving major problems which other subordinates had brought to management's attention. A former member of the editorial management team described how adverse facts were shunted aside and deleted from the final presentation to the Board of Directors: "Sutton listened earnestly as Grum continued with his advice: keep the presentation simple, emphasize the upside, and above all do not dwell on the complexities and uncertainties — the very risks that the task force had highlighted in the January presentation."

Time, Inc. proceeded to lose $45 million on a magazine that ran for only six months. Not only did the board members uncritically accept the optimistic presentation, so did a Wall Street brokerage firm.

Munro and his associates were preaching to an audience that was eager to believe. One of the analysts at the gathering, Alan Gottesman, summed up his reaction to the presentation this way: "Hell, if you hear the company's top men say they've got some new breakthrough computer system to publish the magazine, you're going to believe them, right?"

Wanting to believe is perhaps the most powerful dynamic initiating and sustaining cult-like behavior. Hugh and Clara Robinson accepted Alex Monroe's rationalizations for behavior that they would otherwise have labeled immoral, selfish, or cruel. Along with fear, the need to believe caused them to rationalize their own behavior and continue in Life Force long after the evidence of degeneration was in plain view to the outsider. A similar process seems responsible for the Corvair and TV-Cable Week fiascos. Dissenting voices that could have brought more reality to the decision-making process were ignored or suppressed. Wanting to believe affects everyone, leaders and followers alike.

THE avoidance of dissent is almost automatic where unequal power exists and the leader makes it clear that being contradicted is displeasing, even dangerous. Dissent can only be utilized if the leader and the group value it, understand its necessity and demonstrate that dissent is welcome. In the corporate world, dissent is suppressed the more a CEO is unwilling to occupy an eye-level world with his subordinates and insists on their gazing upward at him.

The leader is not the only inhibiting force, the group as a whole can make its displeasure known if dissent focuses on areas of group vulnerability such as immoral corporate behavior, over-optimism, leadership mistakes, and paranoia. Even if a corporate CEO welcomes dissent, lower level executives may stifle contrary opinion so that it never reaches him or her. Something like this appears to have been responsible for the Challenger shuttle disaster. As described by Henry Cooper, Jr. in The New Yorker, Thiokol engineers voiced their concerns about the safety of the O-ring seal and believed the launch should be canceled, particularly as the air temperature at the launch site was lower than for any previous test measurements. Overruled by company officials, their objections were not passed on to those with final authority for the launch.

Lower-level censorship is particularly likely when leadership wants condensed, simplified reports and summaries on which to base decisions. Unpleasant facts and possibilities are easier to prune and may be given shorter shrift than optimistic, forward-looking statements.

Avoidance of dissent is often confused with loyalty. Author-itarian leaders tend to regard loyalty as the foremost virtue of sub-ordinates. Peter Wyden described how at the final meeting before the invasion of Cuba, Rusk, Nitze, and Bundy all set aside doubts and questions in order to "close ranks with the President" and vote in favor of the invasion.

Only a lively appreciation of dissent's vital function at all levels of society can preserve it as a corrective to wishful thinking, self-inflation and unperceived rigidity.

IN MY view, the most prevalent current treatment of psychosis (in addition to reflecting devaluation of the outsider) demonstrates psychiatry's avoidance of dissenting views, its compliance with group pressures to maintain a particular belief system.

The current swing to a biological view of emotional illness has been described by Walter Reich, former research psychiatrist at the National Institutes of Mental Health, as "Psychiatry's Second Coming." (The first was the oversell of the psychodynamic psychoanalytic approach.) The number of papers of a biological nature published in the American Journal of Psychiatry in 1980 was almost double that of ten years earlier. An even more noticeable shift has taken place in the Archives of General Psychiatry, which is now devoted almost exclusively to biochemical and genetic research. Furthermore, government support for drug research is heavily weighted toward research in genetics, biochemical causation of psychopathology, and drug therapy, while psychotherapeutic investigations receive relatively little funding.

Part of psychiatry's current ideology is that a person diagnosed as a schizophrenic is doomed to life-long social and work disability and recurrence of psychotic episodes unless treated with "antipsychotic" drugs. This belief persists despite studies that indicate otherwise. Loren Mosher reviewed four long-term follow-up studies of patients treated before the use of neuroleptic drugs and found that they " ... give us reason to be much more optimistic than we have been about outcome in schizophrenia. These 20-plus-year follow-up studies... yielded remarkably consistent results; 60%-85% of schizophrenic patients, depending on the criteria used, had achieved good social recovery."

How could there be such good outcomes without the use of drugs? These studies challenge pessimistic beliefs concerning the prognosis of schizophrenia and call into question the necessity and desirability of drug treatment. The most prominent belief of the current biological psychiatry movement is that drugs are the treatment of choice for psychosis. This belief ignores the study by Bockhoven and Solomon comparing the five-year follow-up data of two groups of hospital patients, the first receiving psychological treatment (1947 to 1952, prior to the use of major tranquilizers) and the second group receiving drugs (1967 to 1972). No difference in outcome was found.

"This finding suggests that the attitudes of personnel toward patients, the socio-environmental setting, and community helpfulness guided by citizen organizations may be more important in tipping the balance in favor of social recovery than are psychotropic drugs."

These results were anticipated by Bockhoven's study of the results of "moral treatment," a humane, psychologically oriented hospital treatment program for the insane that flourished in the mid-19th century. Comparison of treatment results with present-day statistics suggests that moral treatment probably did as well or better than what is accomplished today with modern drug therapy.

Keeping these findings in mind it becomes apparent that psychiatry as a whole has avoided dealing with facts and opinions that challenge its ideology. Writing in the Schizophrenia Bulletin, John Kane cautions:

"Given the potential adverse effects that can be produced by antipsychotic drugs, it is critical that attention be given to the overall benefit to risk ratio when these agents are used. Although antipsychotic drugs may symptomatically improve a variety of conditions, they should not be used when equally effective and safer treatments are available."

As the Bockhoven and Solomon research indicates, equally effective and safer treatments appear to be available for many patients. This is also suggested by other findings, some of which I have mentioned, but these data, discordant with the dominant ideology, fall on deaf ears.

When one considers the widespread reluctance of patients to take these drugs because of their distressing effects, the potential worsening of their condition, the disfigurement that may result and the equally good long-term outcome results of psychological treatment, the failure of psychiatry to take the dissenting data seriously is evidence of a cult-like ideology that shunts aside conflicting facts.

As in overt cults, psychiatry's embrace of an ideology limits realism. When a hospital patient becomes more agitated, noisy, combative and uncooperative the standard staff response is to increase the dosage of neuroleptic drug. Rarely is it considered that the patients' disturbance may reflect a conflict among the staff and that attention and corrective efforts should be directed there. Yet as early as 1956 Stanton and Schwartz had raised these issues in their landmark study of "institutional participation in psychiatric illness and treatment." They analyzed and documented many strong effects of hospital dynamics on the behavior of patients. "The most striking finding was that pathologically excited patients were quite regularly the subjects of secret, affectively important staff disagreement: and, equally regularly, their excitement terminated, usually abruptly, when the staff members were brought to discuss seriously their points of disagreement with each other."

At the time the authors were hopeful and optimistic that their research would change the way inpatients were treated:

"It has finally become clear that a mental hospital is a social system and that the meaning of any action taken within it can be known only if the context is known; it has become clear that many assumptions that had previously been taken for granted, such as the assumption that the mental hospital should take the general hospital as a model, are gratuitous and may be damaging... . Built solidly into procedures, techniques, and even the language of the mental hospital is the assumption that patients are mere passive objects of treatment; they are to be 'cared for,' 'protected,' 'treated,' 'respected,' 'handled,' 'controlled.' Psychiatric administrative language consistently speaks of the patient as if he were not an active participant, as if he were an unconscious or half-conscious body upon an operating table.

When it comes to schizophrenia, what Stanton and Schwartz learned seems to have been forgotten; the awareness they hoped would change the mental hospital has not survived the Second Coming. Just as findings contradicting psychoanalytic assumptions were ignored by analytic theorists, so is work such as that of

Stanton and Schwartz or Bockhoven and Solomon largely ignored today. Psychiatry as a profession does not censor discordant information but does ignore, dismiss, avoid it.

Of course, in pointing to those who apply only biological knowledge to the problem of psychosis and neglect the psychological, it should be recognized that there have been some psychiatrists who, drawing on R. D. Laing's ideas, have conceptualized acute schizophrenic psychosis as a "voyage of discovery," a means of spiritual development to be supported and not interfered with. Drugs are seen as only harmful and psychosis is romanticized. Maintaining such an ideology also requires one to ignore conflicting information, associating only with those who believe similarly and dismissing opponents as benighted.

THE WORD *heretic* is derived from the Greek *hairetikos*, meaning "able to choose." All too frequently, administrators of religions consider themselves to be God's representatives and define any choice of doctrine or interpretation but theirs as false or evil. To the extent that religious leaders claim divine authority, dissent is discouraged and suppressed among their followers. Although differences of interpretation of holy writ always arise, when these differences are substantial they may not be tolerated. If dissenters are expelled or leave, a new religion may result; many different sects have arisen in all the major religions. When an individual defies doctrinal authority — becomes a heretic — and the difference in interpretation is deemed dangerous to the faith of true believers, punishment may be severe, barbaric. Muslim clergy tortured and killed Hallaj, the Sufi saint, for saying "I am God." Clergy of the Inquisition tortured and burned Christians who were far less challenging but were suspected of having the wrong beliefs.

Whatever one's position on dissent in the theological domain, it is clear that an authoritarian attitude is incompatible with democratic government. Fundamentalist Jerry Falwell seems to agree, but finds the problem to be democracy itself.

"Today we find that America is more of a democracy than a republic. Sometimes there is mob rule. In some instances, a vocal minority prevails. Our Founding Fathers would not accept the tyranny of a democracy because they recognized that the only sovereign over men and nations was Almighty God."

MEMBERS of almost all groups committed to a particular belief — be it religious or otherwise — are inclined to read and study works that confirm that belief. The dissenting views of outsiders are ignored or dismissed.

Where a religious group's security and the leader's power is heavily committed to infallibility, the extra precaution of direct censorship, including the burning of books, is taken, as occurred most recently in Iran. For centuries the Catholic Church maintained an Index of condemned books Catholics could not read without special permission because their faith or morals might be disturbed. Recently, Christian fundamentalists have tried to remove from American classrooms such diverse works as *Of Mice and Men*, *A Farewell to Arms*, *The Grapes of Wrath*, *1984*, *Catch 22*, and even *The American Heritage Dictionary*. There has been an ongoing battle to curtail the teaching of evolution and great concern with the evils of "secular humanism."

To read or to listen to differing or opposing views is to court disturbance, trouble, doubt. Billy Graham put it thus: "The world longs for authority, finality, and conclusiveness. It is weary of theological floundering and uncertainty. Belief exhilarates the human spirit; doubt depresses."

The exclusion of doubt has a price. Intellectual parochialism may be fostered by restricting contact with outsiders and by building walls of indifference or, in the most extreme cases, hate.

When religions provide schooling for members' children, such schools may isolate the children from other worldviews and facilitate a portrayal of the outsider as evil or inferior. When this educational insulation is perpetuated into adulthood, cult-like abuses may arise. Until recently, the Catholic parochial school system provided recruits for seminaries and convents which, in turn, provide teachers to perpetuate the school system. Although not all parochial schools are repressive, many have created an atmosphere of fear, guilt, and conformity. As one former nun put it, "You are taught that what is bad in you is yours; what is good in you is God's ." The deadening effect of such an education is attested to by ex-nuns' autobiographical accounts.

"I have been becoming more and more aware of the deadness I see all around me — the deadness of tired, tense bodies clinging to a ritual, of people who patch up life's cracks so nothing new can sink in. I see their intensity and I see their seriousness; I see their compulsive concern for the slightest deviation from the Holy Rule. And what is most frightening, I see the hugeness and monstrosity of their commitment to suffering."

Christianity is not alone in providing systems which shield members from outside views. The Lubavitcher Hasidic community in Brooklyn is a case in point. Veneration of its leader approaches worship. The exclusiveness and separation of members from the larger community, enforced by unusual dress, elaborate rules and rituals, and specialized studies and language, can result in an extremely narrow and parochial outlook which is, in essence, cult-like. In a long, mostly favorable article on the Hasidic community, Liz Harris writes of being surprised when her host declared that he did not believe Jacobo Timerman's description of his incarceration and torture by Argentina authorities. Indeed, he declared there was no anti-Semitism in Argentina. The reason for his view was that Timerman was believed to be "sympathetic to the Communists". Since the communists were a godless people who persecuted Jews and Argentina at the time of the interview was certainly anti-communist, Timerman was not to be believed. Harris comments:

"I found it astonishing that one obvious reality, the suffering of Russian Jews, could utterly annihilate another, the suffering of

Jacobo Timerman and many like him. Did it matter to Moshe that Timerman had emphatically denied any Communist sympathies? Or that fuzzy political accusations had brought about the disappearance of thousands of innocent people? The bright light that the Hasidim trained on their communal and inner life seemed to dim considerably when it was turned on the outside world — a circumstance that appeared to strain the quality of mercy hereabouts."

Of course, the more a religion allows debate, discussion and disagreement, the more adaptable and realistic it can be, the less captured by its form. However, this tolerance may threaten certainty, and certainty (as Billy Graham testified) is one of the great attractions of religious belief.

IRVING JANIS, a psychologist who studied presidential advisory groups, notes that in Washington, as elsewhere, the suppression of deviant points of view is often done by subordinates to protect the President from discordant opinions that might damage their confidence. The underlying wish is to preserve for all the fantasy of the Leader.

Unless a leader clearly intends that subordinates should challenge and criticize, his or her views will meet little serious opposition. Hugh and Clara Robinson's story shows how cult followers, even without specific instructions, act to protect the position and views of their leader. In the capacity of protectors, group members may feel justified in employing threats, subterfuge, and deceit.

In our government, as in most, a principal means of avoiding dissent and criticism is through the use of secrecy. Nowhere has this been more manifest than in the planning of covert operations such as the overthrow of Chilean President Salvadore Allende during the Nixon administration and the sale of arms to Iran during the Reagan administration.

Secrecy supports cult-like behavior, as we saw in the Life Force group, where the hierarchy was maintained through limiting access to information. Secrecy functions not only to cover up unethical activities from outside eyes, but also to increase authoritarian control over the larger group. By promoting the idea that the leader or the in-group have special information and expertise, they remove themselves from criticism and justify the exclusion of others from the decision-making process.

In the case of religious cults the special information and expertise is described as divine inspiration or enlightenment. The cult leader's presumed higher state precludes lower beings from judging his or her actions. Similar claims are made in government where special knowledge of the enemy or secret technical information is said to justify decisions that would otherwise be objected to on moral or even practical grounds.

Secrecy is invoked often in the name of national security. Tom Wicker, *New York Times* columnist, comments on the connotations of that term, meanings we can understand in terms of cult psychology:

"But those two words [national security] are magic, an incantation, vibrating with the ideas of power, knowledge, authority, responsibility. National security! — the phrase rings with masculinity, patriotism, heroism. Used in tones of proper solemnity by someone from the White House or the Pentagon, those words can mesmerize most Americans; and a generation of Washington reporters stood mostly in awe of them — not least, I believe, because a reporter who knows something that can't be printed for national-security reasons is elevated himself into that prized masculine circle of power, knowledge, authority, responsibility. He becomes the ultimate insider; and the reporter's deadliest enemy — the desire to be an accepted part of the world of power around him — has won its final victory."

AS AMERICANS, we affirm the right to dissent, consider it of supreme value, make the infringement of dissent unlawful, and recognize it as basic to our political system. However, in actual practice few of us are pleased when someone disagrees with us; at best we tolerate it, inwardly we reject it. Although in our society the right to dissent is constantly affirmed, there is little indication that as individuals or in groups we value opposing views directed at ourselves. In science, within clear professional limits, there may be more appreciation of dissent, more readiness to welcome the opponent, but in general, although we may defend the right of an opponent to speak out against us we are not grateful when he or she has done so. In almost all cases we react to dissent as to an enemy, countering with argument or a patronizing dismissal. This seems natural, just "human nature." Yet, considering how much of our thinking is prejudiced, rigid, and self-protective and how much we make use of inadequate and selective information, dissent deserves to be treated not as an adversary but as an ally, something that can rescue us from selective blindness, make us more realistic and thus more effective. Objectively, we should regard dissent with gratitude. It is a matter of some chagrin to me that even in the process of writing this book I find it very difficult to practice what I preach; whenever my own opinions are challenged my first response is to put up my mental fists and fight back, defending my position. Only then do I catch myself and ask the dissenter. Why do you think that?

Look around at all levels of society. The adversarial approach is ingrained; authors, radio and television commentators, spokespersons for various causes, politicians of every hue, all insist on the rightness of their own views while denigrating the opposition's. Yet life is complex; our perception and information are limited. Indeed, to some degree, everyone is in error.

Just like the members of Life Force, we want agreement for our beliefs so we can feel the security of being right. Dissent threatens that, it reduces our status, our certainty, our claim to privilege. As I remarked earlier, the problem with Reagan's "evil empire" speech was not so much that he was harshly critical of the Soviet government — surely it deserved harsh criticism — but that he did not acknowledge that we as a nation are not free from evil, even if our system is more humane.

In all the deservedly adverse comment that Reagan received for that speech, there was no recognition that similar speeches take place every day in the utterances and opinions of almost all citizens, liberal and conservative alike. Many people regarded Reagan and his conservative allies as the source of evil in this country, oblivious to the irony that in doing so they were engaging in similar thinking. Again, the key issue is not that criticism is undeserved, but that the persons dishing out criticism reserve none for themselves, nor do they acknowledge any validity to the other's position. They are not being artful. They simply cannot accept the fact that their adversary has the same self-righteous feeling as they do because the implications are uncomfortable: our own feelings of sincerity and righteousness do not certify that we are right. To welcome dissent is to accept that fact.

In ordinary life, dissent is restricted primarily by a selective focus on the familiar and the comfortable. At the same time, there may be more restriction by exclusion than we realize. In 1946, when I was in high school, a Russian Communist was invited to address our weekly assembly. I remember that we were unconvinced by his protestations that the USSR wanted only peace. Afterwards students joked, "Yeah, a piece of Poland, a piece of Hungary and a piece of Germany." We were surprised to hear that the American Legion was upset that he had been allowed to speak to us. What are they afraid of? we thought. He hadn't captured our minds.

Some years later, after the Korean War, I heard a talk by a former American soldier who had been a POW and had gone over to the Chinese Communists. They had treated him well, given him a job and even a daily glass of milk, which they understood to be necessary for Americans. But he found the conformity oppressive, became very homesick and returned to the United States. He said he had been susceptible to their arguments because, coming from a small Midwestern town, he had never heard the United States criticized and was impressed that some of their criticism was undeniably true.

Hearing this man, I realized he rebutted the American Legion's concern. Not having been exposed to dissident views, he had been a sitting duck for skillful propaganda; indeed, most of those who were similarly won over were from unsophisticated environments. I thought then how much we needed dissent.

Yet I doubt that many American high schools during the last three decades have invited a Communist to address their assembly. Since the McCarthy period we seem less tolerant of challenges to our basic political principles. The Socialist Party is all but non-existent in America; political statements are tame and court the national consensus; free enterprise is not challenged. We pride ourselves on freedom of dissent but there is not much serious dissent in our politics, nor in the national media. Radical voices tend to be dismissed as lunatic. It's a free country, but we are as free to turn our backs on dissent as to express it.

In ordinary society, the cult processes of censorship and decreased contact with outsiders are often found, but in diminished intensity. Censorship of discordant information and isolation from heretical outsiders is usually done voluntarily rather than at the insistence of the group, although the expression of deviant views is seldom encouraged. Bankers tend to associate with bankers, doctors with doctors, sergeants with sergeants, black with black, and so on. Similarly for various socio-economic, ethnic, and religious groups. These associations provide not only shared interests, but also the security of support for one's views. Furthermore, liberals and conservatives tend to confine their reading to those magazines and columnists whose views are similar to their own; if they scan the writings of the opposition it will be to attack and disparage, not to learn. At their political gatherings one seldom hears a serious questioning of the group's beliefs or any acknowledgement that opponents may be correct in a particular instance. Instead, what takes place is an exercise in mutual support and validation, a reinforcing of the group's belief in the correctness of its views, a strengthening of the fantasy of being true, good and superior.

A *de facto* censorship operates continuously. Whatever the cause of these social ghettos, their effect is to deny a person the benefit of being challenged and contradicted.

SEVEN

Exit from the Cult

ULT behavior is present throughout society but is particularly evident in the military, whose fanatical support of the
arms race has led us to the brink of extinction. The wish of
military leaders for power and their training in destruction cause
them to imagine enemies where there are none and to exaggerate
the aggressive intentions of others. The military cult attempts to
glorify war and is ready to sacrifice millions of lives for the abstraction of victory. Thus, generals and admirals are enthusiasts of
nuclear weapons and think of them not much differently than the
toy guns they fired gleefully as children — the bigger the better. For
this reason, we must be aware of the influence and manipulation
employed by the military establishment in order to maintain power
and promote war. If we can see what is happening to us, we can
take action to prevent them from leading us to nuclear disaster.
We are all susceptible to cult processes.

Did you agree with what I said above about the military? I was
purposefully devaluing them, using the same means that cults employ to define an outside group as evil. The attributions I made
were exaggerated generalizations. Do you know any high-ranking
military officers? It is possible that the paragraph above fits them,
but most likely it does not.

Consider the phrase "the military, whose fanatic support of
the arms race has led us to the brink of extinction." It permits no
distinctions among members of the military, no recognition that
opinions and motives vary from person to person, as in any other
group. Such stereotyping cannot account for statements such as

this one on nuclear weapons:

"At the theatre or tactical level any nuclear exchange, however limited it might be, is bound to leave NATO worse off in comparison to the Warsaw Pact, in terms both of military and civilian casualties and destruction... To initiate use of nuclear weapons... seems to me to be criminally irresponsible."

The person quoted is Field Marshall Lord Carver, Chief of the British Defense Staff from 1973 to 1976. He is not the only powerful military officer to take that position. Admiral Hyman Rickover, the principal force behind the development of the nuclear submarine fleet, on the occasion of his retirement, advocated doing away with nuclear weapons and nuclear reactors as well.

"The most important thing we could do is start by having an international meeting where we first outlaw nuclear weapons, and then we outlaw nuclear reactors, too... I think it would be the finest thing in the world for the President of the United States to immediately initiate another disarmament conference... this is a very propitious time, when the military expenses are eating up so much of the people's taxes."

Nor is Rickover an exception among the American military. Gene LaRocque, another retired admiral, is a leading speaker for Physicians for Social Responsibility and heads the Center for Defense Information, a peace movement organization. And what are we to make of the fact that in May 1982 the entire Joint Chiefs of Staff supported reductions in strategic nuclear arsenals in opposition to Secretary of Defense Caspar Weinberger, a civilian? Around the same time, the chairman of the Joint Chiefs supported the peace movement in its pressure for arms control. "Opponents of nuclear weapons in the United States 'are not a fringe element' but contain many who support a strong military and still want 'to get on with some arms control that is meaningful and results in very substantial reductions.' The military acted as a moderating force when the Joint Chiefs of Staff opposed President Reagan's wish to send a battleship group to South America.

My use of the term "fanatical" denigrates and devalues the opposing view by attacking the character of the opponent rather than addressing the content of what is proposed. A fanatic is "a person possessed by an excessive and irrational zeal, especially for a religious or political cause.'" With the use of this term, advocacy of an arms buildup becomes "irrational zeal," without the writer having to prove that it is so. My demonstration paragraph contains no attempt to understand what legitimate basis might exist for the military's advocacy of an increased arms budget; that viewpoint is only condemned or devalued. The fact is, a general or an admiral might believe that a nuclear war would be an utter disaster for his country, but that an increased arms budget would help guard against such a war. And it is at least possible that such thinking might be correct. Some generals argue strongly for building up conventional forces rather than nuclear arms.

The sample paragraph given above does not acknowledge or discriminate among these possibilities. Instead, it attempts to establish a separate class of human beings, "the military", characterized as wrong or bad — people not like us. The reader is always included in the "us" because in cult communication us means good. We usually do not challenge such an inclusion even though its purpose is to exclude someone else, to lead us to regard them as bad or, at the least, inferior. This is a typical illustration of devaluation as it occurs in everyday life.

The second sentence of the paragraph establishes that the military has bad motives, "The wish of military leaders for power and their training in destruction causes them to imagine enemies where there are none and to exaggerate the aggressive intentions of others." Thus they want power and destruction and are paranoid to boot. The problem with this statement is projection. The sentence implies that the bad traits it designates characterize the military rather than anyone else, not the writer, and by unspoken agreement, not the reader. That implication is certainly false. A keen interest in violence and destruction can be found in almost everyone

— witness the continued popularity of shoot-em-up, beat-em-up television and movie entertainment. In what seems to be the favorite plot, the villain has been so bad that the hero has license to behave brutally, cruelly and vindictively, violating all precepts of fairness or legality in the process. Judging by the ratings, military personnel do not comprise the total audience for such blood-fests.

The capacity for violence, physical or psychological, is present in all human beings. At the same time, everyone thinks of themselves as having good intentions. Indeed, after many years as a psychiatrist, it is clear to me that most human beings, especially those whose behavior is abhorrent, are likely to think of themselves as victims rather than villains, misunderstood by others, not appreciated, treated unfairly, not deserving the hardships encountered. It is doubtful that anyone rises in the morning exclaiming, "Aha! Another day to be evil!"

The wish for personal power is also universal and not confined to the military. As a liberal I have attended many peace movement meetings and have observed that being on a platform brings out the demagogue in many speakers and leaders, whether of the right, left, or center. I myself enjoy giving lectures to large groups of people and still remember one gathering of a thousand that responded with such enthusiasm that I could understand how Benito Mussolini must have felt when he spoke from his balcony. Power, vanity, and greed can flower exuberantly even while high-minded words are being declaimed. (I haven't attended any conservative or right-wing rallies but have observed them on television and read the speeches delivered there. The effect of the platform on the speaker is the same.)

The second sentence of our sample attributes a paranoid perspective to the generals and admirals ("to imagine enemies where there are none"). Quite possibly this does occur in the military, depending on the person and the circumstances, but this too is true of everyone else. Indeed, paranoia depends on attributing to someone or some group precisely those traits one denies in oneself and the reader who accepted the opening paragraph did just that. The paragraph offers a good example of unnoticed, everyday projection, a basic cult dynamic. In this example the generals and admirals are the focus of projection, but just as often the peace movement, the "doves", "the left" are designated as bad, inferior, irresponsible.

An interesting exercise is to consult the newspaper columnists, magazines, or television commentators that are your preferred sources of information and notice the devaluation and projection that is employed — with your tacit approval — when Washington politics, the Soviet Union, nuclear war, or other controversial subjects are discussed. The devaluation reinforces your sense of rightness and establishes a clear source of evil. Also observe the tone of righteousness that accompanies such cult behavior. It signals the presence of projection; They are bad (we are good). You may notice in yourself the fantasy that if you were in power things would be done right!

The last two sentences of the chapter's opening paragraph sound a warning that is true enough ("we must be aware of the devices of influence and manipulation employed"), but that applies to everyone — the military, the peace movement, the Left and the Right, blacks and whites, Christians, Jews, and Muslims, rich and poor.

The military is authoritarian by nature and will inevitably manifest some of the cult behavior we have seen in religions, large corporations, and other social institutions. What is most important is that each of us become more aware of his or her own cult thinking. Only through such awareness can we extricate ourselves from the invisible, everyday cults of which we are members.

THE opening paragraph of this chapter was written to provide an experience of cult thinking by appealing to and stimulating the reader's likely prejudices, fears, and wishes. I used such a device because personal bias tends to make influence and manipulation invisible to those affected. If you are a member of the military or a hard-line conservative, you may not have been swayed; however, for many of us, characterizing generals and admirals as warmongering, stupid, or callous fits our projections very nicely. We consider ourselves, in contrast, to be peace-loving, intelligent, and empathic. We cannot grant laudable characteristics to people advocating very different views without raising the possibility that they could be correct and we in error.

Your response may be: *That's nothing new; I know all that.* Indeed, the concept of cult behavior can be easily grasped, but experiencing it in one's own thinking and behavior is a different matter. Intellectuals in particular, who are trained not to be caught off balance by any idea, may find the concepts of cult psychology overly familiar and yet continue with their own cult behavior and be as ignorant of it as the members of Life Force. If you still feel immune from cult influence, I can offer a checklist of everyday behaviors that you may recognize all too well:

1. Speaking of adversaries or outsiders (e.g., conservatives, liberals, Yuppies, blue-collar, rich, poor) as if they were all the same; characterizing them by negative traits only; attributing unflattering motives to them but not to oneself.

2. Lacking interest and information concerning the actual statements and actions of opponents or outsiders.

3. Failing to consider the possible validity of an adversary's point of view.

4. Not taking a critical look at one's own position.

5. Disapproving or rejecting a member of one's group for departing from the group position, devaluing the dissident, regarding him or her as an annoyance or a problem.

6. Feeling self-righteous.

Exit from the invisible cult is very important because cult thinking has such serious consequences, especially at the government level. In her book *March of Folly*, Barbara Tuchman presents striking examples of both ancient and modern governments that persisted in disastrous policies while ignoring correct advice and countervailing experience. She blames this primarily on "woodenheadedness."

"Wooden-headedness, the source of self-deception, is a factor that plays a remarkably large role in government. It consists in assessing a situation in terms of preconceived fixed notions while ignoring or rejecting any contrary signs. It is acting according to wish while not allowing oneself to be deflected by the facts."

We can recognize here a description of one of the basic cult behaviors, avoiding dissenting views. Correspondingly, in Tuchman's list of requirements for reasonable leadership we see the opposite — a readiness to learn, to acknowledge error, "to keep well-informed, to heed information... if the mind is open enough to perceive that a given policy is harming rather than serving self-interest, and self-confident enough to acknowledge it, and wise enough to reverse it."

The only hope Tuchman sees for averting further government folly is that the electorate be educated to select leaders by recognizing and rewarding integrity of character — moral courage — and rejecting "the ersatz." She is not sanguine about this possibility and concludes, somewhat helplessly, "We can only muddle on."

Actually, we are not that helpless. The study of cult psychology and its manifestations in ordinary life provides a framework with which to understand why wooden-headedness exists, what the behavior of a competent leader is, and how we can educate both leaders and electorate to do more than muddle on. The necessary information is available. If we allow ourselves the awareness of our wish for shepherds, our longing for the back seat of the car, then we have a much better chance of avoiding folly.

BEYOND heightening such awareness, there are some specific ways to reduce cult behavior in society. One of the most effective would be to promote anti-authoritarian education. As I have argued, our initial social experience in the family sets the pattern for the roles of leader and follower and we readily create a parent out of anyone who seeks to lead, teach, or command. We elevate such a person, just as we looked up to our parents who were literally above us. Authoritarian leaders stimulate and intensify this response.

A young child's critical evaluation of his or her parent is very difficult because the child's understanding is limited by an ego-centric view that relates all events to himself or herself as cause. A child cannot comprehend the network of forces affecting parents and their society; furthermore, critical evaluation may be haz-ardous and frightening. When a child accurately perceives hypo-crisy, selfishness, or irrationality in the parent — and says so — he or she risks punishment and the parent's withdrawal. Even the awareness of a parent's bad actions may be intolerable, for the parent is the young child's world and if the world is bad, what hope can be maintained? For this reason, children often regard them-selves as bad rather than see the failings of a mother or father; in adulthood, when faced with the harmful behavior of an idealized leader, reality may again be denied.

The fact is, the capacity for objective assessment of leaders and authorities is not developed in many homes or schools. Although historical figures or current political leaders may be discussed, the role and power of parents and teachers seldom is. Authorities of any kind rarely encourage an objective appraisal of themselves. In consequence, as adults we may be vulnerable to the unrealistic claims of charismatic, authoritarian leaders. But this can be changed, if we wish, and the place to begin is in the schools.

For educational institutions to give up authoritarian power and abandon indoctrination may seem impossible, but the research of Gerda Lederer and others on post-World War II German youth provides evidence that such a goal is achievable. After World War

II, authoritarianism (defined by Lederer as a readiness to submit to authority combined with a readiness to dominate those with less power) was recognized as an important factor in the rise of the Nazis and the willingness of German citizens to follow wherever Hitler led. Beginning in the 1960s, a deliberate effort was made in West Germany to reduce or eliminate the authoritarian attitude.

"Most of the Nazi-era schoolteachers were dismissed because of party membership. Most of the old textbooks were destroyed. Beyond that, educational leaders set out to do what had not been done after World War I, during the Weimar Republic: totally change the atmosphere of the schools so as to practice democratic values as well as preach them."

When Lederer arrived in West Germany to do her research (originally on the difference in math scores between American and German students), she was required to take a month-long teacher training course.

"The training emphasized that the students, not the teachers, should do most of the talking in the classroom. 'We do not use the frontal approach in teaching,' the German instructor said. 'Don't expect your students to be quiet and listen.' The students should be encouraged to talk among themselves, he added."

The atmosphere was so different from the stereotype of German discipline that Lederer felt like Alice in Wonderland. In 1978, using a carefully constructed questionnaire, she found that, in contrast to the findings in 1945, West German adolescents were on a par with American adolescents with regard to authoritarianism. Both groups had shown a significant reduction in authoritarian beliefs between 1945 and 1978, but the West Germans' change had been more dramatic; where there were differences in 1978, the West German adolescents showed a greater support for democratic values than did the American students! (The poll research confirmed the similar findings of a massive, multinational study conducted in 1971 by the International Association for the Evaluation of Educational Achievement [IEA].)

This apparently successful effort on the part of West German authorities to teach anti-authoritarianism suggests that schools can encourage students to examine the roots of their automatic obedience to authority (and of automatic rebellion as well). Considered most broadly, this could be seen as an education in anti-cult psychology. However, it must be recognized that teaching students to perceive and understand the operations of authoritarianism requires more than the establishment of a democratic classroom. I believe that the process of observation and reflection should be applied to the reactions of students and teachers to the social structures of their own educational milieu, of their peer groups, of their families. They would need to learn about the indoctrination and bias present in their society which is communicated directly via news and opinion sources and indirectly via entertainment and advertising. Then they would be in a position to study cults per se, and relate them to themselves. They would begin to understand the forces shaping their beliefs and values. In the words of Idries Shah, "People are widely held to have the right to attack what they dislike. We have not yet, however, reached the stage where it is required that people understand (though they purport to describe) the roots of liking and disliking."

ALLIED to anti-authoritarian education is the fostering of autonomy in various sectors of society, which can also help limit the extent of cult behavior by encouraging the expression in action of multiple individual viewpoints. Autonomy is a mark of adulthood, whereas subservience and automatic deference are marks of childlike dependency. As we have seen, cults regress their members to a stage of dependency on the group and child-like expectations of the leader, who is elevated far above the followers and regarded as if he or she were infinitely wise.

The issue of autonomy is important in the corporate world. The most successful companies appear to have achieved a balance between autonomy and centralized control such that neither dimension gets out of hand. Alfred Sloan at General Motors had such a goal.

"A delicate balance was to be maintained between the freedom of the various operations to manage their business, competing internally as well as outside the company, and the controls necessary to coordinate these operations in the best interests of the corporation's growth and performance."

The Japanese have been very successful at achieving a similar balance. An executive of one of Japan's largest suppliers of electrical products describes their approach:

"Matsushita fosters autonomy and provides enormous incentive for group and individual performance. But... Matsushita exercises extraordinarily tight control over a few variables. The planning process, and in particular the six-month operating plan, are taken very seriously. Matsushita believes that people can be trusted. However, our control system provides guidelines to prevent ruinous mistakes."

Another company, Schlumberger, provides us with clear examples of how autonomy is given employees and how much they value it. In the words of several of their field engineers:

"The thing that drew me here was that no other job gives you the responsibility you are given here right out of school....

"I have much more responsibility than I would in other jobs. The technical side is quite interesting. The engineer has his own unit, his own tools, his own team....

"I joined because I wanted to go overseas and have my own show.... I have the impression that I'm running my own company."

The excellent companies studied by Peters and Waterman all worked to treat their employees with respect, to regard them as adults rather than unruly, lazy children. Initiative, autonomous decision making, and constructive disagreement were encouraged. Sloan's genius at General Motors was to organize independent divisions in control of their own operations but responsive to headquarters' long-range planning. (After Sloan, more and more decision making was taken over by a headquarters staff that had less and less experience in the manufacture and sale of automobiles. Multiple committees intervened to delay decisions and thereby lose both opportunities and money.

THE informed voter is supposed to be the bedrock of democracy, but an interesting study of citizen voting habits done in the 1950s suggests that the rational, objectively interested citizen does not really exist. The researchers concluded that it is the ill-informed, relatively indifferent voters who are essential for a liberal democracy, that only they are responsive to changing conditions, providing flexibility to the body politic. The well-informed, highly interested, involved citizen is usually quite partisan and unmoved by argument; on the left and the right, such stalwarts anchor the political ship, providing stability.

"Highly interested voters vote more, and know more about the campaign, and read and listen more, and participate more; however, they are also less open to persuasion and less likely to change. Extreme interest goes with extreme partisanship and might culminate in rigid fanaticism that could destroy democratic processes if generalized throughout the community."

This somewhat disconcerting finding is due in part to the fact that what informs the citizen is largely propaganda issuing from one side or the other. Radio, television, magazines, and newspapers feature both critics and defenders of a particular policy, but each of these selects facts useful to his or her position, emphasizes certain principles and ignores others, often evoking emotional responses, prejudices, and fears. After reading or hearing such a presentation one may be persuaded, influenced, or won over, but one is not really better informed if what one has encountered is not essential information, but convincing propaganda.

Unless the audience knows a great deal about the subject, one-sided presentations can be very persuasive. In most conflict situations, disagreements are based on differences in interpretation and in the priorities given to different values; but these differences are seldom stated, and, lacking that clarification, we absorb highly selective information, are swayed to one side or the other, but end up no wiser.

As Jacques Ellul points out, whether propaganda is democratic or totalitarian does not matter, choice and discrimination are damaged.

"The existence of two contradictory propagandas is no solution at all... the individual is not independent in the presence of two combatants between whom he must choose. He is not a spectator comparing two posters, or a supreme arbiter when he decides in favor of the more honest and convincing one... The individual is seized, manipulated, attacked from every side; the combatants of two propaganda systems do not fight each other, but try to capture him."

Opposing propagandas do not assist the democratic process but produce partisans, each with the mind-set of a cult member who "demands simple solutions, catchwords, certainties, continuity, commitment, a clear and simple division of the world into Good and Evil, efficiency, and unit of thought. He cannot bear ambiguity. He cannot bear that the opponent should in any way whatever represent what is right or good... the individual will escape either into passivity or into total and unthinking support of one of the two sides."

In order for the citizen to exercise a realistic choice a more searching alternative is needed, a making use of dissent as a way of raising the level of informed judgment without raising the level of partisanship. Let us imagine a debate or discussion the goal of which is to clarify a controversial problem and proposed solutions. The focus would be on the fundamental questions of how the data are interpreted and what values are given priority. The intent would not be to overwhelm or capture the audience, but to clarify the competing values that are involved in the conflict and in the proposed solutions. In this way we could become informed without becoming opinionated. Logically, four areas would be clarified:

1. The key data (Are they disputed?)
2. Interpretations of the data.
3. Value conflicts. (Reason for giving one value priority over the other?)
4. Error indicators. (What events or facts would indicate to each side that their belief or strategy should be changed?)

The best corporate executives promote real dissent even though they may find it irritating. Harold Geneen, who ruled ITT like an absolute monarch, was nevertheless quite clear about the importance of dissent and said that he deliberately fostered it in his search for "the unshakeable facts."

"We cut through layers of fat in our management ranks by putting all the people in one room so they could talk with one another, face to face, regardless of rank, and an honest assessment of any situation could be based upon the facts which emerged.

"But that is only the surface of the matter. Beneath that surface was the clear understanding that we owed each other our honest opinions at all times. People could disagree with me or with anyone else; they could criticize me or anyone else, and no one would suffer as a consequence. I tried to welcome criticism. Naturally, no one likes to be criticized. One's first instinct is to be defensive and fight back. But that is the kind of defensiveness one should try to keep under control. I consciously tried to lean over backwards to avoid bridling when someone disagreed with me. I always wanted someone to point out where I might be heading for a mistake. I never batted down such a man. I listened and we exchanged views... But more important than the encounter itself was that at meetings others observed what was happening and word got around the company that one could speak his mind, disagree with the boss, and be heard."

Geneen's description of himself receives support from ITT executives whom Pascale and Athos interviewed.

"Geneen didn't mistrust people in a misanthropic sense," says one senior-level manager. "But he did mistrust a single source." Geneen disliked relying on one perspective as the means for giving him the whole picture. He believed that people have different points of view and that it is dangerous to listen to a small coterie.

[Referring to the face-to-face confrontations that were encouraged at large executive meetings:] "It was like a tennis match; you could play an aggressive game with your opponent but still have a relationship with him when their game was over."

Jean Riboud, when CEO of Schlumberger, picked key people who were not afraid to disagree with him, people who had "the courage of their convictions," who did not "float like a cork," but "force[d] people to think." Ed Carlson, who was CEO of United Airlines, also valued dissent.

"When Carlson was in accord with his advisors, he might play devil's advocate to see if he could support the opposite side with logic. "He sought the difference of opinion among his executives," said one observer, "and anyone in the group was expected to disagree loudly if he felt so disposed." Carlson's only rule: Disagree without being disagreeable."

Contrast these attitudes with those of the General Motors executives described by De Lorean, or the imperial manner of Henry Ford II as described by Lee Iacocca in his autobiography's or the behavior of key executives during the TV-Cable News fiasco. Inhibiting dissent can be as costly in industry as it is in cults.

FOSTERING dissent and recognizing its value are essential to realistic decision making. It is true that authoritarian decision-makers who dispense with dissent can be right in their decisions; but they can also be very wrong. General Douglas MacArthur showed brilliant independent judgment during the Korean War in his insistence on an amphibious assault of Inchon despite the unanimous objections of the Joint Chiefs of Staff. In that case he was right. However, according to historian William Manchester, MacArthur's equally strong belief during World War II that he would defeat the Japanese on the Lingayen beaches northwest of Manila led him to delay shifting vast stores of food and supplies to Bataan (as originally planned by the Joint Chiefs for a retreat and holding action). Finally, when it was too late to supply the peninsula, MacArthur retreated; but the troops, who otherwise would have been able to hold out for years, were starved into surrender and most died on the Death March.

Today, nuclear weapons have made the stakes of government decision making higher than in the past. Only responsible dissent, voiced and listened to, can offer protection against cataclysmic error. With this need in mind, Irving Janis has suggested adopting procedures aimed at facilitating dissent in government. Among the steps he recommends are:

"Assign the role of critical evaluator to each member [of a policy-making group], encouraging the group to give high priority to airing objections and doubts.

"[The] setting up [of] several independent policy-planning and evaluation groups to work on the same policy question, each carrying out its deliberations under a different leader.

"One or more outside experts or qualified colleagues… who are not core members of the policy-making group should be invited to each meeting on a staggered basis and should be encouraged to challenge the views of the core members.

"At least one member should be assigned the role of devil's advocate."

Janis recognizes the difficulties in implementing his proposals, yet the steps outlined above would clearly be helpful in encouraging constructive dissent and lessening cult-like behavior at the highest levels of government. We can be confident that these procedures are practical because they have been used successfully already.

Following the Bay of Pigs disaster. President Kennedy sought to understand why his administration had blundered so badly, and when the next crisis occurred he put a much different system into operation.

In October of 1962, the discovery that the Soviet Union was installing nuclear missiles in Cuba spurred Kennedy to convene a group of high-level advisors to decide how to deal with the threat. Five of the key men selected had participated in the Bay of Pigs planning group: Rusk, McNamara, Dillon, Bundy and Robert Kennedy. As before, they met under great time pressure, for they believed it was essential to take action before the missile sites became operational.

Rightly or wrongly, Kennedy ruled out a diplomatic approach. He made it clear that the situation was unacceptable and that the group task was to decide on the best form of coercive action to force the removal of the missiles from Cuba.

This time, the team did not try to satisfy an impatient president by obtaining a quick consensus. They reacted quite differently, not only because they remembered what had happened at the Bay of Pigs, but because Kennedy saw to it that their deliberations took place under quite different procedures.

Each participant was expected to function as an independent critical thinker, addressing the problem in its entirety and not primarily as a spokesperson for the agency they represented. Robert Kennedy and Theodore Sorensen were given special roles to guard the group against superficial analysis. No formal agenda was imposed; discussions were free and far-ranging. Outside experts were invited to give opinions and then were questioned closely. If visitors to the group remained silent, they were specifically asked to state their observations and comments. Sub-groups were formed to work independently on the same problem and then meet to compare findings. From time to time, President Kennedy absented himself from the group, especially in early phases when many different alternatives were first considered.

As an example of the results of this different process, Robert

Kennedy, who during the Bay of Pigs discussion had chided dissenters, this time guarded against premature closure of options.
When an airstrike was proposed as the only option, he advised re-
consideration. "'Surely' he asserted, 'there was some course in
between bombing and doing nothing'.... By the end of the first day
of meetings the committee had seriously discussed at least
ten alternatives."

There was no false confidence, no shoving aside of the frightful
risks that attended each option. The participants were encouraged
to challenge each other's assumptions, to speak their minds frankly
and treat each other, as well as outside visitors and consultants, as
equals. Dissent was recognized as vital to finding a way to the most
realistic action.

This process was often stressful for committee members, leading to unpleasant arguments, agitation, and sleepless nights. The discussions went on for days and seemed interminable, but in the end
the blockade plan was decided upon. Furthermore, contingency
plans were worked out in full detail to cope with a variety of possible Soviet responses. Nothing was taken for granted.

"As a result of the thorough review of all the drawbacks [em-
phasis added], the recommendations the group gave to the
President included much more than strategic military guidelines.
The group worked out in considerable detail ways of handling a
variety of political, legal, and diplomatic ramifications, which, if
neglected, could cause a blockade attempt to fail."

The contrast to the Bay of Pigs deliberations is striking. Even
if the blockade had not worked, the chances of success had been
maximized and contingency responses were thought through and
put in place. The practice of welcoming dissent — uncomfortable
and disconcerting as it can be — proved immensely practical.

Unfortunately, it seems that presidents do not always learn from
their predecessors. After the Tower report on the Iran-Contra
affair was released. Senator Nancy Kassenbaum, a Republican
member of the Senate Foreign Relations Committee, commented:

"The underlying problem in all this is a lack of respect for dissent. The president has not been able to hear all sides of an issue. And we saw the same thing on SDI, contra aid. South Africa, and, of course, the budget. People in the administration who challenge policy are just shunted aside. That's the basic flaw in the process.

The Eye-Level World

Probably the most common everyday cult behavior is devaluation of the outsider. As discussed earlier, we do this not only to feel superior, but also as a defense against recognizing those things in ourselves about which we feel ashamed and inferior; human beings tend to see someone else as embodying the defects they themselves deny. This projection of badness interferes with a realistic assessment of another's intentions. Frequently, it serves to justify violence. In contrast, an eye-level view recognizes defects and hurtful actions in the other without adopting a superior position or lowering the other to subhuman status.

In the service of realism, it is important to diminish projection and establish an eye-level perspective, for in our fears, hopes, and capacity for nobility as well as self-deception, we can recognize each other, see that "the enemy is us." Measures that reveal our similarities to the outsider, not just our differences, are very helpful. The reader may object that such perceptions of the hostile outsider must be mutual, that if we perceive the humanness and similarity of our enemies while they do not so perceive us, then we are at a fatal disadvantage. This is simply not so. Perceiving the other person without the distortion imposed by projection permits us to see more clearly, to respond more realistically. That response might be either aggressive or conciliatory, depending upon what is called for by the reality of the situation (not by the product of projective defenses). Such realism is always an advantage, especially in our dealings with other nations, other people — "the foreigner." At such times, cult behavior is likely to be most intense and mutual recognition most memorable. As the

San Francisco Chronicle reported:

> Forty years after the Allied landing in France, an American soldier recalled that time: "Arruda nodded, his hands touching the green napkin with its rough map of a 40-year-old battlefield. 'I'd like to go back to the places I landed, the places I fought,' he said, 'to see the city of Cherbourg...'
>
> "And maybe he could find the spot in a field outside St. Lo where he stood up at the same time as a German officer who was only a few feet away.
>
> "'We looked at each other for the longest time, just staring,' said Arruda. 'I knew he had his troops behind him and he knew my people were back there. I was thinking, Hey this son of a bitch is just like me. And we both of us turned around very slowly and walked away from each other.'"

How can this eye-level perception be fostered? As we know from experience, actual contact helps greatly — if the contact occurs with enough informality for the participants' humanity to emerge. At the international level, citizen exchanges between countries, involvement in joint work projects, and shared living are all moves in the right direction. Unfortunately, the people who participate in such activities usually do not occupy positions in the higher echelons of government, although those leaders need that experience more than anyone else. High-level contact — frequently and for days at a time — is one thing that might cost little but could significantly reduce projection. (Such extended personal meetings resulted in Ronald Reagan's stroll in Red Square with his arm around the shoulders of Mikhail Gorbachev, the "evil empire" relegated to "another time, another era.")

In many situations eye-level perception can be enhanced by using encounter group techniques developed in the sixties and early seventies to increase the depth of communication among group members. Carl Rogers used these techniques successfully to promote understanding between antagonistic national groups. I believe they could be utilized to make perception more realistic between opposing factions at all levels. Increasing the range of tools with which national and international problems might be resolved would certainly be desirable.

MAHATMA Gandhi was successful in achieving political change through non-violent civil disobedience. He served as a model for Kaunda in Zambia, Martin Luther King in Montgomery, Alabama, and many others. Gandhi's principles of action were the opposite of cult behavior. He stressed putting oneself in the place of the opponent, respecting his or her potential goodness, and recognizing that you may be in error. Gandhi was quite explicit about what was required.

"I want you to feel like loving your opponents, and the way to do it is to give them same credit for honesty of purpose which you would claim for yourself.... It is true that they have their ends to serve. But so have we our ends to serve. Only we consider our ends to be pure and, therefore, selfless. But who are we to determine where selflessness ends and selfishness begins?... Immediately we begin to think of things as our opponents think of them we shall be able to do them full justice.... Three-fourths of the miseries and misunderstandings in the world will disappear, if we step into the shoes of our adversaries and understand their standpoint."

These principles directly combat devaluation and aim at establishing eye-level relationships that eliminate all self-righteousness. Gandhi went further and stressed that humiliation of the opponent was not permissible; great care was to be taken to maintain the opponent's dignity and self-respect. At every step Gandhi was concerned that the opponent save face, and this concern was a tribute to his realism. General Smuts remarked after experiencing Gandhi in South Africa. "It was my fate to be the antagonist of a man for whom even then I had the highest respect... He never forgot the human background of the situation."

Unfortunately, the vast majority of Gandhi's followers venerated him as a saint, to the detriment of the eye-level relationship he advocated in dealing with adversaries. They responded to him as to a parent ("Bapu"), with the dependency dynamics outlined for cults. As Erik Erikson's study made clear, Gandhi was quite capable of being authoritarian, tyrannical, and unjust to his own immediate family and disciples. Everyone, even one called saint or genius, is flawed. The failure of Gandhi — like the failure of every great mass leader in human history — was not in having flaws, but in not freeing his followers from cult behavior. The awful violence between Moslems and Hindus that took place during his lifetime and afterwards was a typical product of cult psychology. In the name of religions that advocate justice, mercy, generosity, and humility, the most barbarous atrocities were committed by each group against the other. Gandhi could stop them by fasting, but when Gandhi was gone most showed they had learned nothing.

CHARACTERISTICALLY, cults subordinate ethical and moral standards to the particular aims of the group and leader. These are called higher purposes, usually put in terms of saving the world (as when the needs of Clara's child were made secondary to the needs of Life Force). In political situations in America, "saving the world for democracy," "overthrowing communism," "fighting terrorism," or the "war on drugs" are cited to justify illegal and immoral actions by the government. Undoubtedly, situations arise in which hard choices must be made; but often government officials use "higher purposes" to justify unsavory operations that are remarkably ineffective, if not disastrous: the internment of the Japanese in 1942, the Bay of Pigs, the Tonkin Gulf incident, the bombing of Cambodia, the overthrow of Allende and the sale of arms to Iran, among many others. Cult thinking is seldom realistic.

In contrast, the deliberations of the Cuban missile crisis planning group were guided by a basic approach strikingly consistent with Gandhi's, one which included concern for the ethics of any proposed action, putting oneself in the opponent's place, and being careful to avoid humiliating him. The first days of the missile crisis group's discussions were occupied with the morality of an air strike against the Cuban bases. This proposal advanced by the military was at first favored by President Kennedy and Douglas Dillon. However, George Ball vigorously objected that such a surprise attack would be counter to our own traditions and harm our moral standing. Robert Kennedy agreed, pointing out the loss of innocent lives that would result and that such an action would be a "Pearl Harbor in reverse," going against our humanitarian ideals. Robert McNamara also agreed and in his retrospective account makes it clear that Robert Kennedy's stress on moral values was an important influence which resulted in the abandonment of the air strike option in favor of a blockade:

"His [Robert Kennedy's] contribution was far more than administrative... he opposed a massive surprise attack of a large country on a small country because he believed such an attack to be inhuman, contrary to our traditions and ideals and an act of brutality for which the world would never forgive us."

In practice, realpolitik (which ignores ethical considerations) usually is cult-like in that it is linked to a devaluation of the enemy, to stereotyping and self-righteousness. In contrast, realism requires putting oneself in one's opponent's place if one is to understand and predict the opponent's actions. In typical Gandhi fashion, the Cuban Missile Group did just that.

"Most members viewed their opposite numbers in the Kremlin as no less rational than themselves.... Often the members of the group set themselves the task of trying to predict how the enemy would react to one or another course of action by deliberately trying to imagine themselves in the Soviet leaders' place.... Without denying the cunning and deceit of the Soviet leaders, the group adopted the working assumption that the Soviet Union would not be likely to initiate a war unless unduly provoked.... Rusk and other members... urged the group to choose a response that the Soviet leaders could clearly see offered them a way out.... An important argument that led the group to regard a naval blockade as much more prudent than any alternative military response was precisely that this low-level action could serve as an unmistakable indication of America's strong intention to eliminate the missile bases without confronting the Soviet leaders with a belligerent act that would be 'sudden or humiliating.'"

Avoiding situations that would embarrass the Soviets was an important strategic consideration. Consequently, the first ship boarded was not Soviet, but a Lebanese freighter under charter to the Soviets. At every step, including American replies to Soviet proposals, care was taken to avoid provocative, unduly threatening, or humiliating actions.

Robert Kennedy concluded, "A final lesson of the Cuban missile crisis is the importance of placing ourselves in the other country's shoes."

Gandhi would agree.

Two primary cult behaviors, compliance with the group and dependence on a leader, have served necessary functions in the survival of the human race. They are very important in childhood, where they provide safety, security, encouragement, and support. Groups and leaders have legitimate functions for adults as well. They can stimulate, reinforce, and guide individuals' energies in constructive ways; they provide meaning and counter isolation and loneliness with acceptance and warmth. But the fantasy of parents must be transcended by adults; for us it is no longer functional. Indeed, regressive dependency makes our survival and progress more difficult because reality must be distorted in order to construct shepherds out of sheep.

Adult human beings stand together in a horizontal plane, but they all too often try to organize it vertically. The reader may assume that the eye-level world is his or her basic perspective. It hasn't been for me. Whenever I gave a public lecture I noticed that immediately afterward I felt let down, disappointed, no matter how well the audience had responded. Eventually, I realized that I was preparing my lectures as if the authority figures of my early professional years would be listening. At the periphery of my mind was an image of them seated in the back of the auditorium. There were no specific faces, just a row of sceptical shadows. I worked hard shaping and rehearsing my lectures to convince them of the rightness of my views, to win their approval, their grudging admiration. But when I stepped up on the platform and looked over the audience I could see that they weren't there. They hadn't come.

This fantasy of fathers, this vertical perspective, had been hidden from me until my disappointment alerted me to it. I know I am not alone in this. I can recognize the persistence of what I call the parent-world in the attitude and behavior of my friends, in the implicit views of authors whose books I read, and in the statements of public figures. As a psychotherapist, I find the parent-world in the fantasies of people with normal and useful adult positions — teachers, housewives, carpenters, lawyers, executives, students — people in all the occupations that comprise everyday society. The evidence is strong that all of us show the effects of having been raised in a hierarchical world in which there were those above us and those below. From such a perspective there is always a higher authority.

Perhaps I can bring this home with another demonstration. Morality is usually experienced as a given, as a code whose violation brings punishment or, at the least, guilt. Most people, if they look within, discover a subtle fantasy that someone or something is keeping score of their good and bad deeds and that in the future — usually after death — there will be a settling-up. If you doubt this, try an experiment. Imagine that there will be no ultimate retribution for anything you do, no denial of Heaven to the wicked. Imagine that whether you behave like a saint or a sadist, are kind or cruel, generous or selfish, it will make no difference when you die. How you behave is entirely up to you. Do whatever you want, there are no celestial consequences. Imagining this, what would you do, how would you behave? (Try it now. Take a few minutes to see what it is like.)

The first time I did this experiment it was an uneasy experience. Imagining myself to be the only authority gave me a sensation of wobbly morality. Principles that had seemed rock solid were swaying in the breeze, and in that moment I did not know how I would choose to act if there were no retribution, no reward, no eventual Judgment Day. That uncertainty brought into focus the assumptions and dynamics of my ordinary world and made me realize how my eyes too frequently gaze back over my shoulder at the invisible, hovering parents of adult childhood. When I asked friends to imagine the same parentless scenario I could see it was unfamiliar to them also, even startling and uncomfortable, although they were independent and self-supporting — adult by all usual criteria.

IF GODS do not occupy the heavens, and wise parents do not head governments, if there are no experts without error and prejudice, how can we find our way to a home that is not a dream? The child's home is in the past. We may try to create a home again in the families in which we are the parent. Wife, husband, and children can provide a place where love is given and received. But as adults it is not the same because our reality is different. We are far from being the parent we imagined as a child; pretending doesn't work. Can there be home for us?

The eye-level world is the perspective that arises when the parents in the sky disappear and their images superimposed on other people dissolve and vanish. As you look around, no one towers above you, everyone looks back at the same human height. Although the parents are gone, the landscape is not threatening, it spreads out in all directions, inviting exploration. It is open and calm, in contrast to the world of childhood fears.

The child fears that the disappearance of parents would release anarchy, hatred, and destruction because in the parents' world the child knows no power, no control that is not imposed. In the eye-level world freedom is of a different kind, more responsible than before because the choices are your own, they are uncoerced and unbribed. "Free will is the experience of being the author of the law you obey." This world is different from that shaped by the dependency dream.

Although we have no parents in the eye-level world, when we face each other we find companions. We share the same need for meaning, the same intimations of transcendence, the certainty of death, the saving joy of love. We can sense a new connection, a linking of equals that makes all of us one family, yet individuals. Only in the eye-level world do we emerge as ourselves, true to our own perceptions and strengths, able to respond realistically to the world that surrounds us.

Cult behavior is the expression of the dependency dream. It is a self-deception more serious than may at first appear, for at this point in history problems confront us that threaten everyone on earth: nuclear weapons, contamination of the environment, spiraling populations. To solve these problems we need as much realism as possible, and realism is the first casualty of cult behavior. We must leave the security of the cult circle and move forward into the eye-level world. Whether we are inclined to lead or to follow, let us hope we can see that cult behavior is too risky, the comfort of its fantasy a lie. Reality may be more uncertain than we wish but its freedom is a bountiful reward. When the gods and demons disappear a different world appears, rich in sunlight and storm but without fear. Standing together on that level plain, we find ourselves in a new home, one that is quite real. There are no outsiders. And it is worth more than any dream.

PERSONAL FREEDOM

*On Finding Your Way
To The Real World*

ONE

Who Are the Realists?

SOMETHING is wrong. I've noticed it for a long time, as if there is something odd or unreal about the world. Most of the time I'm busy with what I'm doing and don't notice, but, sooner or later, that persistent nagging awareness emerges again, telling me that something is peculiar about my view of things, and everyone else's, too.

I don't mean that the world seems to be collapsing — starvation, atomic bombs, pollution — it isn't just those things, drastic as they may be. There is something still more basically wrong. It's as if you went to the movies and there was something odd about the projector or something strange about the camera that was used to take the movies in the first place. The images themselves seem normal, but the way it is put together is out of sequence, or taken at different speeds, or the perspective keeps changing. That's what I mean. There is something basically wrong with the structure of the world — as we have been taught to see it — but you might not notice it for a long while. It's not until you really examine your experience that you catch sight of the peculiarities. It just isn't the way you've been told. Let me give you an example:

Time makes no sense. It really doesn't apply to me; it doesn't fit. My hair gets thin and I can't stay up all night the way I used to. But I don't change. At my center I'm transparent; I'm looking out a window at everything that passes by. Time passes (I observe) and I will die (I am told), but these things don't fit that clear place where I am. Isn't that your experience, too? You get older and everyone around you gets older and you see your birthdays clicking away like numbers on a gasoline pump, but I'll bet there is something inside of you that doesn't feel it is changing at all; inside you're like some kind of mirror, reflecting everything without absorbing it. The mirror doesn't change. You watch time pass, and perhaps believe it when people tell you that you'll die — but it really doesn't fit that clear place inside. Time fits my body and the world I see, but it doesn't fit me.

Or consider it from another angle: Time flows like a river, it would seem. Yesterday, today, and tomorrow seem like a road stretching far behind and far ahead. Yet outside my window is an actual road, and on that road any place seems the same as ten feet ahead or ten feet behind — but it's not that way with Time. Ten seconds past and ten seconds ahead is nothingness, just smoke, whereas Now, this moment, where I am, is clear and bright. On either side in Time, there's nothing similar to Now, only memories (the past) or imaginings (the future). The place you were ten seconds ago has vanished, and what is the place ten seconds ahead? There is nothing there. It's very odd. Doesn't it strike you, now that you notice, that something is wrong? The "road of Time" is a thought — and the thought doesn't fit.

You have been told that you are fundamentally alone. "We enter the world alone and we exit alone," and so forth. Just you, confronting the universe. And what is the nature of the universe? Our scientific "realists" tell us it is a fascinating, orderly biochemical machine composed of electrical charges, but meaningless, purposeless, and indifferent. So — you are alone in an indifferent world. You are a highly sophisticated "biocomputer" in a highly sophisticated "hyperspace." Congratulations!

But is that your actual experience? Remember those times when you were touched by something impalpable emanating from that "outside" realm of people and things. Music, nature, sports, prayer, sex, insight, drugs, encounter, friendship, or love — a moment when you felt connected, merging, exalted. I'm talking about those special times when you felt a joyous reverence and gratitude and mystery and recognition, at finding yourself, once again, at that place. Of course, you can "explain" it and nothing need change. The mechanical puppet cosmos can clank along forever; just tell yourself that those experiences, "mystical" or otherwise, are the infantile derivatives of wishes, fears, and early memories. It's simple. But is that what they feel like? Talk to children and see if they experience such things. Consider carefully whether those special moments really fit the vapid formula; "Infantile derivatives." Isn't that explanation something you have swallowed, force-fed, like an infant, indeed, but have never been able to digest? It's indigestible because it doesn't fit, that's why. It's another swindle, like Time.

You are told you are basically alone — in empty space. Yet, when you love, are you alone? When you look, unguarded, into another's eyes, clear place to clear place, are you alone? When you wholeheartedly engage in work or play, are you alone? There is only one way to be alone: by thinking about it. The thought creates the aloneness; the concept is the problem. "Aloneness" does not fit experience.

When mathematics and chemistry define your world, it has no meaning; the world dries up. But, for you, as you walk the streets, engage others, live your life, your world is charged with meaning, filled with purposes, conflicted or aligned, at every level. Do the words "random" and "meaningless" really fit what you feel, what you experience, moment by moment — or are they something you have been told, something you now think?

Let's go a step further: Who or what are you?

If I ask myself that question and take a look to see, it's very curious indeed. I thought that I was happy, that I was thinking, that I was seeing, but when I pause and look inside it seems as if I've been looking out a window at "my" feelings, at "my" sensations, and at "my" thoughts — such as this one. If I'm looking at them, how can they be me? There is some kind of awareness, something basic that observes everything, and, although I usually don't notice because it is drowned out by all the noise, it's always there. If I turn back to find myself, look inward to the deepest, the very heart of me where I actually live, that awareness is me. It seems to have been there always, just as it is, while everything else changes. Try an experiment, right now. Close your eyes and ask yourself if you have disappeared. What's your answer? Now, cover your ears so sounds are absent — have you disappeared? No matter what part of the world or your thoughts or your feelings you make go away, you stay there. Now, what is that you? That's what I'm talking about — that place. And, in fact, it's not even a place, it's you. That's what you are and that's what I am. Until I ask that question. I'm a psychiatrist, a male, a husband, Arthur Deikman. But when I ask that question and look to see, I'm that window, that lookout, that awareness. It isn't just a theory; it's what my experience actually is and yours, too. It's really very obvious, but you were told nothing about it through all your years of school. The most basic factor of your existence, the one thing you experience indisputably, your own aware self, is never mentioned. Everything else is: the everything else that is not you.

Let's look at the wisdom you've been taught, your guidebook to the human condition:

SAMPLE 1: Satisfaction doesn't last. We're used to that principle and accept it, but isn't that a strange arrangement? You work for a goal that evaporates when it's in your hand. "True, so true, that's the way life is...." What an odd life!

SAMPLE 2: Nothing's perfect — particularly you. Everything's flawed, everything's a little off. How come? It's not so obvious that life must be defective. Would you have constructed it that way? No. So why would God? It doesn't make sense.

You see, you've been taught that that's the way everything is. You're even annoyed that I bother you about it. But stop, consider what you've been taught; time, aloneness, dissatisfaction, imperfection, identity; are they really logical? Are they facts? Are they "realistic" or have you been swindled, conned so well that it feels like home to you? It's almost funny! You thought you were being mature, adult, strong, looking life straight in the eye, hardly flinching. Maybe you've been duped. Maybe you've been living in a crazy house all this time.

Let's look around. (Perhaps there's a door.) Let's be curious and ask, "How did I learn about reality? Who are the realists?"

TWO

Learning About Reality

IN THE WOMB

WE BEGIN as awareness floating in our mother's ocean. We are warm and at ease, but do not "know" it. Slowly, we grow and move and sensations flower: pressure, vibrations, motion. In the beginning, there are no needs, no wants. Food comes to us continuously, permeating the blood. There is no need to breathe; oxygen, like food, flows effortlessly through us and our world. The temperature is even and the fetus is supported by the womb. There is neither satisfaction nor dissatisfaction. Movement occurs, vibrations are transmitted, and chemicals may change, but, by and large, the womb world is a constant one with little stress with which we must contend. We are called a fetus at that stage but we are really a part of our mother's body, not more separate than her own heart, held back from merging completely with her only by the placental membrane through which we "breathe" and "eat."

Not at birth does awareness begin, but months before. While still in our mother's womb we become aware. Consider:

Infants may be born prematurely, one or two months early, and yet they function psychologically, even though, by the calendar, they have not yet been born. The capacity for awareness does not depend on emerging from the womb nine months after conception. Inside the womb, the fetus senses the world and can respond. For example, a loud noise will cause a fetus to stir. If you tap on the mother's abdomen at the same time, the tap and the noise will become linked; the fetus will then move in response to a tap; it has "remembered." Microscopic studies show its nervous system is not fully developed, but a nervous system is there, responsive to a degree we cannot determine, as we have no idea of what systems of perception and response may exist without neurons, or with use of neurons we call "immature." Premature infants are responsive, and we must conclude that the human organism before its birth is very much alive, in mind as well as body.

"Well," you say, "we may be aware and capable of 'learning' in our mother's body, but who can really remember what we learned?"

There are many kinds of memory. For example, our bodies remember. Our posture, shaped by tension, our rigid jaws and tight bellies — the "armoring" of Reich — encode the pain and fear of early years. Release the tension, soften the armor, and the past floods forth in emotion, images, a word, a gesture. Yet, what our bodies had remembered every day of our lives, our minds had not recalled.

The very pattern of our life remembers. We may choose our "luck," the style of our mates, the form of our work, our personal myth, in order to repeat, to remember the past. We react in old patterns — the "transference" of Freud — remembering by emotions. With these strategies, we repeat without awareness the pain and fear of early years, controlling and preserving them at the same time. How early are those memories? Very early, before words, sometimes; so early that a tingling in the lips may be all we can recover. The memory is there, but it guides our life without our knowing.

If you agree we are aware within the womb, "listening" to life, "remembering," you may still ask, "How can we be taught; what is the route whereby we learn?"

Our mother's speech, her laughter, her crying, her anger are vibrations transmitted through her body as well as through the air; they pervade the womb as well as the outer world. Vibrations speak in their own way: the fetus knows no words, but it can feel. In India, sounds are used to transform man. Mantras — syllables and words — repeated endlessly, are said to reach each cell, stilling the mind and setting free the energy of bliss. Mystic masters, scientists in their own right, claim each sound has its own vibration energy, producing its own effect, to be prescribed according to the need and possibility of each human being.

In daily life we can sense the meaning of a muffled conversation. Anger, joy, and sadness sing their own songs, without need for words. We feel them — why not also within the womb? An experiment: Subjects are asked to imagine emotions, then press a delicate button that records the subtle pattern their pressure makes, forward and back, strong or soft, wavering, increasing or declining. The different subjects give the same pattern for each emotion; we touch in the same way. Deep in our being is a code of feeling, of touch, vibration — a language in our cells.

Our mother spoke to us in many ways, months before we left her: the rich vibrations of her voice conveyed her feelings; her hormones signaled stress; her muscles tensed and changed the pressure of our world. Were there yet other languages and channels for our pre-born mind? Pure energy may be a route for knowing. Acupuncturists say an energy permeates and flows throughout our bodies, affected by pressure and by heat at key points along "meridians." Kirlian photography shows pulsing zones of "bio-plasma" surrounding living forms, responsive to emotion. Electrical currents on the skin change with emotion and can be measured to indicate the meaning charge of words. Salamanders grow back limbs, guided by the change in their limbs' electric field. And if ESP is real, what barrier can exist between a mother and her unborn child?

We were bathed in energy within our mothers, pulsations rocked us in our sleep. Hormone messages came by blood and sounds vibrated in our cells. Information perfused our first world.

What did we learn? Much more than we believe. The serenity, agitation, or depression of a mother goes quickly to the womb by all the messengers of body and mind. Subtleties of voice and movement paint a portrait of the world. Some persons shine with an aura of joy; calmness and easiness streams from them like light. We feel good in their presence. They say, without words, "The world is okay"; "No cause for fear"; "I'm with you"; "I like you"; "We're one." From another person comes alarm; posture, voice and odor warn of pain, of danger stalking the world. Distrust speaks: "Stay away"; "I'm afraid"; "I dislike you"; "Bitterness is life." Basic messages, day by day; cosmologies of feeling transmitted through a chain of generations.

As we flowered in our mother's womb, we were learning, listening to the messages that told us of the world, how it is, what we could expect, how we should approach our swelling life.

And then we were born.

THE PELVIC JOURNEY

Although we think of emergence into the world as the first great shock, it must have been tremendous relief after the inconceivable stress of the pelvic journey. When birth begins, the world of the womb is utterly transformed from placidity and ease to utter violence and chaotic tension. The contrast with the previous state is so great that it will probably not be matched during the entire period of life that follows. The uterine muscle contracts with enormous power, and the pressure upon the fetus multiplies many times. Its body is jammed and twisted into the pelvic tunnel with such force that the head may be molded to accommodate the passage. The mother herself is in a state of maximum stress, mobilizing all her reserves in order to cope.

Within the womb, the world has gone mad, convulsing and churning. A contraction ceases, and there is a period of quiet and rest — and then it occurs again and again and again and again. Each time the forces and pressures are stronger and the fetal functioning more compromised. The once free-floating world becomes totally constricted until all freedom is gone; the arms are pinned to the sides and the head is twisted, stretched, and bent in its journey through the pelvic outlet. During that passage, the umbilical cord providing oxygen and food may become compressed and occluded, or the cord may be wrapped around the neck and shut off or decrease the oxygen needed by the brain. Thus, suffocation may be added to the onslaught. The turmoil reaches a zenith and then resolves with great suddenness as the head pops free; the body follows soon after. Initiation of breathing and the security of the mother's arms mark the beginning of the next phase.

Is that really how it feels? Perhaps I've given an adult's view of something that is only a physical process, with no mind or memory to take notes. We don't remember being born, so how can we tell?

True, we think we don't remember, yet there may be memories deeply buried in us. They may be memories of a different kind — not in terms of vision, but in a physical form, in sensory patterns different from those forms that develop later in maturity. When patients were given LSD, week after week, for months, they showed a similar pattern of experience. It seemed that each person re-experienced his birth. Mentally and physically he portrayed the pelvic journey with all the features that go with it: suffocation, pain, strain, and rest. Trapped, compressed, in endless chaos, the journey ended in explosive, expansive bliss, in utter quiet and flooding light. These "memories" were so explicit, so correct in detail, they suggest our birth creates a pattern around which we group events of later life. Birth may be a way of classifying life.

If that is so, what could we learn from being born? Such an overwhelming journey might begin a "need" to escape and to expand, a need for power, to control, and a fear of helplessness. Linked with these needs and fears may be the "memory" of serenity, of paradise, of a state without confusion, pain, or struggle. From the moment of our birth we may begin a journey toward a goal whose initial form lies behind us, but whose path will carry us to something we have never felt before nor seen.

THREE

Lessons Outside the Womb

AUTOMATIZATION

Now begins a process that is both the magic means and the relentless curse of our lives: automatization. Whatever we do becomes a pattern — automatic — no longer needing our attention. Watch an infant struggle to its feet, intensely focused on its basic task; it sways perilously, staggers forward, sways again, and falls back solidly on its rump. Totally absorbed, it tries again — and falls again. Yet, two months later, it stands without concern and toddles rapidly to its mother, all attention fixed on the bottle in her hand. An adult, learning to drive, sweats to make the clutch and shift work together, looking up desperately to steer and looking down to do the gears. A year later, he or she drives down the freeway, sixty miles an hour, chatting with a friend about a party the night before. We learn to move and grasp and drive a car and a thousand other skills and, having learned, run off with our attention fixed on something else.

We learn everything. We must even learn to see. The first world of mixed-up colors, changing shapes, and shifting brightness required our attention, too. When adults, blind since birth, have sight restored, they do not see a world suddenly found. Light and color in pure confusion assault their minds. Weeks of effort finally yield success: a pencil can be recognized, held up and down. But shift the pencil to the horizontal and it is lost again. Another lesson must be learned. So much work is needed that adults with newfound sight sometimes refuse the gift, retreating to the world of sound and touch already fashioned since their early years.

Our bodies teach us, too. The mouth informs our mind with openings and closings. A man holds out a box, lid closed. "Open the box, baby!" It's a problem for the baby's mind, and he turns the box, puzzled. Finally, he opens wide his mouth, then he opens the lid. His body functions lead his mind, providing patterns for his thought. Those pattern modes respond to need — and to reward, reward determined by his culture's need. Many forces teach us how to live.

Learning, learning, every minute, every day, learning about reality from those who learned from those who learned, back through the generations. Learning patterns, layer on layer, building up our world. From one pattern to the next we move, each lesson filed away, programmed now to function automatically without awareness of the process steps. We are automatized, our attention freed for other things. Freedom, yes, but slavery, too, for a curse is latent in the power: the first encounter cannot be regained. What was it like to stagger to our feet and, lurching, take our first steps across an enormous room? What was it like, that first movie, concert, beach? We pay a price: the freshness and the richness of our "beginner's mind."

We learned to hear, to see, to think in a world of objects, and we could not learn about the object world without selection. We are taught to be selective, to pay close notice to the shape of things. A mother holds a ball and says a word; baby repeats the sound, reaching for the bright, round color, "Ball, ball!" Day after day, the baby learns. The ball, the mother, and the world are jealous beings. They demand subordination of all competing things: the background must subside so they can stand forth, commanding recognition. Objects and their meanings rule our day; as we grow older, form, shape, and boundaries crowd out the sensual. Color and texture recede from sight; no longer chosen first, they fade in intensity. The world changes as we learn, according to our lessons.

Selection has a price, and we forget what we left behind. Our infant years are blank, and early childhood, too. We seem to have emerged at five or six into a world already there, not remembering our creative role, not recalling how it was before our school began, not knowing that we learned it all.

THE DEVELOPMENT OF THE SENSE OF SELF

Imagine the infant's world: Shifting fields of sensations within shifting levels of sleep and waking. Swirling mists of warm sleep giving way to bright color and simple patterns, mixed with gnawing feelings, persistent and demanding; then muscle tensings and crying sounds; then warmth and pleasure and the smell of mother, liquid warmth and mouth tensions; then dissolving into darkness; and then the light and color, discomforts — beginning patterns — on and on. Memoryless, the flow holds all attention. Gradually, the patterns form: mother's smell and comforting pressure, activity of eyes and mouth, hands grasping, mother's sounds.

Sensations separate the baby from the world, those that go and those that stay, becoming "inside" and "outside" much later on. Now they just come and go; pain, hunger, touch, and smell are the teachers. Pain draws a line around the edge of fingers, and vision tidies up the clutter of light. Together they teach the body as the baby's will begins to command. Grab the bottle; grab the nose; pat the face that smiles. Crawl to the warmth; pull back from the fire; grab the food; stuff the mouth; drop the glass; move the fingers for the eyes to see. Pain, loss, and intention separate the world into us and them. Mother leaves, but pain remains; the arm can be moved, but the crib stays still. Yet the separation of "inner" from "outer" is really not so clear. Crying can summon others and thus affect the inner pain; the baby may not be able to move from the holding arms. What is cause and what effect comes later. For the moment, patterns rule the day and may continue, if the culture wills, without an automatic road of Time. At first, experienced only in the moment, the world just happens.

THE HUMAN OBJECT

We objectify our world and others in it. "Others," indeed! "[Eighteen-month-old children] mostly treat contemporaries as physical objects or disregard them completely. Five in one room may each disregard one of the others. If two were together near an object, one may just push the other out of the way impersonally, as though he were an object... one as [he] climbs, pushes a second, who falls on a third. All ignore this. Or two may try to climb up in exactly the same place. Both struggle with each other, but merely for the space, not aggressively, as later. Child wanting to sit on chair filled by other child may either sit on other child or may spill him out. May walk around or just bump into other child." [Ames]

What a startling observation! So much skill has been acquired, so many lessons learned, and, yet, still no Other. No Self like you in all your world because you know no Self — you, the person, are not there — although your memory, thoughts, and sensations make up all the world.

Your unselfconscious will is in the service of acquiring. It is possessive and slow to emerge. At twelve months of life, about to walk, with words to say and understand: "... even the sense of personal possession is practically absent and he makes very meager distinctions between himself and others." [Gesell] Possession comes late and precedes Self; possessive pronouns are used first. "Child grabbed from may hang onto object; and may let it go and cry; may just let it go; may shout 'mine.'" [Ames] At twenty-four months of age, "Pronouns, mine, me, you, and I, are coming into use approximately in the order just given." [Gesell] "Mine" leads to "me" (the object) and "you" (the object) and finally to "I," an "I" whose shape and meaning are ruled by the possessive mode.

FOUR

The Action Mode

WHEN we see and when we think and walk and eat and breathe we serve ourselves, our purpose. The purpose guides the rest. In the beginning, floating in the maternal ocean, we allow the environment in and are nourished. Indeed, we should not say "allow." Allowing is an adult decision. In the womb we just exist in a state of permeation, perfused with the blood and vibrations of our world. Then, during the cataclysm of birth, we struggle for the first time. What had been a world of comfort is now pain, and we contract to shut it out, to gain control, to act and so to change the turbulence back to peace. With the first breath, and the first breast, peace does return. The infant body loosens, relaxing as the warmth flows in, allowing what is needed to enter once again, receptive to the world. In the early weeks all is intake, relaxation, sleep, and food. Briefly, however, between feeding and sleep, eyes focus on the world; they are active, following, reaching out in interest rather than in pain. The motive differs but the function is the same: to act upon the world. A mode of living has begun: life as acting on the world, doing things to all the objects of the object world so as to bring about possession and relief from pain.

The lessons, bottle, ball, mother, nose, are lessons in possession, in reaching for what is shiny, bright, warm, and safe. Name what's good and squeeze it with the fingers, draw it to the mouth, and take it in. The baby reaches for the bottle, eyes focused, brain intent, arms extended and waving with excitement. Into the mouth pops the nipple — and what a change! The body softens, eyes cross, lids droop down, arms relax. And then — sleep. All functions are eased, immersed back into a resting world. The action mode yields to the receptive mode, phasing back and forth. For a brief while, at the beginning, reception dominates the infant life. It will recede as we acquire the world.

School continues. More and more the action mode rules the day. With practice and reward it grows in scope until, with symbols, it creates thought to plan its action. Then thoughts detach from sensations, becoming self-sufficient, independent, and, finally, absolute. The abstract world is born; thoughts seem real. Memory builds a Past and imagination creates a Future; between both they establish Time. The action mode sets priorities: "mine, me, you," — in that order we learn. Possession shapes the Self and the world.

As our bodies teach our minds so our minds instruct our bodies. Desire for the ball will focus eyes. The broad, impressionistic world narrows to a central stage whose sharp details and clear edges separate the ball from all the rest, which now recedes, vanishing into background. Muscles tense and capillaries shunt the blood from gut to muscles; adrenalin executes the change. Breathing hastens and the chest expands. Eyes and neck and body synchronize, directed to the target. Watching the ball roll, learning what it does, teaches object logic: A is not B. Object thought is born with the rolling ball. The ball, an object; the ball, a thought. They are linked together, welded tight, until our thought blankets our perception.

Thinking is for action, for acquisition and control. Thinking guides effort until thought itself is effortful. The knitted brow, the intent look, the tensing of the eyes, all partners to a single purpose, a mode of being in the world. "Me" and "you" and "I" are sharpened, suitable for object games. "Mine" is the favorite, and clear boundaries are the rule. Day by day, body and mind coordinate, learning control, learning to manipulate the world. The action mode becomes the norm. Reception, where we started, is used for sleep and food and comforting.

As conscious doing is the essence of the action mode, allowing is the essence of the receptive. With the action mode we divide and conquer our environment. With the receptive, we take in, receive and unify. It is the difference between breathing out and breathing in. Try a sample, now. Take a full breath; breathe in and then breathe out. Notice the difference in your state of mind during those two phases. On inhaling, mental contents become diffuse, thinking tends to stop. On exhaling, energy flows out, the vision sharpens; thinking, too, is sharper on exhalation, boundaries more clear.

When manifesting in the action mode, when striving in the world, the electrical currents of the brain are fast and short.

The big muscles tense and eyes focus; the sensual recedes. But in the receptive mode, the senses unfold. Vision softens, muscles relax, alpha waves may appear; slow, irregular, and higher waves, they indicate a change in attitude, something subtle, beyond words.

And words themselves, where do they belong? Our words are from the object world, the world we made by separation, in the action mode. Words are the tools of that mode. With them we discriminate, with them we divide reality into pieces, objects, things, which we can grab with minds or bodies. The Eskimo has many words for snow, the skier several, the average man just one — according to need, according to the word's function in the action mode. Although objects may have many names, sensations have very few, but not from the dullness of our perception. We can discriminate a thousand hues of color but not name them. Feelings are the same. How many forms of love have we to match against the one word? Love is experienced in the receptive mode. It is the action mode that separates with forms, boundaries, words, logic, and the Road of Time. The receptive mode unifies, is sensory and diffuse; receptive time is instantaneous, all at once. In that mode, the self merges into Now. What do you call relationships where A is B? I-Thou, Buber named it. I-It is in the action mode.

The function, the goal we set, controls the mode. What's the goal? Is it combat, control, and capture, or receive, synthesize, allow? It is not activity versus passivity. "Allowing" is an action but of a different kind. We say "I-It" and fire the bullet so it intersects the racing deer. We say "I-Thou" and receive our lover's embrace. We need both modes; each has its place and function. Merge with the infinite and you lose the deer. Calculate your "making love" and it becomes another task, depriving you of re-creation. Yet they can blend. You can work in your garden, uprooting the weeds, one by one, while being receptive to the breeze and the soft earth.

Infants and children must perform their biological task: survival in a biological world. That primary need begins in the womb and pervades the childhood years; it has trained us all too well in the action mode. The receptive comes occasionally, hardly at command, as if it were an alien being. That which should be familiar we come to perceive as strange. Years later, as adults, we may go to special schools to learn receiving, to regain the mode with which our life began. Until then, the receptive mode goes obsolete, latent, receding from the repertoire, but not forgotten.

> There was a time when meadow, grove, and stream.
> The earth and every common sight,
> To me did seem Apparelled in celestial light.
> The glory and the freshness of a dream. [Wordsworth]

Glory? Not likely in the child. But when adults recover their receptive mode and grow to a new wholeness, recruiting to the soft, wide span of childhood vision the complex meanings of adult thought — then glory, then, perhaps, a dream transcending the dreams of one-eyed man.

FIVE

Consequences

SELF, TIME, ANXIETY

THE action mode creates a world. That world has dimensions of its own, distinctive features, normally unquestioned in their status as elemental facts. Who does not assume a separate self and the flow of Time? They are the pillars that uphold that world, but they were not given: they grew or were made.

The self grew, for the organism has its plan. We started as pure happening; we were what was occurring in the womb. With the birth process, intention formed to direct action: fear and desire took their roots, then grew in strength like other parts. With intention, the body self took form, for the body is the agent of intention and executes the biological plan: possession. (Mine, me, you, I — in that order.) The body is the source of pain and pleasure, qualities that dominate our sensory world. They are so compelling, they define what is "personal," what belongs to self. Their authority is never questioned.

Memory and symbol engage sensation, organizing objects and object laws. Others see your body as an object and that helps you do so, too:

"What a pretty smile you have!"

"Come here!"

"Wave your hand!"

The body possesses and possession is the game:

"Here is your bottle."

"Give me the ball."

"Want the doll?"

What the body hugs belongs to self; what it does not touch may disappear. First the ball, then the reaching arm, then the body of the arm, and then the reaching wish produces "me" — all objectified into the landscape of the object world, seen from a window. The window frames the world and in the space behind the window an invisible object forms: "I." Gradually, a solitary Self is born.

Memory creates Time and orders objects in a Past. Images and words create a Future, ordering the objects yet to come. Between the Past and Future, laws are found, connecting both in a smooth path on which walks the form of Self. Like a cage of tigers, the trained objects stiffen to the whip of logic and take their places in an even line, arrayed in demonstration of predictive power. Wild applause greets success, but when the noise subsides, another character appears: Anxiety. What if the tigers all jump down and in disordered rage make a bloody meal of the maestro? These shadows of the future, cast by the past, can overwhelm the bright display. The scene of gaiety and pride may give way to troubled dreams.

The action mode has welded past and future into an arrow. As it flies there can be no rest, for Now has disappeared.

Zeno's paradox is lived by us. By the action mode we acquire Self, gain power, and survive. But Past and Future, joined by Anxiety, has no room for Now. Scurrying in memory, images, and thought, we have no time to stop and be nourished by the world. A hunger grows: dissatisfaction. Forgetting how to eat, we begin to starve at the banquet. Believing what we're taught, we cannot fit the world.

MORE school, defining Self: boy, girl, good, bad, fast, slow, happy, sad, strong, weak, pretty, ugly, smart, and dumb. The Self stands like a sculptor's armature, and the others fire away, heaving globs of clay to spatter, stick, and lump together as the self-shape grows.

"Tommy is a good boy with blond hair, a nice smile, smart and fast."

"Jennie is a pretty girl, delicate and sweet, with brown hair, a merry laugh, and very understanding."

"Jim is a roughneck, not too bright."

"Helen has black hair and big feet; she's homely but kind."

Animated sculptures taking shape, sitting in rows in school. Eyes peering out of the hardening clay.

Adolescence, we are told, is the time of identity. Teenagers intimately converse: "Who are you and who am I?" No wonder the question is asked. Awkwardly, the clay figures stagger around the room, trying to walk after such a difficult new birth.

"You tell me and I'll tell you." (Maybe we'll find out that way.) "You are really very sensitive!" (Not much help, just more clay.) Some rough places are smoothed and a hole or two filled in. Adult statues serve as guides and they are so stiff they have forgotten what the young ones can still feel: that something doesn't fit. "It looks just fine!" (But it doesn't feel right.) The clay binds and cramps in all the wrong places. A memory of freedom haunts the room.

HOW DO YOU SPEND YOUR DAY?

On waking in the morning, things are unsorted. The first stumbling steps informed by a foggy vision give way to clear reentry into the familiar. You wash your face, brush your teeth, enjoying without realizing it the sensations of your present moment. Before long, your thoughts begin: remembering, planning, drifting briefly into fantasy. Thoughts of the day's work, yesterday's events, wishes for the future, all perform an act of transmigration, and you fly through your breakfast world, only occasionally aware of the taste of the food and its texture, or the colors and light of the room. Your day of fantasy has begun.

The morning paper may complete the job. The same news you read yesterday, a day further along, absorbs attention with a thousand details, none vital, but all arousing concern, fear, and desire. It would not matter if you had been away for months, your newspaper would sound the same. If not the paper, then the radio, television, bringing the morning news, the weather, and the ads. A familiar noise — it fills the spaces between thought and memories.

So into the car or into the bus or train and go to work. Busses and trains hold rows of people at morning prayer, or so it seems, heads bowed over their texts, swaying together in silent, somber attention. Inside those heads the movie film unwinds. A few pairs of eyes look out the window, some seeing, some in dreamland.

Finally, the job. Absorption in a task is some relief — and even satisfaction. But symbolic satisfactions set the pace. Victories of effort allay fear, promote pride, provide assurance of control and worth. Success means all the dreams will turn out fine, all the fantasies and images are warm and bright. The thousand faces of the Other, mounted on swivel necks, in neutral position while the issue is in doubt, at the moment of success swing toward you with smiles and admiration. You rest a while, savoring the glow, but it does not last long. The heads soon swing back to neutral, threatening, should you falter, to swing the other way and be transformed into a crowd of departing strangers.

Yet a task is good; it may demand you focus your attention, eliminating thoughts and images as you exercise skill, immersed in the process.

The effort continues, tiredness ensues, and then — lunch, usually a social event. With the others you can talk and laugh, without demands. But did you taste your lunch?

Back to work — wrestling with the future in the landscape of your phantom mind. During the day, if you were lucky, a brief suspension of concern and will took place. Your energies flowed, converging on the task; and with just the lightest touch to guide the stream, something whole emerged, new to you, not exactly yours. The creative moment was complete; it filled you, solid, there. You felt its difference from all the rest, its flowing life, that magical appearance of something more than you — from you.

But that moment may not come today, or for many days.

The housewife is the same. The morning cleanup, helped perhaps by radio or television. Live a thousand fantasies while the vacuum cleaner sucks up dirt, its noise washing out detail. The dishes done in reverie, the grocery list prepared, the washer filled. And in the afternoon, perhaps a gathering of friends for talk and stimulation in the abstract world. What was the texture of the cup? What was the feeling in the eyes that touched briefly?

The end of day, at home again where everyone converges with his or her hunger, not just for food. Man, woman, and child gather there to receive, for so much effort wants reward. Husband and wife greet each other to be filled; so do the children. The supper meal, biggest of the day, designed to fill, can give some joy if not washed under by the daydreams or the talk. Then television, the paper, cards, or a gathering of friends for talk, for words and con-cepts, memories, private thoughts. Finally, sleep. Perhaps sex before sleep, a touching and a sensing of what is Now, but much entan-gled in the will. Concepts, planning intrude on sex; doing, rather than allowing, may be the mode, and in the doing fantasies take part, instructions from the latest book: "Fantasies are good. Remem-ber all the zones — take your time — relax — don't worry." Is she ready? Should I tell him? Sex can become another task, prior to sleep, but mixed with satisfaction, still. The charge of body energy brings you home for a moment, dissolving the structures of the mind and leaving in its wake peace and joy — a little. Not often, perhaps. Indeed, sometimes never.

Then sleep. For some, a pill to gain control, even here. The drug most used in all our land is a tranquilizer.

The weekend. Work around the house. Go to a restaurant, to eat without demands. The service and the expectations are more important than the food. Relief, indeed. Perhaps a movie. Three hours of symbols, fantasies, emotions, nothing you have to do but surrender to someone else's world. Afterward, let's be social: talk, anxiety, alcohol, and games. That loving feeling underneath emerging for a moment, now and then.

Then, religion, dependency fulfilled. A contract, sure enough, for work performed, for control, for faithfulness, the promise of eternal care. Father and mother fantasies above the clouds, accompanied by organs and emotion, and singing all together for the comfort of the group. Yet an echo of something else may pervade the hall. Something may be touched, some reminder. "Oh yes, I must come more often." Out into the day, for greetings, talk, and home.

Perhaps sports, pure play (unless a task). Performance measured by the number may spoil that, too, but there are times when the miraculous happens. The body flows into the ball, the skis, the wave, and once again a light turns on. "Oh yes! I had forgotten — I want more." You forget again, the memory drowned out by all that's different. Sports may mean to watch, in stadium or on television, giving oneself up to another dream. At the end you are elated by a vicarious victory or angered by defeat but, either way, a little drained, a little fuzzy in the head: the sign of fantasy.

All this may seem extreme, an exaggeration for poetic style. You and I are not like that, not living in a phantom world of abstract symbols, strung together into an enormous net with a mesh so fine that as it covers up the world hardly a speck shows through. "Not me!" Are you sure?

Consider: **Every thought you have is unreal.** Each one is an abstraction, a shadow of the thing that is. Your future is not real (imagine a purple cow). Your past is not real, for the past is memories. (How can you fit your memory of the ocean inside your living room?) Memories are images of where you are not, so how can the past be real? Concepts are not real. Write "One million dollars" on a paper and take it to your grocer. Good luck. Thinking is not real. It's a tool. Would you lay a loaf of bread upon a scale, then eat the scale? Bon appetit! Every thought you have is unreal, every memory you have is unreal, every imagining you have is unreal, all your anxieties are unreal, all your hopes are unreal, all your desires. All that which you remember having, all that which you imagine will come — all are unreal. So what of the day that you just lived in fantasy — in abstraction, concerned with past pleasures and future problems — how much was real?

"All this is crazy; you go too far. It's semantics, tricks with words — that's all!"

Have you ever noticed how they do the news whenever a war is on? Do you remember those reports? "Fifty-five enemy soldiers killed!" They didn't say, "Fifty-five husbands, brothers, lovers, fathers, sons were killed today by our efforts." Curious, isn't it? "Fathers" evokes the real. "Enemy soldiers" evokes a dream. If we evoked the real, what would happen then? Consider. Billions of your dollars go for war. You are not the only one. Billions of Russian rubles go for war. Billions of your dollars go for killing a husband, a father, a brother, a lover — or defending yourself against Them doing that to you.

Our resources are ending, that is true. We take the dwindling energies and precious metals and fashion machines to destroy cities that we will be unable to rebuild. Working hard, creatively and well, we have accumulated bombs and poisons in such vast quantities that their use would destroy all life. We breed viruses never seen before; their military potential is truly staggering. To minister to our fantasies, to entertain us, we give to a man or woman a hundred times the money we give to him who grows our food. There is not enough food, but more babies are produced. We are poisoning what we breathe and what we drink and what we eat. We are waiting.

It is the nature of ideas and fantasies and symbols that they have no guiding wisdom of their own. The action mode is out of control, and we are dreaming a symbolic world, only briefly waking to what is real.

At the same time (in the nick of time?), if we are lucky we are stirred to a saving action, for as we grow older our fantasies of power may lose their credibility. Death approaches and the dissatisfaction that gnawed from time to time now mixes with anxiety and causes us to look around for a way out. Activities and

fantasies will not do. What else is there? Where, in all this enormous room, is there a door?

SIX

Spiritual Doors

THE mystical, spiritual, religious life has always been here. From the corner of your eye you saw the churches and processions, you read of "holy men" and fat Zen beggars full of enlightenment. Western scientists have proved that meditation rests the body, but yogis have been chanting mantras for three thousand years. From India, China, Japan, Arabia come strange tales of strange people hinting persistently that there exists a way. For Christians, there's the image of cowled monks, a cross, and Saint Teresa. "Lord Jesus Christ, have mercy on me"— the West has mantras, too. Western meditation is called "affective prayer" and "contemplation," and asceticism is nothing new. It's all in our tradition, but few think of it as a door. Religion mostly isn't. Crusades in many forms kill for Christ, or in the name of Allah or a Hindu god. Yet the texts go back three thousand years and the men who wrote them do not seem like fools. For example: Buddha.

Old age, sickness, and death — these were what the young Buddha saw when he was not the Buddha but Siddhartha Gautama, a prince with wealth, a beautiful wife, and a young child. Old age, sickness, and death. He realized those three things could affect him, too, even though he was a prince and the sun shone on him. Dissatisfaction with his life suddenly flowered at that moment, and he abandoned his royal way of life to seek an end to his dissatisfaction, an end to the anxiety that these realities aroused in him.

Six years later, he said he found it. Not through mortifying his body, although he did that, not through living as a hermit in the forest, although he did that, and not through practicing the special meditations through which he achieved strange states of consciousness. He did learn from all these things, but what he learned was that they were of no use, their effects didn't last. Time after time, Gautama must have found himself still back at the human position, still dissatisfied, still anxious about the prospect of old age, disease, and death. So he gave up. He gave up his efforts, he gave up his austerities, and he gave up his disciples — the ones who came to him because of the fame of his self-mortifications. He sat under a tree, for there was nothing else to do. It is said that in that state of cessation of striving he gazed upon the morning star and was enlightened as to Truth. This Truth set him free — free from suffering, from dissatisfaction.

There were Buddhas before Gautama and Buddhas after him, Buddhas in the West as well as in the East, men and women who found a way and a door — or so they said and left instructions for others to do the same. The instructions haven't been a great success; the world seems as bloody-minded now as it ever was, and Buddhas are not numerous. Yet so many Buddhas point to the same door we would be foolish to pass it by. At least we can understand what they are talking about even if we decline to go that way.

"IF WE keep ourselves free from the things that are outside us, God will give us in exchange everything that is in heaven... itself with all its powers." [Meister Eckhart] "Binding the mind stuff to a place is fixed attention... focusedness of the presented idea on that place is contemplation...." [Patanjali] "When this active effort of mental concentration is successful, it is followed by a more passive, receptive state of samadhi in which the earnest disciple will enter into the blissful abode of noble wisdom." [Goddard] "For if such a soul should desire to make any effort of its own with its interior faculties, this means that it will hinder and lose the blessings which... God is instilling into it and impressing upon it." [Hilton]

These are instructions for you, instructions in opening a door, the "spiritual" door. They are very interesting instructions if you notice that they are basically the same, even though they come from men who spoke quite different languages, lived centuries apart, and went their own way. The instructions can be summed up simply: practice "renunciation" and "meditation."

Renunciation. There's a heavy word! All those images of self-denial: the wild-haired, skinny, bearded old man in the desert cave; the beautiful nun hidden away, entombed within convent walls; flagellations of the body and the spirit — we confuse means and ends. There is another definition of renunciation: "Renunciation... is not giving up the things of this world, it is accepting that they go away." [Suzuki] Allowing, letting, nonattachment: renunciation means relaxing the grasping hand — the opposite of the action mode. Have you ever done it? Have you ever quit, really taken a vacation? How hard it is to stop! In the national parks the visitors stream from busses, cameras ready, kids in hand, naming the flowers and the trees, stunned for a moment by the first view but soon hard at work looking and doing.

All the while, the mountains stand there waiting to speak if the noise would just die down. Sometimes it does. Sometimes one person's mind, blessed by fatigue or sudden shock, just stops; his eyes are open, he is listening, and the world comes in. That's meditation. That's contemplation. That's renunciation: when you stop. The door is not "religious," not exotic, full of incense, robes, and symbols. It is not alien, not strange, not secret — just un-practiced. Buddha taught: "One is one's own refuge, who else could be the refuge?" "He said that there was no esoteric doctrine in his teachings, nothing hidden in the 'closed fist' of the teacher." [Rahula] Nothing hidden, nothing secret — just forgotten.

Perhaps you don't believe me. Perhaps you grew up thinking meditation meant crossing your legs, chanting Sanskrit, fingering beads, looking holy, or just being a freak. Enlightenment meant your troubles were gone, you could fly through the air, read minds, and avoid reincarnation as a frog. Spiritual meant religion: bishops and rabbis, solemn-faced priests and ministers, and an endless line of organs playing hush-and- glory music. Okay, but set all that aside for a while. Let's go to a monastery and see what actually goes on. Monasteries are schools where you learn to be "spiritual." Perhaps we can understand what they do, and why.

IN MID-CALIFORNIA, some twenty miles inland from the Big Sur coast, is Tassajara, a Zen monastery. It was a hot springs resort, so it doesn't look like Shangri-La. Everyone in it is American and rather young. Yet it's very Japanese. The gateway entrance is traditional, and time is regulated by the notes of bells and wood clappers resonating impressively through the quiet air. The men and women wear black robes, and the men, and some women, shave their heads — definitely exotic. And when you look in at the zendo (the meditation hall), you see them sitting in cross-legged rows like a picture out of the National Geographic. The students are doing "zazen" meditation. They have been told to follow their breathing or to count their breaths one by one and not to get in-volved in thinking or daydreaming. They are instructed to keep their backs straight and breathe from the belly. Pacing slowly along the rows is a robed figure carrying a stick, and every now and then one of the seated students presses his palms together, bows forward, and gets whacked on the shoulder. Strange indeed! They do that for forty minutes at a time and then get up, walk slowly around the hall, sit down, and do it again.

The students have their meals in the zendo, too; the diet is vege-tarian. Mealtime is more ceremony than eating, full of wrapping and unwrapping howls, placing spoons and chopsticks in ritual order, and chanting verses in Japanese. Sometimes, in the evening, there is a lecture about Zen. It's philosophical, in English, full of paradoxes, usually a translation of everyday events into Buddhism.

"There are perhaps three kinds of creation. The first is to be aware of ourselves after we finish zazen. When we sit we are nothing, we do not even realize what we are; we just sit. But when we stand up, we are there! That is the first step in creation. When you are there, everything else is there; everything is created all at once. When we emerge from nothing, when everything emerges from nothing, we see it all as a fresh new creation. This is non-attachment." [Suzuki]

Try zazen. If you sit cross-legged for forty minutes you will get pains in your legs. The students are told, "Be the pain, watch it, don't move, don't complain, accept it." If the student is disappointed with his meditation, he may be told, "You have a gaining idea in mind." Thinking, daydreams, and emotions are described as intrusions, as distractions to be patient with until they go away. The student should not strive for enlightenment, he is told, because if he is truly "just sitting" he is enlightenment itself. The person meditating is not supposed to do anything except be sitting. "Be" is sensory-perceptive, concrete.

Like monasteries of other systems, Tassajara is a communal society. Although there are some status rewards, there are certainly no profits in the monetary sense. The work is shared in rotation, and the daily routine has little variety to it. Each activity is represented as being equally important as any other; washing dishes is supposed to be as "good" as walking in the woods.

There are no televisions, no radios, no movies. Three times a year, there is a week of intensive meditation called sesshin, in which the students spend seven days sitting in meditation in the zendo from before dawn to late at night. Occasionally, they have an interview with the Zen master.

That's it. Tassajara is a Japanese Zen Buddhist monastery sitting in the mountains of California, attended by young Americans. What does it mean? Assuming there's something to it, what is that something? How do we make sense out of it? What does it contribute and what are its limitations? One cannot judge too well from the outside, but an interesting consistency emerges when one thinks of the rituals as techniques pursuant to a goal: teaching the receptive mode.

To begin with, zazen, "just sitting," is the opposite of everything we have learned to do. We learned to move our minds from
sensation to thought. In infancy we were an arm reaching for a
spot of color. The muscle and the color became one. Over and
over again we reached until we saw only an object, the ball, and
we saw the shape before the color. Finally there was only the ball
and we hardly felt the reaching of our arm; it had become automatic. Our minds were free to think ahead and know where the
ball would land. We learned to move and see and hear and touch
automatically, freeing energy for thought. Now we can think and
be only half aware of sight and touch and sound: thought dominates our conscious life. But when we meditate, what are we
doing? It doesn't matter if it's a yogic, Zen, or Christian form. The
meditation de-automatizes the generation of our thoughts by sending us back along the developmental path: sensations receive our
attention while thought is ignored; the attention energy withdrawn
from abstractions is reinvested in perception. Breathing, chanting,
saying mantras, or "just sitting," the focus is the same: sensation.

Whereas the action mode controls, the receptive mode allows
— and meditation is allowing. Hour after hour, sitting in the
zendo, the students learn the receptive mode, the one they started
with but set aside and now, belatedly, renew. True, it's very exotic,
very mysterious, very Japanese. Fundamentally, however, it's a
functional matter. They didn't wear wristwatches in medieval Japan,
so they had bells and wooden blocks they struck with mallets. But
they still use them. Clocks and watches would stimulate minds into
the Western mode. Bells and chimes are better. The penetrating
sound stops thought and hangs there, shimmering, teaching the
mind to follow it into silence. Long robes slow you down; a deep
bow stops you. The ritual at mealtime receives full attention,
and silence helps shift our organismic program from the abstract
future to the sensory now. Linear time, the pillar of our usual
world, is undermined by hours of sitting and counting breaths, by
the merging of one day into the next through unvarying routine,

by lectures convincing intellects that their intellect is wrong.

The gospel preached aims at your motivation. Our motives program our perception; our purpose organizes our world. So acquisition is the first to go, the primary purpose of the action mode. The self is fired at by sermons teaching ego is illusion, by standardizing clothes and posture, work, and meals, by minimizing speech. Death, the focus of an anxious life, is discredited, declared to be a product of delirious minds. Pain, the prod that taught us boundaries and motivations, is challenged and dismissed in meditation. You are told to "be the pain" and keep on sitting. "Endure, don't run; experience, accept!" Pleasure, too, must lose appeal, lose its beckoning power, to bring about the shift in mode. If you "accept," "let go," and never seek the memory of the past, how can pleasure serve to guide your acts? So open your hand. "Renunciation is not giving up the things of this world; it is accepting that they go away."

And when, in sesshin, you sit for seven days counting breaths, following sensations, it does its job. The stoutest defender of the action mode will waver somewhere in those seven days. The carrot of enlightenment is dangled before the goal-seeking mind, dangled forever out of reach, yielding in the end frustration and moments of collapse of mode.

It's all scientific, planned. There can be more to it, of course; there probably is; certainly at one time there was. The monastery was a tool, an instrument to help in opening an unseen door; it had a function once, in a certain country, at a certain time. From the outside it's hard to tell what's happening now, but this pattern, at least, can be seen: the monastery works to shift the organism's plan — from control, manipulation (the action mode) to allowing, receiving (the receptive).

You see, there is nothing "mystical" here at all; it could be done by other means, without robes, without sutras, without the lotus position and the rice and bowls. After all, if you are Japanese, it isn't exotic to be chanting Japanese, or sitting cross-legged eating rice, or bowing fifty times a day. Indeed, what we need now may not be something foreign which existed in an alien time.

The religious monasteries understood their tools quite well, when they began. In western lands we have a training, too, where students sit in a small space, confined to concentrate on dull, repeated stimuli, restrained from movement hour after hour, reciting texts of gospel. We call them public schools. Their original purpose was to turn out scribes, clerk machines for the upper class. They're changing now, but we have our purpose and means confused and don't quite understand the mode we use.

SEVEN

Other Doors

I F YOU were a yogi, would it be different? "The Truth of Atman is revealed when a qualified aspirant instructed by an illumined teacher practices the disciplines of self-control, meditation, and inwardness of mind." {The Upanishads.) Not much different. Some paths devote you to a guru or a god. What sort of "refuge in one's self" is that? But the texts go on to say, "Worship the guru until you know the guru is yourself." "I am God," said Hallaj. Dependency is turned around, merging the parent and the child until the human being stands forth.

Renunciation, acceptance, selflessness, the notes are played on different instruments but yield a similar melody: Change your goal and your world changes. Change your inner attitude, change the purpose of your life.

You see, it's a functional matter. Body-mind obeys your commands. Set your goals to act, acquire, or fight, and lo! Time is born, enabling prediction. Symbols fill awareness, creating plans, giving meaning to an abstract future, A self is built to focus and reflect the plan. Fear and Pain assume command, adjusting your response. Vision sharpens on strategic forms. The incidental drops away; the sensual is set aside so the target can be clear.

Now change the goal, shift to Being. Receive the world and be nourished. The gaze will soften, vision diffuse, maximizing entry of the sensate world. Time dissolves and Now emerges, accompanied by satisfaction. The Self subsides and the world enters. Muscle tension eases, breathing slows, judgments fall away. Beyond fear, beyond pleasure. Now is. All questions are answered — for the questions have disappeared; they are the product of another mode, the action mode, another world. The mode of Being, the receptive mode, serves a different function. It is not "higher," not more "spiritual"— just breathing in instead of breathing out. Half a breath cycle is not enough. We need both to live. We need both modes.

You didn't have to learn to breathe, your body knew how. It knows the way to another world, too. Those moments happen all the time, without a monastery, and you don't call them spiritual, but you probably think of them as special. They are. Specially desirable, pleasurable, motivating you for a brief time to try to stay with it, come back to it, have it more. If you play golf, they are the moments when you let the club hit the ball and just watch, transfixed by the perfect flight following the perfect, easy swing. In tennis, pressed to the limit, running full tilt, you whip your body into the ball with a smooth, complete, unthought motion, and the ball flashes across the court for the point. You couldn't repeat it if you tried, particularly if you tried. Skiing, basketball, running — it doesn't matter — there are those times when you go "beyond yourself" and "something else" takes over, transforming all to smoothness, delight, and performance "above your head." There are books now that you can read, showing sports as something more than play, recreation in the original sense, perhaps.

Sex will do it. If love is there, enough tenderness to make your partner real, you may become a flow that takes you "out of yourself" and carries you someplace from which you later know you have returned. Drugs can do it for a while, even alcohol sometimes provides a foggy feeling of an opening door, but as drugs wear off the door slams shut again, and it may be harder afterward to return, and harder still to live the vision in your daily world. Church can do it but it's very hard, since you are so flooded with emotion and all that canned music from the choir. With saints and sinners, bad paintings, and boring talks, it's a miracle the door can open at all. But it can, for true devotion can change the inner program. Service will do it: the performance of an action because it needs to be done — not for gain, not for reward, not for anything except itself, just doing it. Just doing is meditation.

Creative work is a door for many. To be creative, you've got to stop, to lay off, to sit back a bit, to take your chance and let the thing flow. No matter if you're writing, composing, building a house, teaching a child, cooking a meal, there's something in us that does it better than we can consciously do, and when it happens we are satisfied. Satisfied because it's so complete; there's nothing else to want.

So it isn't just big moments, great discoveries that you read about in books, with inventor/mystics leaping wildly to their feet, spouting verse and ecstasy. It can be something small, something no one else would know or notice; the movement of a hand in setting three flowers in a glass, or the instantaneous and smooth turning of the wheel that slides your car across an icy road to safety.

But you're not a saint, you're like a child with a bicycle who gets it going for half a second, then lands on his head. The moments are too infrequent and the range too narrow. The self dies hard; it hovers in the background even when we think it's gone. We take that special moment and cash it in to keep on playing our usual game. "Wow! That was great! If I could do that often. I'd be the star. I'd earn a lot of money. I'd win the Nobel Prize — and all those women [or all those men]." "Spiritual materialism" infests the land like a strain of virus combining the common cold with athlete's foot. We're the carrier. But, still, we have our moments and in those moments, during that split second, or make it two or three, you're in a different place, tantalizing in its promise of something wonderful that is always there.

In those moments you become No-Self. You haven't disappeared, you've not gone anywhere, nor has the world, but it's different. The fantasies are gone, the symbols are not there, the net that has covered all the world has been removed and you are free — whatever it is you are. Unlike the world of self, there is nothing to be added, nothing to be done, nothing incomplete. At that moment the world is you and you're it. Enlightenment? Not yet. But it's a step through a door; so congratulations, John Doe — you're a mystic now and then.

EIGHT

Dependency

Now and then is not enough, and that way is a door, not a destination. Realizing that, you may decide you need to go to school; you ask around, applying to the one that sounds the best. Looking for help, being ignorant as hell, you jump in, sign up, and take the vows — whatever they may be. Then, full of hope, you pack your bags and off you go to school, to spiritual school, to be enlightened.

Unfortunately, you took along (unawares) a stowaway. Between the underwear and the toothbrush, your old companion sneaked aboard and went along: dependency.

Spiritual schools are for the dependent, too. Prayers and mantras, lots of kneeling, robes, incense, and relics — magic to summon power from the Big One to make you immortal, unafraid, blissful forever. Dependency-greed finds a home: "Satchitananda! I'm told the chicks in the ashrams get pretty horny after a while and it's good hunting. But if you hold off on the sex, you can get a really big orgasm they call enlightenment. It's far out! And I kind of like the Sufi dancing — it really gets me high. Did you get zapped by Muktananda? He's better than Guru Maharaji. See you around! Have a good one!"

Spiritual schools are still schools and schools have teachers and teachers become parents to learners who become children. "One is one's own refuge; who else could be the refuge?" said the Buddha, but all the eager heads, mouths open, nod in admiration and reverent wonder — then swallow it down, open their mouths again and wait for more. "To study Buddhism is to study the self.

To study the self is to forget the self. To forget the self is to be enlightened by the ten thousand dharmas... ." [Dogen] "Yes, yes! Tell us more!" Mouths open... waiting.

The list of the seven deadly sins has left out the worst one. For if you want to know reality and act in it with your creative power, dependency will do you in. Perhaps it's not listed because it's so often hidden and has so occupied our perception that we are not aware of how tyrannically it binds our lives. What we are told is dependency is a caricature: the man or woman still tied to the mother's apron strings or dominated by a spouse. Dependency is more subtle and disguised than that: it is just the wish to have parents.

Dependency is a fantasy. In that fantasy parents know what you should do; they give you what you want and what you need. They are powerful. With their power, parents can control what you cannot: love, anger, and fear; sickness, age, and death. They give attention and esteem and love you no matter what you do. They make no demands — except submission. Parents will provide if you bend your knee. In dependency, tyranny is sought, not overthrown; for the more tyranny, the more comfort in the parents' power.

Who are the parents of our adult years? Anyone will do. Husband, wife, son, daughter, boss, America, city hall. Neighbors, policeman, the company, the bar. Doctor, lawyer, senator, judge. The President of the United States of America. We all kneel.

Dependency is a disease, an insidious fantasy of protective power looking down, guarding you, judging you, rewarding you, punishing you. The disease has symptoms: helplessness, envy, vanity, jealousy, and admiration; blaming, exploitation, and reproach. "You're supposed to love me no matter what I do, for I've done my part [submission, feeling small and frightened], now you do yours!" Consider the justified anger, the sweet despair, the mournful longing, and the upward gaze, or the sullen pout that says, "I can't do it, I have no choice. You're supposed to do it, so give me what I need!" And when the fantasy seems true, when parents play their role just right, you're "blissed-out" with "God" or "life" or anything at all.

Perhaps you thought you left all that behind you when you left your home for college, job, or marriage. Not likely. Remember the moment when you said good-bye? You didn't really. Let me sketch the scene as, psychologically, it really was — and still may be, now.

The local band is playing outside, children, dogs and the ice-cream man, noisy in the street. The whole neighborhood is gathered, cheering with a banner: "Good luck to you! Come back and see us some time!"

Inside the house, the moment has come. Mother and Father are standing there, tearful and proud. The suitcases are packed and ready by the door. The rest of the family gathers around. You kiss them all and shake their hands, embrace Mom and Dad one last time. The band strikes up the final number, you pick up your bags, open the door, and then march — round and round the living room!

The band is gone, the street is quiet. Mom and Dad have gone to bed. But chances are, you are still there, marching around the living room of your childhood home.

It's very difficult to leave — and yet we must. Dependency is so commercial; it's nothing but transactions from morn to night. Security agreements, barter, bribes, and threats, manipulation and maneuvers of a hundred kinds. And all that accounting and the double set of books, the strong-arm squad collecting debts, for in dependency the parents can't say no, they must pay up, there is no dropping out of the parent game. Your own task is clear: bind the parent person and lock the door. Once you've got the parent caught, he or she must be fed; he must be satisfied to play the game. Yet it isn't that easy to detect his needs, to give him what he wants so you'll get yours. You must be good at watchfulness and care, with one eye guarding the inner road on which your energy may flow. Guard that road, for the unrestricted outflow of yourself may take a form unpleasing to the Big One. You see, it's not an easy business, living in dependency. It costs a lot.

Then are you never to be cared for? Are you never to relax, let go in the arms of lover, friend (or the world itself), feeling cared for, at peace? Of course you can, such letting go needs no fantasy and no parent — only trust: trust in yourself, that your need will end, that you will want to work again and care for others, that your emptiness can be filled; trust in others, that they receive in the act of giving, that they need you to need them. It is an inward process through which you turn to others, as they are, to receive that which you must have. You do not need parents now, and you do not have them (as you had them then, or wanted them to be). To resurrect parents requires fantasy, and the price of fantasy is high.

You pay with fear. Pretending you are helpless, imagining you are small, feeling needy for protection, you scare yourself. It's part of the game, to be afraid. And having summoned parents, you become more fearful, for you harbor treason: wishes for the parents' power, anger at the parents' needs, resentment of the role of humbleness you must adopt. The treason is concealed but it poisons trust, creating loneliness.

You pay with greed. The child is needy, and feeling needy, in want of something from outside, how reasonable to seek possessions, love and power, money, sex and food. But the fantasy of needfulness turns pleasure into possession and power into tyranny. The acquisitions are symbolic: A millionaire will seek more millions, beyond consumption, for the emptiness will not be filled and the desire for security is not appeased. That hunger can consume the world, yet the appetite stays sharp. So your greed whips you on: to acquire clothes for vanity, thus building loneliness; to acquire homes for grandeur, in which you feel smaller.

You pay with vanity. You must be special and attractive in your body or your mind to catch the eye and hold the person who must save you. It's competition to the death, to win the prize from all the others. Fame entices in the hope that all-out war will capture entire populations of providers. And if you win? The people crowding toward you have dead eyes; they are blind, grasping,

dependent, and self-centered. Throwing their own ropes of fantasy, they tie you to the book, performance, reputation — whatever object you have created. You have summoned angels to
provide and find yourself with vampires that feed their own vanity
by possessing you. In consolation, they leave piles of money on
the floor. You gather it up thinking money means more pleasure,
except that pleasure done too often fades away; and so you find,
instead, the death of pleasure.

It is as if we saw the enormous animals of sickness, age, and
death roaming wild across our land. Grasping power and fame like
a bit and bridle in our sweating hands, we go chasing madly to fit
them over the terrifying muzzles. But the animals are too big; they
cannot be controlled. Sickness, age, and death tower over us, gigantic, while we scurry on hands and knees to harness their shadows.

So the house becomes emptier than when you began. That
emptiness is born of your abstractions, and the fantasy of emptiness
engenders fear. Fear drives you to the Future, and the satisfaction
of the Now recedes and further disappears. Rising in its place are
more abstractions, more desires, jealousies, envy, more vanity —
more hungry ghosts rioting in the shadowy house within which
you march around the deserted living room.

Dependency exacts a further price: it murders creativity.

Creative action plays with the unknown. But as the child fears
the dark, full of big dogs and mental monsters formed from fantasies, the adult child will be fearful, too, faced with the dark world
of the unknown mind, with vast concepts looming enormous
just beyond the front yard. Peering out, he sees no parents in the
darkness of that land where he has never been. The unknown is
uncontrolled — no strategies exist that will enclose the endless
territory of the new. Only trust in yourself and in this world can
carry you past the watchdogs of your fears and out of the iron gates
of the already-known. Dependency locks you in, secure.

In order to create, you must move forward into what you cannot see and urge it into being. You cannot do that in submission,

doing what you're told — nor, in rebellion, not doing what you're told. In both, the focus is the same: turned back to Them. To be dependent, you stay a child. To stay a child, you stop reality's forward motion, roll back to a past time and freeze it there, preserved forever. It's "transference," the reliving of the past in the midst of the present, the casting of all newcomers into the roles of the dead. Time stands still, stagnant. When transference is finally given up, a person mourns the departing ghosts, who slip back into their proper graves, leaving that person "alone" — in the world — Now. But while the wax museum holds sway, nothing new can enter. Information needed for creation is made to pass a censor, whose job is preservation. Thus the past is reinforced to keep Now from flowing, for the flow will carry your parents away.

So to keep a fantasy, do not peer too closely at the world; fuzzy vision suits you best. Your creative power, turned away, is aimed inside to juggle fantasies, to solve the problems of a child's intrigue. Thus, "What am I? Who am I?" the cardinal questions of our life, are never asked. These guiding questions direct creation in a thousand cultures; they are the points by which we navigate our voyage, carrying us as far as we will leave the land. They do not orient our lives in dependency. Aborted in its course, the creative thrust misses the world.

Dependency kills us, for it is the unknown that gives us life. The unknown flowers when we are receptive to it, allowing it to enter. The unknown carries us to the constantly forming edge of the world where light, beauty, and ecstasy are found. There is no other path to the spiritual, to the creative, to reality.

THE STORY OF THE CAPE

A woman came to Rabbi Israel, the maggid of Koznitz, and told him, with many tears, that she had been married a dozen years and still had not borne a son. "What are you willing to do about it?" he asked her. She did not know what to say. "My mother," so the maggid told her, "was aging and still had no child. Then she heard that the holy Baal Shem was stopping over in Apt in the course of a journey. She hurried to his inn and begged him to pray she might bear a son. 'What are you willing to do about it?' he asked. 'My husband is a poor bookbinder,' she replied, 'but I do have one fine thing that I shall give to the rabbi.' She went home as fast as she could and fetched her good cape, her 'Katinka,' which was carefully stowed away in a chest. But when she returned to the inn with it, she heard that the Baal Shem had already left for Mezbizh.

She immediately set out after him and since she had no money to ride, she walked from town to town with her 'Katinka' until she came to Mezbizh. The Baal Shem took the cape and hung it on the wall. It is well,' he said. My mother walked all the way back, from town to town, until she reached Apt. A year later, I was born."

"I, too," cried the woman, "will bring you a good cape of mine so that I may get a son."

"That won't work," said the maggid. "You heard the story. My mother had no story to go by." [Buber]

In the Eastern disciplines, in the old times, you might have sat for days before the monastery gates or, having entered, failed another test and been sent away. Many were called, but few were chosen. Why? "Be free from greed!" "Be humble!" "Have courage!" How? In all the Vedas there are only exhortations: to meditate, to be sincere, to lead the virtuous life. But how? "Do not grasp!" But why do I grasp? Why is it so hard to let go? Self-reliance is essential, say the texts: "One is one's own refuge; who else could be the refuge?" Why do I look to the guru, instead of inside?

In the West, we have some understanding of our own. We have a science of psychology and have learned of motivation and defense. We can provide help for the disqualified. We understand that opening the fist is more complex than sobering a drunken monkey.

No external role can free us from dependency. It can adapt to any form. The explorer in the arctic or the sailor on his solo trip across seven seas may still be voyaging in the world of his childhood, watched and applauded by giants in the sky. Dependency is inside, hidden in motivations. It is supported by belief in the badness of one's being, by fear of the wishes and emotions we sense bubbling potently in some inner volcano. We mistrust the natural energy and are convinced we must control it. Otherwise, it seems, the universe would take reprisal if we were unbound. Fearing ourselves, we fear the world and search for parents to control us and It and Them.

When we are young, our parents cause us pain, inevitably. To master this and maintain hope, we manufacture meaning as best we can. But the meaning we construct has only two compartments: good and bad. "Are they, my parents, bad?" That's a catastrophic thought, for parents are the world, and what hope can I maintain if the world is bad? "Am I bad?" That brings the hope that badness may be controlled, for if it's me that's bad, it lies within the circle of my will. So the badness that I felt without, I take within, and make into myself.

Internalization, it is called. Anxiety is calmed, but the price is great. Assault from the outside mobilizes anger to repel the threat. When the enemy is outside, that anger can be released. When the internalizing choice is made — "I am the bad one" — the anger is entrapped and breeds mistrust of self. From the cauldron of that anger, demons emerge and monsters stalk the cellars of our mind. We grow into maturity watchful of misshapen creatures locked in secret rooms within. Let go, indeed! The legend of Pandora's box bespeaks our answer. We'll let go, all right, down to the first floor, perhaps. As for the depths beneath — the key stays in our pocket.

The hidden anger is denied, then "projected" back to the outside world, onto safer targets. Paranoia is our basic tool, transplanting the dangerous from us to Them. A hostile world is created by our anger and by the misinterpretations of the past. Who then can trust the world? One needs parents, allies, armies. Imagine this scene. Sunday at the beach: skywriting against a blue sky, a small plane glints in the sunlight, wheeling and diving. Its white path forms expanding letters and one by one they spell the words, "You need no one to take care of you." The statement shimmers in the air, viewed by the crowds below in utter disbelief and rage. "The world is full of murderous wolves!" they shout en masse. "We need a leader, to protect us from the sharp teeth!" Dependency thrives on fear and hostile vision. The child clings to the parent and will not let go.

"Letting go" means giving up control, allowing something else to be in charge. In any person it requires trust, but trust may be withheld. We know reasons why. The shock of being born, the transformation of a world of peace into suffocating chaos, may root distrust. The infant's world so open and so helpless cannot be free from trauma, and pain will raise suspicions of an evil force that needs to be controlled. The urge to master, to control, ensures our biological life; it is trained and reinforced in all our different schools. The first control is ordering sensations by selecting some and blocking out the rest. Then, control of body, control of objects; acquisition and defense become the master plan. Success produces parents' smiles; there are frowns for failure. Objects, persons, urine, feces, walking, eating, all, we learn, should be controlled, for helplessness invites disaster.

When we were young our parents were the world and their anxieties and pain mark our memory. The mark endures forever, it would seem, providing energy for the tight fist.

The infant child clings fiercely to its mother, for the comfort of the breast is supreme. Let go of that also? Letting go of the world is all right, when you fall to sleep in comforting arms. But let go of those arms? Let go so they can hold another? Let go to leave for school? Let go when death commands? Not easily, not willingly, not while strength lasts.

Control of time feels so urgent. Let go? Letting go allows the wheel of life to turn and gather speed, permitting change and loss, permitting death. We feel that world swirl by when our grip opens, when we surrender to the flow of change.

All things remind us of the possibility of change. Holding on to what has passed, inevitably we turn to face behind us, witnessing departures. Yet letting go permits our turning forward, into the flow of new arrivals, the stream of gifts from the unknown. Facing backward, how can we receive?

Males are taught that letting go is weak and passive. Passivity is female, so the lesson goes; it is the female who receives and pays with sexual submission. Letting go of feeling means "hysterical" and letting go too far will mean "insane." So we don't let go.

Finally, if letting go takes place, if the receptive mode prevails, the sharp boundary of the personal "I" may blur and dissolve, arousing panic at the emergence of an alien world.

Thus, the fist stays clenched despite a thousand exhortations to "let go."

ONE DAY an atheist was walking along a cliff when he slipped and fell over the edge. As he plunged downward, he managed to grab the branch of a small tree that was growing from a crevice in the rock. Hanging there, swaying in the cold wind, he realized how hopeless his position was. Far below were jagged boulders, and there was no way to climb up. His grip on the branch was weakening.

"Well," he thought, "only God can save me now. I've never believed in God, but I might be wrong. What have I to lose?"

So he called out, "God! If you exist, save me — and I'll believe in you!"

There was no answer. He called again.

"Please, God, I never believed in you, but if you'll save me now, I'll believe in you from now on."

Suddenly, a great voice boomed down from the clouds, "Oh, no you won't. I know your kind."

The man was so surprised he almost lost his grip on the branch.

"Please, God, you're wrong, I really mean it. I'll believe!"

"Oh, no you won't. That's what they all say."

The man pleaded and argued.

Finally, God said, "All right. I'll save you. Let go of the branch."

"Let go of the branch?!" the man exclaimed. "Do you think I'm crazy?"

NINE

Psychotherapy

A SECOND-LEVEL school is needed, to learn what you have never tried to know: the process of your thought, the way you lie and hide, and what is hidden — the secret workings of your fantasies, the forms of your fears. Our science helps us here, with information on development and psychological defense. We have a second-level school, born of that science which has become an art: psychotherapy. It doesn't go as far as Eastern schools, the eye of "I" is not examined, and after Body and Mind, the catalogue is blank. But it's a second-level school: Dependency and Letting Go are studied there. Perhaps you should enroll and take a course or two, in preparation.

Annoyed at the idea? Disappointed? In a hurry for a saffron robe? Be reassured: psychotherapy embodies Western wisdom, but its school has rules so close to Eastern thought you hear Freud in the Vedas: "The truth of Atman is revealed when a qualified aspirant, instructed by an illumined teacher, practices the disciplines of self-control, meditation, and inwardness of mind."

Let us examine this prescription and see what it can show us about this second-level school of the West, what it does and where it meets the East.

"The Truth of Atman" — "Who are you? What are you?" These questions return again and again. Their answer is the enlightenment sought through spiritual paths. It is the justifying goal of a bewildering number of techniques and procedures that have been used as far back as we have history. Is there a different goal for Western science? Not really. The physicist and the biologist go deep into life to know what life is and what we are.

Atman, the True Self, is obscured by ignorance, the Vedas say, by misinterpretation of the sensory world, by conditioning of false assumptions that support the culture but imprison the man. The path of Freud also seeks "The Truth of Atman," the nature of the real self, and, for all its deficiencies, it has more explanations than the Vedas do for "ignorance." It talks of demons, too, of grotesque figures, the demons of fear, guarding the treasure of real knowledge. Illusion, too, is the foe of psychoanalysis, creating the illness of isolation. Self-inflicted blindness, said Freud, creates its own world, producing "transference" and the paranoid view. The psychotherapist knows that fear of what's inside, and fear of the body's death, creates a special world for reassurance. Sufism knows it, too:

ALL YOU NEED

"I'll have you hanged," said a cruel and ignorant king, who had heard of Nasrudin's powers, "if you don't prove that you are a mystic."

"I see strange things," said Nasrudin at once; "a golden bird in the sky, and demons under the earth."

"How can you see through solid objects? How can you see far into the sky?"

"Fear is all you need." [Shah]

The activity of Western psychotherapy holds up a mirror to the patient's mind, showing him his mental life. In the process, he dis-identifies. You cannot be your emotion when you look at it, when you examine its flavor and notice its beginning and its end. Something happens when you observe, when you join the therapist in watching, in noticing, with moral judgment set aside and replaced by interest and by awe at the creative madness of the fearful mind.

Ramana Maharshi prescribed observing until the "I" was there and everything else was gone. Zen hammers at the "I"; Hasidism, too. Observation is a strong solvent; it dissolves identity. "Who are you?" Look and see. If my name changes, am I gone? Am I "psychiatrist," "American," "male," "tall"? The object words come thick, fast-flying through the air, like someone throwing rubber balls at a Plexiglas screen in front of you, who are watching. Lying on the analytic couch or sitting in the "hot seat," Gestalt style, the objective is the same: discovering a pattern that you didn't know you thought was you. "The Truth of Atman is revealed..." only under certain conditions.

"An Illumined Teacher" — East or West, you must have a guide, someone who knows the way, the way to freedom, back through the eye. The therapist should have traveled the path before you, for he cannot show you what he himself has never seen. He must have reached a treasure on the road and, knowing it is there, persist until the patient finds it too.

He must be acquainted with demons, knowing how they're pumped and stuffed with air, seeing how it's done — inflation and deflation both. It's an "illumination" of a sort. When the patient's demon jumps out from behind a tree, making horrifying sounds, the therapist should be less afraid than the patient-child.

The therapist, too, must practice self-control, to avoid feeding the patient to the therapist's own demons. Abstinence is the therapeutic rule for both. Not chastity, but abstaining from gratifying the demons: the need to teach, to cure, to save (perhaps the most dangerous of all). Abstinence from being Daddy, from feeding a gaping mouth.

SOMEONE said to Bahaudin Naqshband:

"You relate stories, but you do not tell us how to understand them."

He said: "How would you like it if the man from whom you bought fruit consumed it before your eyes, leaving you only the skin?" [Shah]

Neither may the therapist protect himself; he must be free to act, not blocked by considerations of self-esteem or fear. He must stay open so that understanding can expand, so that he can be a channel producing the "good hour" when everything flows, when he acts without acting, when a process contains and extends him at the same time.

The therapist can see what the patient cannot — the free person shining, like a flower seen through weeds.

"Qualified Aspirant" — What qualifies you? "Sincerity," say the spiritual guides; "Motivation" say the psychiatric texts. Sincerity — wanting to know in order to be free. Motivation — the wish to know, stronger than fear.

In psychotherapy a war is fought with Fear. When you are a patient you find that all is smooth until the armies meet, then comes the chaos. A traitor schemes within, in league with the old life, advising flight no matter what the cost: "I think I've got as much out of this as I can at the moment. I'm thinking of stopping after this week." "You can't help me anymore, I need a different kind of treatment." Or — silence. Then, you don't return. You get close to something so important your mind tries to run away.

The problem is not new: "When you feel least interested in following the Way which you have entered, this may be the time when it is most appropriate for you.... You will always have doubts, but only discover them at a useful time for your weakness to point them out." [Shah]

Courage, trust, humility — priceless qualities in searching for Atman, on the couch or off of it. Who is qualified? In ancient times, you sat seven days before the monastery gates. Psychotherapy should test more; money and time are not enough as indicators of sincerity.

"Self-Control" — The patient must not run. When monsters and witches rise from darkness, he must stand his ground in order to observe. No action prompted by anxiety can rule his mind. The gratification of dependency must be relinquished, as difficult to do as unclenching sticky fingers from around a lollipop. There should be no commotion, no noise. Only in stillness can one observe, like the stillness in the eye of a hurricane.

"Just sit," the Zen master instructs. "And then what?" asks the eager student. "Just sit" is the reply.

"Meditation" — Just sit, become the Witness, or call it "free association." Let go interpretation, analysis by intellect; allow the stream to be itself and watch. "There is my fear (I am not that)." "There is my desire (I am not that)." "There is my concept (I am not that)." Stillness, watching — meditation. Not different for the therapist. His action is to still the clamor of his ego and in that stillness allow intuition to be heard. "Free-floating attention" prescribe the psychoanalytic texts.

"Just sit!"

In psychotherapy, patient and therapist together watch the mental stream flow by. They learn dis-identification. They are so intent, so busy, they don't turn and glance ahead along the road they are traveling. The road leads to two mirrors standing face to face; it leads to a stunning fall into infinite space, shattering theories and pretensions. At ease in Objectland, unaware, therapist and patient dance along an exit to another world. "The patient learns to identify with the observing ego of the analyst." The observing ego, you say? Show it to us. ("Show me your true self," the Zen master cackles gleefully. "Who is it that has the thought?" asks the saintly yogi, cackling inside.) Pursue the "observing ego" and it steps behind you, out of sight and out of reach. No object can you find. Chase it madly, hunt it with the intellect, try to catch it with your rational mind — your sanity wavers, the Fiftieth Gate yawns wide. My mind fails, too. I cannot tell you what I do not know, and those who know cannot speak of it with words. The action mode is helpless here. Our minds can only show us that our minds have failed.

"What can I do?"

Be still, watch, listen.

The information of the second-level school will not be heard unless the eyes and ears are open, and they are closed for a reason. Resistance and defense, the illumination of Freud, requires a "journey" to the hidden jewel. One by one, resistances must fall apart, each lollipop dropping away until the hand is fully open to receive a different food. If you read the lives of the yogis, the Zen masters, the Sufis, and the Hasids, there comes Satori, Enlightenment- — followed by more years of work, more meditation, and the everyday life. It is not Saturday night but Monday morning that is the time of journeying. Stage by stage, level by level, understanding must penetrate like water soaking steadily through a packed, dry soil. It's an inward journey, and meditation is an attitude.

There is no sudden transformation, all in a moment. Growth needs time.

"Inwardness of Mind" — The patient journeys inward to find his true self. Inward into the ego, into the "I," to understand how he has made his world, his demons, his gods, his form of perception. The therapist is inward too, listening to his inner life to tell him what he cannot see. Intuition, the voice from inside, becomes refined, but he must listen to his emotions too — all inner promptings showing the patient and the therapist in one continuous stream.

In ordinary life the intellect sits like a lid, covering and containing the interior force, the nutrition of change. After all, that's its job, to keep a focus on the outer world. Preoccupation with the self and inward journeys will not secure food. It is with outward energy that we master the biological world. Our intellects are tools for a certain function, marvelous in use, but it's hard to use a hammer to clean your hands; so all the disciplines say, "Put it down — for now." When the patient journeys inward, he sets the intellect aside, decommissioned, as it were, until a later time. Techniques can help: deep breathing, relaxation, free association, and imagery are used in East and West. Psychosynthesis, Gestalt, Reichian are therapies built on a bypass, routes that skirt the intellect, providing access to the interior.

The inward journey is a journey because the path is long. The intellect does not resign. What once was servant now rules the house and must be gradually restrained until, once again, it serves our needs, and those only. So we travel inward to freedom, inward until, perhaps, inward and outward are the same. "Where id was, there shall ego be," said Freud. Ego may be a bad translation. The word Freud used in German was "ich" — the "I".

Psychotherapy School and Spiritual School —
Congruent Principles:
1. The truth will set you free, so understand yourself.
2. Increase the scope of your awareness, ("Where id was, there shall ego be.")
3. Confront your demons. Learn thereby they are your own creations, at your command.
4. Free yourself from attachments to the past (assumptions, conditioning) and from desire for the past (transference).
5. There is nothing to be afraid of.
6. You create your world; therefore there is hope and responsibility.
7. Flow with the flow, for you are alive and the organic is formed by interaction, as well as by design.

When the sufferer is the agent of his suffering, the doctor has a different role. Someday all body ills may fall under the same dynamic and there will be no division in the healing arts. Now it is psychotherapy that sees the villain and the victim in the same person and, therefore, does not "cure." The therapist points to the Self, the Other, the World, bringing them into the light of awareness. He and the patient hunt the origins of those ideas, hunt the motives, forces, energies maintaining them, feeding the "illness" that is the patient's creative work, his master plan. Those forces, fear, love, and guilt, must be examined so the door of the cage in the dark basement can be opened wide. Out of that gloom there staggers forward to greet us a small child, fearful, loving, bewildered. Psychotherapy can be a hand leading the child, who then finds the hand (his own) that leads him to sunlight.

There is something else that happens that cannot be defined: a transfer, a conduction of something good, of something healing, of something for which the therapist is source and channel both. Not to be measured or defined, it is there, felt over time, experienced beneath awareness, like air to us, water to the fish.

Psychotherapy school and spiritual school part company along the way. The teacher/therapist cannot teach what he does not know. The teacher/therapist will not see in the patient what he cannot see in himself and in the world.

The psychotherapist is limited in what he sees and knows. He may trust reason and intellect to define the world, and intellect does not go far enough. It must be left behind at some point to open the door for a different kind of knowing.

THE FIFTIETH GATE

Without telling his teacher anything of what he was doing, a disciple of Rabbi Barukh's had inquired into the nature of God, and in his thinking had penetrated further and further until he was tangled in doubts, and what had been certain up to this time became uncertain. When Rabbi Barukh noticed that the young man no longer came to him as usual, he went to the city where he lived, entered his room unexpectedly, and said to him: "I know what is hidden in your heart. You have passed through the fifty gates of reason. You begin with a question and think, and think up an answer — and the first gate opens, and to a new question! And again you plumb it, find the solution, fling open the second gate — and look into a new question.

"On and on like this, deeper and deeper, until you have forced open the fiftieth gate. There you stare at a question whose answer no man has ever found, for if there were one who knew it, there would no longer be freedom of choice.

But if you dare to probe further, you plunge into the abyss."

"So I should go back all the way, to the very beginning?" cried the disciple.

"If you turn, you will not be going back," said Rabbi Barukh. "You will be standing beyond the last gate: you will stand in faith." [Buber]

Ordinary reason cannot be trusted to carry you all the way. Nor can ordinary emotion do the job. Such feelings cannot be used to plumb the world; they are mixed and rooted in a world gone by: the past.

Most important of all, psychotherapists stand on a plain whose basic dimension is the separate self. Discontent arises from that separate self, but the solution cannot be found because the ground of the self on which the therapist stands is not open to challenge — he does not see it, it is too close and too big. The universe viewed from that Western stance is mechanical and meaningless, for it is based on abstractions and abstractions are empty. Meaning is not a product of language, or object logic, of the action mode. Meaning is experienced and therefore outside the mode and outside our science.

Finally, at some point the patient must go alone. What he needs to learn by his experience cannot take place in dependency on the therapist, on a guru, or on God. Psychoanalytic theory was brave, indeed. By design it plotted to give back parental power to the patient, to analyze the "transference" until the power that was projected was reclaimed. No other Western institution has this goal, not government, not church, not school; but practice differs from the theory. Therapists, and spiritual' teachers, too, may fail in that transfer, and the patient/student stays behind.

Dependency systems are all the same; they cannot pass you through the door. No matter how grand the vistas they survey, the view is from the doorway of the living room, and the living room, exotic and brilliant though it may be, is still the child's home.

TEN

Third-Level School

PSYCHOTHERAPY school is a school for the lower grades, a prep school for the next stage: the third-level school that teaches What You Are. Its curriculum, "death" of the "self" and awakening of "intuition," is taught by no school that you would recognize. It, too, begins with unlearning.

UNLEARNING THE SELF

The strangest part of this strange world is yourself. There are so many varieties of you, moment by moment, state by state, that only a very selective memory allows the illusion of a constant, continuous self to be maintained.

Think about all the various conditions that constitute your life. Sometimes you are in a state of remembering and ninety per cent of you is — at that moment — memories. Sometimes you are emotional, angry or ecstatic or sad, and ninety per cent of what is you is that emotion. At other times you may be what you see, or what you fantasize. Sometimes it's a mixture, fifty-fifty; it really doesn't matter.

Through all these variations, all these changes, you assume that you are there. Indeed, sometimes "I am" may be your only feeling, very powerful, very "spacey." Most of the time, you're too busy, so it's ninety per cent of something else.

You have so many selves: the thought self, the body self, the I-am self, the I-want self, the emotion self; perhaps the left-brain self, the right-brain self, the limbic self, and the mid-brain self. So many, so changing, not continuous at all. Each self appears and disappears, fades from view while another takes its place. So where in all this are you? If you are your experience and that experience always changes, what makes you think you have a self at all?

What of the times when the "I" is zero, when you are engrossed in a movie or performing some action too quickly to permit thought? You assume, nevertheless, that you have been there all along. That "I" is discontinuous, but your memory fills in the gaps, just as your eyes create an optical illusion by filling in the "correct" line.

"What's the difference?" you may ask. "Other people are witness that I don't disappear." You are right. But the "I" they see and the "I" you mean may not be the same.

When you began, aged zero, you did not assume that "you" were there or that anyone else was there when he had passed from sight. "Out of sight, out of mind," and out of thought, as well. Maturation enabled you to find the pea under the shell of memory. Once you remembered, you could predict, and soon your existence needed no proof — because existence itself had changed. Where once it had been all sensation, now thought and memory had become real, most real of all. "Mine, me, you, and I, in that order." In that order we create ourselves. Emotions become "mine." Thoughts are "mine"; whose else could they be? Desires are mine; what is more me than my wants? And fear is "mine," for who else will die? Mine becomes "me," the social object, collector of labels, possessor of things. "Me" encounters "you," the object, the Other, who tells us we are objects, too, and tricks us into categories that enclose us like snug beds: man, woman, Indian chief.

"I think, therefore I am."

No, you are not your thoughts. Your thinking tells you that you exist. The structure of your sentences implies an "I." The logic of your thought points to a subject, even when the subject isn't there to see. Have you ever looked at a picture that illustrates "perspective"? Dotted lines emerge from houses and from trees, marching to a focus straight off the page, aimed at you, the viewer. The picture says you're there: "All these objects point to you —

so you're an object, too!" The linear perspective in our thoughts converges backward to an empty space. So you fill it in. And color it.

What do you color the object you? Color it with more thinking, with emotion, with desires, and with fear. Use all the "inside" colors to make it bright and clear.

"What about emotions? They, at least, are mine!"

Emotions are signals for response of body and of mind. They program the physiological circuits for the pre-set plan. Sadness, for example, slows us down, "depresses" us. Our depressions follow loss; the loss of mother meant the threat of death for the child. It had to wait for the mother's return or for a substitute. Depression serves a purpose: to conserve life. This theory is confirmed by research with infant monkeys, separated from their mothers. First they are active, searching and crying. Then they huddle, non-moving, "apathetic," and withdrawn. The heart rate slows, the metabolic rate falls; conserving its reserves, the organism waits. Efficiently, it meets the threat.

Anger mobilizes for defense, not against abandonment but against attack. The heart rate quickens, breathing is fast, and vision narrows to the threat. The strategy is counterattack. The emotional signal, like Paul Revere, storms through the physiological streets, wakening the citizens to armed action.

Joy releases tension. It halts stress responses and remotivates the organism for creative life. Joy kills fear and catapults you outward to embrace the world.

"What about love?"

Love opens you, decreasing barriers to union, relaxing muscles, eyes, and mind, and permitting a flow of energy outward and inward for nurturing of growth and creation. Yet there are different kinds of "love," perhaps for the different functions of mother, lover, teacher — and different systems, too: self, species, life. As the function varies, the means will vary, too, requiring many kinds of love, some not emotional at all.

Fear tells you that you are there. When all else fails, fear will rise in panic to sound alarm at the approaching end of the object self. So loyal in your defense, so faithful, watchful, at your side — you trust him most of all. Yet, he's corrupt. Without you as object, fear must go. He shrieks: "Look out! Don't listen! It's a trick!" His job's at stake. Without an object self, what cause for fear? Fear protects itself.

We do not realize with what efficiency we function. For instance, we feel sad and do not know its purpose. And it's more complicated now. Our emotions have been elaborated and woven into a symbolic world. Threats of abandonment or attack can now be more abstract than a monkey can conceive. Our rage can turn within, killing us; our grief can slow us down to a dull coma, conserving energy against the return of a lost bank account we do not need. "Love" can short-circuit, turning our energy back to us, never passing beyond our mental skin. Yet the roots are the same: functional signals. Ignorantly, we bow to our emotions in mindless awe because they are so "personal." Yet, we are not them. Emotions serve us, or should.

"What about desire? I want, therefore I am."

When you want two things at once — in conflict — is that you? Or do your urges answer to biological needs, to patterns in the genes and to lessons learned at home, buttons in the psyche that anyone can push behind the scenes: "Don't take that lying down!" "He stole my idea"; "Her blouse is unbuttoned, I can see..."; "It's transformed my life, do you want some, too?" "She snubbed me"; "I climb a mountain because it's there"; "All you can eat!"

Possessing gives life to the object self, to the Thing. "I want," the energy of possession; "I have," the locus of possession, of substance, of mortality; "I will," the energy of intention put to work collecting; and, then there is "me," the social object, staggering forward with all my attributes in a huge bundle on my back, like a peddler.

Possession creates suffering, and pain hurts because it's "mine." Pain, old buddy, what happens when I step a pace away, look you squarely in the eye, inspect you head to toe like a new recruit? "What's your shape, mister? What color are you? Hot or cold? Thick or thin?" Pain — old buddy — you begin to change, learn manners, drop your eyes, turn in your badge of power.

Behind pain, in a line, stand all the others: vision, hearing, all the senses — a whole company of pseudo-selves. After inspection, they're more obedient to your command.

There is no end to object-making. Go to India, climb the highest mountain, and sit cross-legged observing all the other objects, all the inside colors, until you become, finally, the Witness, the finest object of them all.

"Then the next stage is concentration upon the idea of limitless consciousness. Here one does not dwell on limitless space alone, but one also dwells upon the intelligence which perceives the limitless space as well. So ego watches limitless space and consciousness from its central headquarters. The empire of ego is completely extended, even the central authority cannot imagine how far its territory extends. Ego becomes a huge, gigantic beast." [Trungpa]

Most of us are content with the usual "I's": young, old, handsome, dumb... and on and on. What a collection! Look at all we think is part of us: joy, anger, calculations, desires, objects, labels, fear, and "soul." Look at that merry-go-round, the way it spins, and then, watching it go round, perhaps suddenly you'll ask, "How do I know it's me?" The question seems absurd and never does get asked aloud. For we have entered Objectland. We have become a Thing and reap our reward; identity with all the Others, the reassurance of our kind. We need that reassurance now that we are objects.

THE VELVET CROWBAR

Spiritual school goes beyond psychotherapy school when it teaches the unlearning of these selves. The self of thought, the self of emotion, the self of desire, the self of sensation — all must be unlearned. These conditioned selves cling to you as shells and vegetation cling to a tide-washed rock. But the schools know what to do; they have many ways to clean the stone. Meditation is a velvet crowbar that pries thought-mussels loose, leaving the bare surface to be bathed again by the sea. The crowbar slides beneath emotions, too; those clumps of feeling, those subtle forms of memory, open and close like the carnivorous flowers they are, all mouth and color — now separate from the rock, afloat in the wash of the tide. In school, in meditation, sitting like a rock, just sitting, you let sensations spatter like the spray and drip away, polishing the rock until it reflects back the sun.

Desires are the last to loosen. They are lodged like petrifications in the heart and must dissolve away. Many things are tried: the ascetic life; koan dynamite; the hypnotic energy of dance and the deep chant, resonating in the center; the teaching story, holding a mirror to the form of desire; and, finally, the Teacher, whose radiant vibration shakes the atoms of the stone into harmony and peace and praise in the rhythm of the sea.

The mirror of the School shows you many selves, shifting, changing: the I of intention, the I of I am, the I of emotions, the I of possession, the I of the body, and the I described by Others. These selves have functions; you need to use them all for living in the world. Unlearning is a step to freer use. But you cannot use what is weak or hidden. Our Western culture, like an obsessive tailor, has spent so much time on the intellect-jacket it has yet to get around to the emotion-shirt and the body-pants. No wonder we are a spectacle, displaying our new clothes, annoyed at the laughter of children, yet haughty.

Not long ago, some new tailors set up shop in California, where East meets West. Now, there are so many tailors they don't know whose needle they are using, but, back then, the Esalen shop opened a new frontier: fitting the shirt and pants. The emotional self and the body self were taught in class. Encounter by the sea, massage and sex, here-and-now orgasms for "intimate strangers."

How ridiculous! The New York tailors almost died from laughter but were saved by indignation at the sight of so many customers discarding jackets in California. The colors of the shirts were often weird and the pants let it all hang out, but at least they were clothes that gave warmth to the heart and to all that land below the waist. Although Wilhelm Reich, a tailor of the body self, died in prison (he opened up his shop too soon), times have changed, the body has returned, although it still is seen as an appendage to the head.

Esalen is more than laughs; how strange to find one's state of mind sparkle like a fresh-rinsed glass when it receives a body bath. The emotion self emerging from a Weekend smiles with delight to see the sky again. Strange how the wrinkles disappear and the face is young, how the thinking slows and senses sharpen when the rediscovery is made. Catharsis and the body, old-fashioned clothes, indeed, to be selling so briskly — but that's the Frontier West, you know, no sophistication, no culture, no tradition.

Yes, the body has returned, bringing with it sensual life and feeling. Just in time. The spiritual schools teach letting go of self — but not to babies, or adolescents, or psychic cripples, deformed beyond belief. The Western student knocking at the door presents a gigantic inflated head, spindly legs, and a sunken chest, and announces with intellectual fervor, "I surrender!" What a prize! There cannot be a harvest before the crop is grown. Before the self is ripe, what can you dare to give away? When the conceptual self disappears, when the head is gone, the intellectual has little left. "It's Death!" shrieks the swollen head, watching itself vanish in the mirror of the School. "It's Death!" it cries, and flees or goes hysterical. Without the body self, without knowing you are there, in your breath, in your belly, in your thighs and chest, what will rescue you from panic when "you" "disappear"?

No wonder the Schools have strange routines, depending on the students who stumble to the door. Weird diets, heavy work, incense, singing, meditation, dancing, breathing, postures, flowers, swords, or sex may be prescribed. Five or seven chakras, say the texts, form the path and source of energy that needs to flow without constriction. So open all the chakras, one by one. Until you are fully there, in all your strength, you do not have the power to surrender. The many routines work, but for whom are they correct? The druggist lines his shelves with little bottles; a doctor must prescribe. Which medication is right for you? Maybe none. Go to a doctor, if you can find one. The diagnosis should be made before the treatment starts and you've been ill a long time. Leave the drugstore, you don't know what the labels mean and it isn't candy on the shelves, despite the bright colors. Go find a doctor (teacher). Now.

"Where?"

"Try the Yellow Pages: 'If you are really sincere, you will find a teacher.' 'The door is always open.' 'You are already in the Teacher's hands.' "

THE TEACHER

So you look around and find there are so many teachers of so many things; the first problem confronting you is to choose. The advertising is unrestrained. No FCC to limit claims; each one says it will take you there, to bliss, to peace and kundalini. enlightenment is in the bag; just follow the guru, roshi, rinpoche, pir, baba, buba, reb, swami, reverend, or hippie saint, clothed in white, yellow, blue, orange, red or brown. Take your pick. That's the problem. How do you know if this or that one is for you?

Let us imagine that you see a poster: "Teacher is in town!" You go to hear him. He's younger than you'd thought or wanted. It bothers you. You say so. This is his reply:

"What you're really asking is whether I have the Big Truth. If I had a long white beard you'd think it more likely. You want me to have it in my pocket; then all you have to do is kiss my feet, be a good boy, be a good girl, and I'll finally pat you on your nice little head and give you your reward: Enlightenment! You're afraid I'm not old enough to have it in my pocket, that's your problem.

You're a conniver who's looking for an angle you can play and so you come to me — the mark — to rip me off in perfect sanctity with your eyes rolled up to Heaven, counting your beads and muttering your mantra. How does it go? 'Lord Jesus, Krishna, Allah-kazam, seven-come-eleven for the promised land.' Well, it won't work, and if I fell for that baloney I'd be a bigger fool than you and all the others like you, with your flattery and coyness and preening and tears and awe and all that damn emotion."

He leans forward. "What do you want? Do you know? Do you want me to take care of you? Well, I won't, it doesn't interest me, I have children of my own. So that's out. Do you want Enlightenment? Why do you want that when you don't even know what it is? What do you think will happen when you get it? Answer me!"

You manage to reply, "I don't want to be afraid of Death and I want to be content and happy — like the time I had a mystical experience. The books say you can be that way all the time, once you're Enlightened."

He groans in mock pain. "My God! Didn't it occur to you that solving your problems comes first!? When you examine all your problems and see what's going on, when you figure out why you're scared of dying, when you start being happy, and when you cut out all this crap, then, perhaps, a Teacher might have something to show you — if you still needed anyone to show it to you."

"Then what's a Teacher for?"

"To get you to work on yourself — the last thing you want to do, because you're lazy or you think it's hopeless or it will take too long."

"But I do need help, even for that; and what if I make a mistake and choose you when you're not the right one or I don't choose you and it turns out you're the one I need — then I've blown my chance and it will be too late!"

"You'll miss the Good Ship Lollipop! Too bad! There it goes, your last chance, sailing away toward the bright horizon, leaving you unhappy and forever alone on the cold shore. Now there's a fantasy to keep you scrambling like a beetle for your whole life!"

He pauses, thinks, then continues, slower: "Look, it's not finding some Big Truth that's the issue, but your growth. You are like a plant in the ground that is growing: if you are three inches high with three leaves poking up out of the ground, you are not going to be an oak tree three months from now. Indeed, the attempt to be an oak tree would destroy you. You must grow from where you are. Furthermore, you may really be some other kind of tree. We need more than oak trees in this world, you have to allow your own growth to take place.

"For instance, if what I'm saying is helpful, then you are using me as a Teacher. If what I am saying is not helpful, then you are not able to. No big deal! No tragedy! We both are doing what we can. All you can do, and all you will do, is to learn what you are ready to learn. And all that takes is an interest in learning, in watching, in seeing, in trying to understand your own nature. The activity is lifelong and interesting. In its own way, it's a delight.

"We are in the position of looking around from where we are standing to those areas we do not understand, that are still unknown. That's the position of all of us; and that position provides freshness and the joy of discovering the new, the yet unseen, the yet uncontrolled, that which is the aliveness of growth.

"Don't be afraid that you will fail, that you will make a mistake and not guess under which cup the pea is hidden. There is no pea for you to find. There is only the process of becoming more sane, more real, truly alive. If you look, you will see exactly what your eyes are able to see and use at that time, and if you can have some trust in that process, you will enjoy your life and growth and be free from the fear that holds you where you are now.

"So you see, there is nothing to be afraid of, and there is nothing to lose. There is only the experience of learning, of freedom, of interest and wonder at the vast reality, beyond anything you have seen, to which you belong."

ELEVEN

The Path as a Multi-Stage Rocket: A Speculation

You enter your path of learning before you are born. By just being, you begin — for the first stage of your journey is pure experience — the self of happening, the unknowing experience of the maternal flux. No adjectives we now use will fit, for words need memory to provide comparison.

Gradually, the happenings of pressure, movement, and vibration come into focus, increase in depth and shape as discrimination grows. But, still, you are not there. Reality glows with consciousness, yet unselfconscious still. The stress of birth, and later shocks, stimulates intention — a direction for energy and the birth of a new happening: action. The organism moves, in purposeful response to the urgings that are triggered by discomfort and threats to life. Action spells the end of the pre-self world. The action mode, as it selects and shapes a world, selects and shapes a self — you are born a second time. Danger, pain, and desire release energy, and the body grows, and the world grows with it. The personal self is shaped like soft clay, then fired in the kiln of social life until it hardens; it can be changed a little, here and there, with pressure, but the basic form remains.

Everyone goes thus far along the path. From happening to action to self — we go that far, seeking to expand, but the clay shell of the self does not yield and we feel trapped. Dissatisfaction in a hundred forms erupts like weeds, converting the world's garden into a ruin. Yet dissatisfaction is our energy, too, and if its pressure has strength and the shell of the self is not too thick, cracks appear through which we catch a glimpse of light, tantalizing and remote. Psychotherapy can thin the shell and widen the cracks if it treats dissatisfaction as an ally, as a live force pounding on the door asking for health. The Teachers of the spiritual schools stand on the other side, in the light of the space beyond self. They can tell you there is freedom, they may even reach a hand that you can grasp to help step through; but no one takes that step, save you, and at the self's threshold there may be no light that you can see. You have just an urging from within, as you struggle with fear.

We may travel a long time approaching the threshold. Our path is like a type of rocket-to-the-moon, with several stages. At birth the earliest desire was set in motion, an urge for freedom from an enclosing form. An archetype of evolution, it sets the course for freedom. In the same birth is born control, the urge to master the changing world, preventing the return to chaos. So we grasp the world to take command, striving to achieve control, to travel at a comfortable pace to a destination we select. Struggling with objects, we become an object, gathering the power we will need to make our journey.

With intellect, with skill, with culture, with science, and with the time won from biological needs, we build a ship for traveling upward — through space — to the destination plotted in our bones. The journey's end is unseen, but it draws us from within.

Stage One, the stage of self, may take a lot of time developing the thrust that sets you free from gravity, from the earth's pull. The action mode has built a great engine, the object self, and dissatisfaction is the fuel. It finally sets the ship in motion, blasting off the pad with great commotion. And off you go, gathering speed, nosing through the clouds and heading for your rendezvous with a "spiritual" school, a way station in space, orbiting our world, between the earth and the stars. It may look different from what you thought. The pictures of the old Schools do not help in recognizing the new; their forms change to suit the times. But if your fuel lasts and your engine doesn't falter and your radar stays true, you make your rendezvous, connecting with a Teacher and a School.

Then the work begins in preparation for your further flight. That work requires energy, too; and at first you use dependency for fuel. The wish for parents shifts to guru or to god (mother and father can take many forms). In the beginning you are delighted and encouraged by what you find, doing all those "spiritual" things. Blissful sensations abound. Time and space alter, as you do what you are told, and the self rejoices at these victories. So much hope arises that joy and love come bubbling forth, and utter satisfaction permeates the room. As Time is shaken. Death is shaken, too. Aging loses terror and aloneness fades away. Enfolded in the presence of the Teacher, trust returns and the hands of Buddha-Jesus-guru rest lightly on your head. Your fantasies have come true, it seems. Reunion with the Parent is achieved — you think. "At last. I've come home!" And indeed you have. But that kind of home is not much different from the original, and so the joy doesn't last or is succeeded by despair. In the end, for most, it's blissful enough, for their energy of growth is not so strong and dissatisfaction subsides; the shell of the self may be so thick that the interior disturbance is contained and the voyager stops there. Everyone around may confirm what seems to be completion of the trip. Joyful eyes reflecting joyful eyes seem evidence enough. The "blissed-out" student- child, watching himself on the stage of his fantasy, sees himself dressed in all the traditional clothes. "I'm happy and carefree — like a Zen monk." "I'm ascetic and pure — like a yogi." "I'm full of love — like a Sufi saint." The energy of growth still hammers from inside the shell but is not noticed with all that song and dance going on outside.

The schools are smarter than you might think. They know that action and dependency will go only so far, and then a different kind of power must be used. Receptive energy begins to build be-hind the scenes. Communal living, meditation, chanting, dance, robes, texts, and lectures do their work: they undermine the action mode, teaching the receptive. The Teacher says "stop," "sit," "be," and, finally, you do what you are told — you quit for a moment or a while. Then: more bliss! More joy! "I've got it! I'm enlightened! Wait until I tell my friends!" But, still, it doesn't last and if you're lucky, your eyes won't stay crossed in bliss. When it goes away, a new hunger will be born: you want it back, you want more. You want to make it permanent, that brief experience of "grace," "enlightenment," "peace."

"Fine," says the Teacher, "just keep on sitting, dancing, working, reading... keep working! If you have any gaining idea in mind, however, that will ruin it; so just be aware of all your greed. And if you are afraid, that will block you, so don't run away; experience the fear. If you have pride, however, the spell won't work, so taste your vanity and spit it out." Under such scrutiny the object self shrivels, little by little. Greed is turned against itself.

"Teacher, I try and try, it works for a while and then I'm back again where I began. It's no use!"

"Then give it up! Cease your striving; just sit, just be, just do; allow, receive."

Exhausted, you let go, you stop, and something else begins to move. Nonstriving energy now begins to work, receptive power lifting you above the school, away from structures of the object self, into the space Beyond Self. The fantasies of dependency and possession that have led you to the school have been used, if you are lucky, to upset your plans. The lure of dependent dreams has led you to a destination you had not foreseen. Separation from Stage One has begun, using a new fuel, the power of surrender.

The hollow cylinder of Stage One that housed spiritual striving, the object self, dependency, and its defenses turns in empty space, and you watch it shrink, receding. It takes a long time to disappear from sight, but the distance widens as you gain speed.

What do you see beyond self? What can be said beyond self? Words are from the object world and the syntax of our language is bound by its rules. Perhaps our rocket metaphor will carry us further, and speculation, while not itself the truth, can point the way or stir an awareness that needs no words.

We started with the self-as-happening and then became an object self. Mixed in were moments of the self-beyond, when attention, usually gathered around the object self, like iron filings at a magnet pole, was able to detach itself and cluster on the opposite pole — the world. When we detach from the object self, the world comes in, occupying the space that had been us. In our ordinary lives, the self-beyond is a momentary thing, but in that moment may be endless time, no-time, eternity.

Life is not fixed and nothing in reality stands still. Cessation of the object self is but a doorway, and on the other side is still a self, the self-beyond, an intangible locus from which the universe is seen. That locus is alive. The self-beyond is process, in a world of process that has no end and is not you and is not me. You see, my words are failing here, becoming mush. In this realm, paradox is king. You've heard the classic puzzles, the teasing insult, the slap at equilibrium, the lure: "Why did Bodhidharma come to China?" Answer: "An oak tree in the garden." Or: "Surrender to the guru until you learn the guru is yourself." Meaningless words to the object self but what more can be said? Beyond self unifies the doer, the doing, and what is done. (More word mush.) The unselfconsciousness energy of the self-beyond moves mountains, does "miracles," and connects the stars and you. (Mystic mush.)

I see Stage Two spiraling upward above my head; it turns so fast and the light glancing from it is so dazzling that it blurs my sight, but I can see the outline of its form and see the connecting wires where they broke away. Higher and higher it goes until there is another sound (or is it a sound?), and then it disappears and cannot be seen at all from where I stand. Are there other stages? I don't know; it has become invisible. Has self disappeared into everything? I cannot see it anymore, so I cannot say.

TWELVE

Watching

I T IS not necessary to understand everything from where you are; just realize what sort of journey you are on. The realization eliminates despair and guides your energies. The trip should be enjoyed; don't be afraid. "There is no cause for fear. It is imagination, blocking you as a wooden bolt holds the door. Burn that bar... ." [Shah] Enjoy the trip. When it's all over, you may wonder why you were in such a hurry, why you were looking so far ahead.

Meanwhile, the world is very real and there is so much to do. With some idea of the problem, we can begin to talk about solutions, something practical for John Doe, who is worried about the price of eggs and gasoline, who reads of terrorists with atomic bombs, who is asked for money to save the millions from starvation, and who cannot see the mountains because the smog has raised a gray-brown curtain, obscuring and poisoning his world. What's he to do with his dissatisfaction and his fear in a world that's spinning toward the grandest crisis of them all? John Doe-me, John Doe-you, there will be no Messiah; there is just you and the rest of us like you. What can we do? After all this talk of schools and mystics, selves and rockets, what's a realistic person supposed to do — now?

If you haven't found a Teacher and your job is nine to five, you may wonder what to do, how to begin to shake loose from the clay shell that sticks to you and makes it hard to breathe. There's a lot that you can do, plenty to keep you busy, and it turns out that you are the one who finally has to do the job. Start now, don't waste time. It's like a battle in the old days, hand-to-hand. Your enemy

.g, so unsheathe your sharpest sword, the one you have
∤s carried but seldom used — watching.

You need to watch to see who's been in charge, because up to
now you've been an automated slave. Part of your training is to
think, "I'm free! I'm free!" while your robot circuits buzz and the
gears click and your head bobs like a puppet.

There are buttons sticking out all over you waiting to be pushed.
There's one called "Don't let him get away with it." Try the green
one: "Selfish!" There's also, "Hurry up, you'll miss your..." How
about, "You're wonderful!" or, "You understand, not like the rest."
See the pink one? It says, "You're sexy — here's your chance!"
There's a purple one, "You deserve it, don't listen to them," and
a brown one, "Work hard, don't quit." The biggest button says,
"What will they think of me?"

No, you're not free, but you can be. Begin by watching. Watch
the things that seem to be most you: your feeling states. For example, try depression, if that's your style. Watch it rise so gray and
foglike, so sad and soft and comforting. It's like an old pal, arm
around your shoulder, leaning heavily on you in a narcotic embrace. Its gray fog blots out all disturbing details and leads you
straight to bed and helplessness. What a relief! You've worked
hard, and now, with all those savings of resentment and doubt, you
can retire. Watch yourself become a child. Sink into bed. No effort
is required; no effort is possible. Just suck your lollipop and wait
till mama comes home. You've been deprived of what you need
and are defective, and the world is a big bully. There's nothing to
be done. Just watch the negative thoughts do their dance: "It's the
same old thing"; "What's the use?" "I'll never make it"; "To hell
with it"; "No one gives a shit"; and on and on. Watch them twirl
in a ludicrous ballet. Watch — and walk away. You'll probably
see depression trail behind, nagging for attention like an irritable
child. Keep on walking — pat its head, understanding how it feels,
but you're not going that way today. Don't try to throttle the rotten
brat; just watch its antics with an interested eye. Compassion goes

a long way.

What about falling in love? That's a feeling state, too. Should you watch that also? "I'm most gloriously me when I'm in love." Okay. But watch it; just watch the ecstasy while your eyes cross or bulge with delight at having found the one person who meets your needs — all of them. What a relief! To have found her/him after all that anxious waiting; now everything will be all right. Your delight assures you it is so. The excitement is so alive you vibrate with joy. Watch it. But don't start watching it until the merry-go-round has gone on long enough for you to tire of the thrill, and find out what falling in love is. When you've had enough, just watch — and step off, for that you will be able to do.

Watching is a powerful sword. It cuts through fantasies with one clean stroke, and feeling states, too, and the social reflex, and the thousand selves answering the buttons, saluting the commands.

Watch your usual self. Which self are you? You're a housewife. Fine! Which housewife on television are you? Or are you the housewife in a book you read, or are you just your mother? There's sure to be a picture flickering on the movie screen behind your eyes, telling you what to see and do and think as you play the role. It's Method Acting for everyone. You're a professional, although you didn't know it. Step back and watch the idiot perform — be interested, admire all your skill in being someone else. How well you learned! Admire all your friends — they do well, too; everyone's playing in their theater-in-the-round.

You're a bright young man. Fine! You know the part: you watched it, read it since you went to school. There you are, intent, setting all else aside, just like that guy in the movie you saw years ago. In the film, there's a wise old man who is watching you, looking out for you and passing you the power, 'cause he's the one who finally informs the world you're great, a Father who rewards his son — together you defy the Rest. (There's a Girl somewhere among the props.) You've a good role, you're some-thing special with unlimited potential, and you'll never grow old, only up.

Or be the wise old man — now that's a part! Gentle, kind, firm, and loved, while all admire your gray head and bend their knees in true submission. Pretty ones, too, when they're not screwing, will come to you with trust. Serene, above it all, you comfort them.

Or be the citizen: do your duty! Or the black man: defend your pride! Or the new woman: don't let the bastards put you down! Father, mother, sexpot, wife, he-man, real man, victim of life. The curtain is open, the audience never goes home — you're on! Every day, all the time. Watch your own show.

Once you watch it you're off the stage. So join the audience and you're almost there, another step will take you out the door.

"How do I know when I'm on stage?"

"By how you see."

There are some special kinds of vision when you're on a stage. I think you'll recognize them all:

Painter's vision. Your eyes sweep the scene like an artist's brush, splattering emotional paint on the canvas of your world. For example, when you do Justified Anger, you use a solid red with brown and purple flecks in an even wash that leaves the details clear, but with all perspective gone. Edge to edge, hostile power binds the canvas in dynamic unity. The painting is from a classical school, but prime examples can be found at every age. No first-rate collection is without one. Another kind of work is Spiritual Glow. This school of portraiture employs a shimmering golden blue; the brush strokes are pointillist, little dots of light radiate throughout. In the most intense examples of its kind, it creates a kind of glare. The finest examples employ glow-behind-the-eyes and include some works in the best modern style. I've Got a Secret is typical. In this ingenious masterpiece, the letters of the title are formed from all the elements of smile and eyes and radiant concern that are the focus of this spiritual scene. The paint's a special blend, transparent yet opaque, so that you're never sure if what the artist is doing is revealing or concealing. If not done well, of course, a delightful ambiguity turns vulgar; spiritual paint requires the utmost taste.

Almost everyone can learn to use Depression paint. The cool gray tones create a monochrome whose power resides in the subtle variations of the depth of tone, a kind of visual smog that infiltrates the world so that the gray vision of the artist encloses the spectator without his even noticing. Everything dissolves in aching peace, somber, but, in its own way, brilliant!

Reverse vision. The eyeballs turn around and focus all perception inside the skull on fantasy and remembered dramas. You become engrossed in the scene inside. You're like a man sitting on a donkey, backward, convinced you're facing forward because the scene you see is in the direction that you are looking. It's dreaming out of bed and it has the quality of dreams: the details aren't really there, the scene is vague for all its vivid emotional charge. After you have watched it for a while, you may feel a strange sort of pain, a kind of subtle headache telling you you've been too long at the movies.

Limbo vision. This is the commonest sign of the actor. Not here, not there, you're somewhere in between. Your vision stops before it reaches the live reality of the face, the tree, the scene confronting you. Only outlines register upon your radar screen, enough to identify a friend or foe, to name, respond, and move away. Your focus hovers in the air, suspended between worlds — not here, not there — floating in between, receiving signals from both globes, but safely disconnected. You may not know you're out in space until you make the effort to connect, and as you draw closer to the ground the details of the world appear. With marvelous concreteness something live emerges and you can feel the energy come out to you, filling up your empty space; space, you realize now, that was horribly cold.

THIRTEEN

Rebelling

I T ISN'T enough to watch. At some point you must act, defiantly. You're like a city that's been enslaved so long you think the army camped outside is for your protection. Once you see what's going on, it's time to rebel. It will be a fight and you'll stand alone, for your most trusted men — your words and thoughts — are in the pay of the enemy. They must be overthrown, for it is they that keep you trapped within the city walls, creating a maze in which your energy is drained and you are led back to the same point from which you began.

Words and thoughts evolved to help us manage an over-whelming world. As an algebra for experience, we use them for rapid calculations and for building complicated plans to ensure survival in a savage world. Indeed, the biological world is a gaggle of mouths, one devouring the other until all are swallowed in turn. By abstracting from this world a code of language, we have become the largest mouth of all. The symbolic mouth, worked by hidden levers, does a fine job indeed; in fact, it's big enough now to swallow the world, but we have forgotten who it is that's working the levers. It's as if the Wizard of Oz had become so engrossed in the puppet head he made that he prayed to it for help and forgiveness.

For example, consider the white matter of the brain. Neuro-logical books, heavy and full, contain precise descriptions of the "organ of the mind," the brain, and the white matter which is a part of it: "The white matter of the cerebral hemispheres is shown to best advantage in horizontal sections of the brain.... It is then seen as an

apparently homogeneous mass filling all available spaces between
the surface gray matter (cerebral cortex) and the subcortical gray
matter (basal ganglia and thalamus)." [Didio] The white matter
is evidently "real." But let's imagine how its discovery was made.
You be the surgeon and we'll look through your eyes, although the
process may not sound like anything you have read — until now.

As you begin, you experience a field of sensations which you
have learned by practice to see in stable patterns called "table" and
"body." In the center of the field, you experience a familiar pattern
that you symbol-name "a brain." Using sensations linked to the
symbols "muscles" and "knife," you bring about a regulated change
in patterns of visual sensations, a successive alteration in the "brain"
configurations; you label that orderly change "cutting." Eventually,
you experience a pattern of sensations not previously symbol-
labeled and, therefore, "new." To this pattern of sensations you
give the symbol name "white matter," and, characteristically, you
automatically regard the pattern as more "real" than the actual process by which you discovered it, that process being labeled "mental."

The "brain" is derived from sensations and thought — not vice
versa. Yet, haven't you been taught that the brain and body are
"physical" and real, but your thoughts are "subjective"? Haven't
you been taught that the world is more real than you?

THEORETICAL PHYSICS: THE SUBVERSIVE SCIENCE

We are educated in precision. Ambiguity is the sin of science.
It had been cast out, or so we thought, until we had to grapple
with the ultralarge and the ultrasmall. Then, the more precise our
scientific terms, the more error they led us to, for they were further
from experience. The physicist Heisenberg writes:

"Furthermore, one of the most important features of the development and the analysis of modern physics is the experience
that the concepts of natural language, vaguely defined as they are,
seem to be more stable in the expansion of knowledge than the
precise terms of scientific language, derived as an idealization

from only limited groups of phenomena. This is in fact not surprising since the concepts of natural language are formed by the immediate connection with reality; they represent reality. It is true that they are not very well defined and may therefore all undergo changes in the course of the centuries, just as reality itself did, but they never lose the immediate connection with reality. On the other hand, the scientific concepts are idealizations; they are derived from experience obtained by refined experimental tools, and are precisely defined through axioms and definitions.... But through this process of idealization and precise definition, the immediate connection with reality is lost."

Heisenberg goes on to emphasize the fundamental stability of the concepts of natural language such as "mind," "the human soul," "life," and "God"; and he concludes, "We know that any understanding must be based finally on the natural language because it is only there that we can be certain to touch reality, and hence we must be skeptical about any skepticism with regard to this natural language and its essential concepts." But even the concepts of the most natural language are nevertheless constrained by the logic that rules any language. Eventually, we forget that language is not experience but is a selective description and a basically inaccurate, biased description, at that: "...we have to remember that what we observe is not natural itself but nature exposed to our method of questioning."

Another physicist, Bridgman, comments:

"It has always been a major bewilderment to me to understand how anyone can experience such a commonplace event as an automobile going up the street and seriously maintain that there is identity of structure of this continually flowing, dissolving and reforming thing, and the language that attempts to reproduce it with discrete units, tied together by remembered conventions.

"An essential distinction between language and experience is that language separates out from the living matrix little bundles and freezes them; in doing this it produces something totally unlike experience, but nevertheless useful. That is, language as language is divorced from the activity which is the basal property of all our experience."

Thus, not only do we grant our symbols more reality than the experience that underlies them, but the abstract arrangements of those symbols and concepts create a picture of the world that is grossly in error. For example, we see boundaries where there are none. Your skin is in exchange with the blood and air. It excretes your wastes and absorbs the sun. You see it as a line — stable, fixed, a separation — only because the clock of your perception ticks at a particular rate and the microscope of your eyes is adjusted with a particular lens. Look more closely at the skin and the boundary line dissolves. Speed up the camera and the skin changes steadily like a sunset. Do you regard the sunset as an object? Only when it's frozen in a photo or a painting. Otherwise, when you stand beneath the late afternoon sky and experience the vast incandescence of reddening light, you are aware of change and color sliding inexorably toward darkness.

How stable are the mountains! Yet set your movie camera to take one picture in a hundred years and the mountains will flow like ocean waves.

Where do you stand in the infinite scale of time and space? Look behind you, as time slows; the world congeals in static shapes. Look ahead in quickening time; forms dissolve in motion. Shrinking space discloses atomic speed; infinite distance shows a single point of light. In quickening time and microscopic space, the biological body loses all form: "As a result of its metabolism, which is characteristic of every living organism, its components are not the same from one moment to the next. Living forms are not in being, they are happening." Bones and muscles are not more fixed than blood: "What are called structures are slow processes of long duration; functions are quick processes of short duration. If we say that a function, such as the contraction of a muscle, is performed by a structure, it means that a quick and short process

wave is superimposed on a long-lasting and slowly running wave."
[Bertalanffy] Shift our scale and the "inorganic" enters the stream
of life. Our world is a world of gradients, not boundaries. Activity,
change, and process are the "substance" of our world.

Scientists tell us now that their truth is relative, and, in
important respects, their earlier "truth" has led us astray.

Consider Time

"The time of the mathematician seems to have got itself
ineradicably embedded in the thinking of modern civilization, for
apparently we all nearly always think of time as a homogeneous
and unlimited one-dimensional sequence, all past time on one
side, all future time on the other, separated by the present which
is in continuous motion from past to future. What could be more
unlike the time of experience, apprehended with true freshness,
which consists of a blurred sequence of memories, culminating in
the budding and unfolding present? [Bridgman]

Consider Matter and the Particle that is supposed to compose it:

"According to modern mechanics [field theory], each individual particle of the system, in a certain sense, at any one time,
exists simultaneously in every part of the space occupied by the
system. This simultaneous existence applies not merely to the field
of force with which it is surrounded, but also its mass and charge.

Thus, we see that nothing less is at stake here than the concept
of the particle — the most elementary concept of classical mechanics. We are compelled to give up the earlier essential meaning of
this idea; only in a number of special borderline cases can we
retain it." [Planck]

"Before Clerk Maxwell, people conceived of physical reality
— insofar as it is supposed to represent events in nature — as
material points, whose changes consist exclusively of motions....
After Maxwell they conceived physical reality as represented by
continuous fields, not mechanically explicable.... This change in

the conception of reality is the most profound and fruitful one that has come to physics since Newton. [Einstein]

Consider Causality:
    "The objective world simply is, it does not happen. Only to the gaze of my consciousness, crawling along the lifeline of my body, does a section of the world come to life as a fleeting image in space which continually changes in time." [Weyl]
    "In man's brief tenancy on earth he egocentrically orders events in his mind according to his own feelings of past, present and future. But except on the reels of one's own consciousness, the universe, the objective world of reality, does not "happen" — it simply exists. It can be encompassed in its entire majesty only by a cosmic intellect." [Barnett]
    Concepts that we created to be our instruments in managing the world have become our masters: the tail wags the dog.
    We are so under the sway of our cerebral Frankenstein that we usually do not perceive the difference between our phenomenal world — the world of being — and our meaning world. So as we live, we shroud the world in the gauze of our abstractions. This dome of abstractions, like an old-fashioned cake cover, encloses reality. It does so by altering our perception to fit our concepts, by selecting from the stimulus array that which our ideas expect, and by trapping much of our attention in the colorless monologue of our thoughts. As a result, we see only the world's shadowed outline. What is the world like when we lift that cover? Quite different, say the physicists, and the mystics, too. A contemporary sorcerer, Carlos Castaneda, has described "stopping the world," ceasing the activity whereby we create our conceptual gauze. When the conceptual activity stops, the phenomenal world breaks through, vivid and flowing:
    "I turned around and examined an extraordinarily new world. The lines were visible and steady even if I looked away from the sun.
    "I stayed on the hilltop in a state of ecstasy for what appeared

to be an endless time, yet the whole event may have lasted only a few minutes, perhaps only as long as the sun shone before it reached the horizon, but to me it seemed an endless time. I felt something warm and soothing oozing out of the world and out of my own body. I knew I had discovered a secret. It was so simple. I experienced an unknown flood of feelings. Never in my life had I had such a divine euphoria, such peace, such an encompassing grasp, and yet I could not put the discovered secret into words, or even into thoughts, but my body knew it."

Rebellion begins with the realization that you are in that conceptual and perceptual cage of your own making. The cage has covered you. Realizing that, you need not be gulled into buying shadows. Anxiety, loneliness, and death, the monster companions of man, are a product of your abstractions. Experience does not contain them. They are born in thought and memory, never in the Now. Bridgman writes: "... our insistent attempt to visualize death as some sort of experience is set against our intellectual realization that death is not experience. I suppose that our inability to think of death except in terms of experience has had more social consequences than any other vagary of the human mind." Without the concept of the object self, there is no loneliness. Without the phantoms of imagination, anxiety retreats and disappears. Time, Death, and Self have no power, except that which you confer upon them. Reclaim your power. They are servants, unworthy to command. It's been a swindle, all along.

"You've duped yourself. What made you give your power to The Boss?"

"Well, he's the boss! If I don't, he'll fire me."

"What then?"

"I'll die! I won't have any money and I'll starve, my family, too."

"You're smart enough to keep away from that. You'd find a way to get some food."

"There aren't any jobs."

"What do you want to do?"

"Man, I've got to eat."

"What else have you tried to do?"

"I haven't had the chance; these are hard times."

The conversation could go on a long time. Paralysis scents the air, plus helplessness and fear. The questions seem unfair at first, the answers obvious, and yet you sense a squirming and a sliding, a sideways glancing of the eyes, as you abandon one outpost after another, always in retreat, defending: "What can I do?" — the battle cry of dependency. Who is that person sneaking through the grass, scurrying through your mind, throwing back plaintive justifications to hamper pursuit? Haven't you noticed him before? You've paid him good wages to sit by your door making sure you're not disturbed by certain visitors. Now get him by the collar and hold him! Grab his chin and turn his head to face you (even then he looks away).

"Who's paying you off? What's his name?"

"Ah, give me a break, please — I'm afraid to be alone." "Who said you'd be alone?"

"They all did. They said if I didn't join, they'd throw me out in no-man's-land and let me die."

"What no-man's-land?"

"There — outside the walls."

"What's it like?"

"How do I know? I haven't been there, but everybody knows it's hell."

And so you drop the wretch and turn away, struck by that last phrase, "Everybody knows it's hell." Isn't it strange? No one in the city has passed those walls and yet they know it's hell. You were told that, too, remember? Your parents, warning you of destitution and abandonment: the old fears, back through the generations.

You learned from childhood, the terror of the nights so filled with your own frightened passions. And all those times your mother disappeared and you felt hunger and pain, without defense. And then, when she returned, it was so comforting being held while the soft voice murmured of the dangers outside parental arms. In elementary school, there was the punishment of isolation. Dunce! Sit in the corner! Later on, in high school, at the dance, you could stand by the wall and learn what it's like not to be chosen, not to be one of the crowd.

The needs of the child are preserved intact and used to establish laws for adult years, as if the needs were still the same. Societies, groups of every sort, conspire to a single overriding plan: preserve the group. "No member is allowed to leave; it weakens us!" So you are bribed (we'll comfort you), and threatened (leave and we'll kill you), and trained (serve your country, for in unity there is strength). All the institutions sing the same song: "You need us. Outside our sheltering walls is loneliness and death. Be one of us and we'll take care of you." From the United States of America to the latest yoga commune, no one gets to leave scot-free. "Insane," "bum," "commie," "freak," or "uptight," "fascist," "middle class": those are the clothes the Other wears. Take your pick; they smell the same and carry the same tag: Outsider. No hunting license required, no limit, take by any means: Thorazine, jail, contempt, and spit. Eat 'em up, lock 'em up. "Let 'em know that we won't stand their kind here!" "They put out bad vibes." "Serves them right!" "That'll teach 'em."

You've seen a lot of examples paraded down the main street of our town, or given the treatment in the ashram, in the newspapers and the neighborhood bar, and in the country club and the convention and Local Ordinance Number 666. Yes, indeed, they teach, "Outside the walls is hell!"

But what is it really like outside the walls? Suppose it isn't bad at all, suppose it is green grass and soft breezes, lots of sun and good things to eat? After all, some people have gone outside and said it's fine, even better than behind the wall. Of course, they're crazy — mystics, you know, foreign freaks mostly; what do they know without science training? Still, why not take a look? Rebel that far; consider that out there "alone" might be nicer than you have dreamed. What have you to lose? It's gotten awful stuffy in the town and there are rumors of a plague. Time to leave.

Shibli was asked:

"Who guided you in the Path?"

He said: "A dog. One day I saw him, almost dead with thirst, standing by the water's edge.

"Every time he looked at his reflection in the water he was frightened, and withdrew, because he thought it was another dog.

"Finally, such was his necessity, he cast away fear and leapt into the water; at which the 'other dog' vanished.

"The dog found that the obstacle, which was himself, the barrier between him and what he sought, melted away.

"In this same way my own obstacle vanished, when I knew it was what I took to be my own self. And my Way was first shown to me by the behavior of — a dog." [Shah]

When fear departs, the encircling army melts away, but ignorance may still remain. There is much to learn. There is also much to do.

FOURTEEN

Quitting

ONE TIME, not too long ago, I was discontented, agitated, and depressed. Something was wrong but I didn't know what it was, so I decided to go into the woods and think. I followed a trail along a stream bed that led through a spacious world of trees, with huge boulders and mossy banks, which created a succession of pictures, very composed and still. I walked, noticing the beauty, but my distress continued, as if hiking with me on a parallel trail. Finally, I stopped, sat upon the ground, and rested, gazing rather blankly before me. I was enclosed by trees that sheltered everything beneath them, creating a roof of green leaves and light in place of the sky.

A fantasy came to my mind. I saw myself as a troubled, intense, and angry young man who had gone to see a Teacher. I told him of my disgust with the world, how people hurt each other, did stupid things, and wouldn't listen when you offered help. No matter what I did, I told him, the same old thing happened, and even when things seemed to improve a little, sooner or later they went right back to where they were before.

Parents abused their children, creating more parents who would abuse their children and on... and on. People were obstinate and self-centered and kept ruining every chance they had. The misery of the world kept increasing, not decreasing, and Buddha and Christ have made no difference. Education hasn't made any difference, nothing makes any difference — it gets worse and worse, and more and more horrible.

The Teacher listened. Then he asked, "You hate the world?"

"Yes, I hate it, it's so mean and stupid, it destroys everything; and the more beautiful something is, the quicker it will destroy it. I'm fed up. I've had it. I don't know what to do now, there seems no point to anything, and I feel awful!"

The Teacher was silent for a while and then he said, "I have an idea of something that might help you, but I'm afraid it may prove too severe a task for you."

"No it won't, not after all the things I've done, how hard I've worked, how desperate I am. I care nothing about myself now. No matter how difficult or painful your task might be. I'd do it if I thought there was some hope."

"Very well," said the Teacher, "but I'm afraid it may be too difficult for you. It is this: Whatever you do you must enjoy, or you may not do it. No matter what it is, if you find that you are not enjoying it, you must stop right at that moment. It doesn't matter if you are driving your car, or eating, or doing your work, or doing anything else. If you are not enjoying it, you may not do it. It is up to you to find a way to enjoy anything that you do. Nothing is exempt: you may have to give up your work, you may have to stop in the middle of the street, you may look to others like an idiot, and you may sit on the floor and starve to death, but unless you enjoy whatever you're doing you may not do it. Do you understand?"

For a moment the young man's eyes were wide, incredulous, then they narrowed and his brow wrinkled in annoyance and disbelief. "That's impossible!" he exclaimed. "No one can enjoy everything and, besides, there are damn few things that are enjoyable. You're trying to trick me or having a joke!"

The Teacher smiled. "I was afraid it would be too difficult for you, and now you see what I mean. Nevertheless, I know of nothing else that would be of help to you. You must go away now. See if you can do it for a year and then come back."

A year later the young man returned. His face was open and glowing. "Good," said the teacher. "Now that you love the world, perhaps you can be of some use to it."

WHEN I returned home from my day in the woods, I told my
daughter the fantasy I had had. She said, "Do it! Do it for a year
and then we'll celebrate." And so I did and I learned that I could
enjoy anything. Then, after a while, I would forget. Sometimes,
enjoying things no longer seemed so important. It had become
my choice, a choice of how I wanted to be at any particular time,
depending on my purpose. Often I forgot about enjoying things
because I was just too busy.

How did I do it? I "stopped," "I quit." Each time I was unhappy I found that I was centered in my thoughts, my worries and
concerns. For example, traveling to work, bored and restless in a
long line of commuting cars speeding over the Golden Gate
Bridge, I found that if I stopped and opened my eyes and ears
and nose and touch (all the sensual channels), if I allowed that
reality of smells and sounds and familiar color to fill the space
of my attention, displacing thoughts as if my mind were hollow,
then, with "me" gone, the sensate world entered suddenly, like an
enormous guest who took up all the room but none of the space —
and I enjoyed it. It wasn't "happiness" — happiness comes from
me; enjoyment is in the being of the outside world, when it comes
inside. Enjoyment comes with the flavor of the thing; it came with
the car's qualities, its metal life, its special presence, noisy voice,
strong being, hurtling character, the comfort of the seats, and the
slanted shape of the glass. Its being spoke in sensual words and in
something else more direct that senses. Around the car, the bridge
unrolled, sending me an iron message, gray beneath the red and
cold, yet soft and telling me its self. Nothing different than it is,
nothing special. It's always there, waiting outside for me to open
the door of my room and ask it in.

Do you know what I mean? Possibly not. You may be out of
practice — so let me show you.

Consider: How long do you work? Eight hours? Not likely.
Chances are you work every minute you're awake, and part-time
while you're asleep. Consider all the orders you receive and all the

ways you labor to meet the stream of commands. From your boss: "Finish today"... from yourself: "Make it neat"... from your leg: "I hurt — move!"... from the waiter: "Choose"... from a sign: "Buy me"... from a centerfold: "Screw me"... from the radio: "Remember this!"... from your spouse: "Listen to me"... from your mind: "How?"... from your desires: "Fantasize"... from your fears: "Worry"... from your skin: "Scratch me"... from your car: 'Fix me"... from your room: "Clean me"... from your mind: "Talk with me"... from the golf club: "Swing me".... from a bottle: "Drink me"... from a problem: "Solve me"... and even from your vacation: "Enjoy me!"

Would you like to try quitting? You may never have done it before, never really taken time — any amount — just for you. You may never have said, "The next ten minutes are just for me," and stopped doing. Consider: ten full minutes in which to be aware, just for yourself, not doing anything, just being aware of your existence. Do you know what it is like to stop and give it all to yourself, to have the whole world just for you for as long as ten minutes? Find out. Try it now. Realize that no matter what problems are facing you and no matter what work you have to do or what people need you or what your body wants, for ten minutes there is nothing you must do. That's true. Realistically, no matter what your situation is right now, it can wait for ten minutes. The Bump may be coming, but the next ten minutes can be yours.

So set the alarm clock or ask someone else to let you know when the time is up so you don't even have to worry about that. Then quit. Sit comfortably. You needn't be solemn. You don't even have to close your eyes. Just quit. Feel how tired you are of saluting all those commands, or placating all those anxious messengers, so threatening, so seductive with their flattery and their bribes. Rebel. Does your foot hurt? Say to it, "To hell with you, I won't move!" Does your nose itch? "Sorry — go scratch yourself." In the middle of a thought you may suddenly realize that you've been thinking — well, just sag inside, let go of the thought and drop it to the floor. It's too much work to finish the thought, too much effort even to be annoyed, just too much. But don't go to sleep; that would be a swindle, that's what they're always doing. Every time you start to stop and see what it's like, they send you to sleep so you never get to know. This time quit and stay awake. Be curious: What is my experience when I stop doing? What is it like when I'm just being? Try it now. Just ten minutes. Stop reading. Stop. Quit now.

WHAT WAS IT LIKE? You probably didn't stop just now, but kept on reading. You may have felt that you didn't have time, that you wanted to finish. That's the whole point: you are driven. So stop now and do it. Even if you have done "meditation" and think you know all about quitting, it is important that you stop — now — and do it, anyway. Don't go on reading. "Quit" now, for ten minutes, right where you are.

YOU MAY have found a world emerges that seems different. When the outward pressure of your mind relaxes, it leaves space that can be filled. Don't be afraid. Let the world move in and fill that space. See what it's like. Savor the color and the fragrance. Experience the rich, massive presence of the emerging world. Later, realize that Time was gone and so was your personality. Some part of self may have stayed to register anxiety or ask questions in your mind, but only from the back row. Satisfaction is the main event. How complete is the moment world! When you let it in, comparison collapses, for memory is gone, displaced by the fullness of the chair, the tree, the air, the sounds. You have been peering out the door at the world and now, in the twinkling of an eye, the world jumps into the room. Let it stay. Get acquainted with your guest. He won't stay too long; he's very sensitive to the host's concerns and will be gone before you voice the thought. Enjoy him. Be entertained. Even rest your head a while on his strong shoulder. Then you can come back to thinking, to doing.

That's how it seems to me, when I quit. You will have your own description. Back and forth you go, from being to doing, the two realms complementary, side by side — a biphasic world.

Want to try it again? Go ahead.

ONCE, in a Zen sesshin, after five days of focusing on my elusive, disappearing, watching self, I let go. Before that, during the first few days, the Zen master had said, "Show me yourself, find it, look for it, and bring it to me!" I tried. It can't be done. You may try, too. Twist and turn as fast as you can, you cannot see the eye of your awareness. As you struggle, as you watch the contents of your mind, every thought and every feeling, separation grows. You realize you are not them. You, the watcher, become more clear. And so you turn to find the watcher; and there is nothing here. Fear rushes to defend the empty citadel. Demons huff and puff in blustering dance. Just sit. Is it so bad, not being there? Touch a toe in the water; see, not so bad. A little longer, now.... Okay? Look around a little. You've been holding your breath — relax. Ready to jump in?

We chanted in the early morning. The words were printed black on large sheets of paper that we held before our eyes. Day by day, the words acquired life and vividness, until that morning of the fifth day they marched across the page not needing me at all. The world existed and I did not need to be. "Let go!" it whispered in my ear. "Disappear — the world will still be here, let it be without you, see what it's like when you aren't here; let go, let go, jump! Die."

Okay.

At the moment that I let go and vanished from the world, it changed. Abruptly, sharply, suddenly, at the moment of my "death," the world was something else — transfigured. All the students, robed in black, were Buddhas, perfect, radiating their perfection in awesome beauty. The bell sounded and the tone, like full silver, shone, pulsed, and vibrated from the heart of the bell, sounding its name. All was transfigured, godlike, fourth-dimensional.

I don't know how long it lasted. We rose and walked in line from the hall. Outside the birds spoke their note, their beingness shimmered in the sound. As I walked, it all faded, and when I reached the cabins, it was gone.

I don't know what it really means, except the suddenness stays in my memory. Exactly when the self was gone, the radiant world appeared. They didn't overlap. The world emerged when I left. Well, who was there? Something remained to be the vantage point in space and time. Something experienced the room and moved outside. No one saw me disappear; my body stayed intact before the eyes of the man who was chanting behind me. What happened? I can't imagine. Psychologically, I "left" the world, relinquished my existence, and at that exact moment the world changed.

When you "quit," a short while back, did you feel the same — in a minor way? Were there moments when time had stopped, self-consciousness was gone, and everything was Now — as you realized only later when your thoughts and you and time and restlessness had returned? The hand is open or the hand is closed, you cannot "keep" the world of the open hand; the closing action of your mind's hand transforms you and the world. You cannot "know" it and have it at the same time, for the "knowing" needs a "you" to know. Now appears only when you leave. Perhaps that's why we seldom stay long — in the Now. We miss our object self.

The action mode and the receptive mode create two worlds. In one, the object self rules, served by linear time and thought, dedicated to control, but spawning anxiety. In the other, beyond self, perception replaces thought and Now replaces time. In that world, receiving is the goal, allowing the means; satisfaction results, and nourishment as well. We live in both worlds but possess only one, for it is the self that possesses. And so we easily forget that the other world's there; we fill in the gaps between the world of self with memory and finally believe that the object world is continuous, unbroken, supreme. Yet, if we quit, if we stop. Past, Now, and the Future can sound in harmony. That complete music restores the soul, for what was held apart is brought together, allowing selfless action and purposeful existence.

Have you ever been a "channel," performing action with such effectiveness and grace, with such a matching of need and answer that "It wasn't me that did it!" arises in your mind? "Allah did it!" exclaimed the runner, fresh after twenty-six miles, doing push-ups in exuberance, the gold Olympic medal his, but not his, he said. Or "the perfect hour" of the therapist, when the action is a dance between two minds in tune. "Like a spider upon the water, his mind moves upon silence," said Yeats of Michelangelo. "Allah did it!" because we think we are the object self that consciously controls. When the worlds unite in harmony, the flow of power that results feels different from the self that only knows the strain of willing. When you let go the object self, when the "ego" is not you, perhaps you'll know that power to be your own, for you'll feel no boundaries to restrict you from your rightful home.

FIFTEEN

Realistic Action

"BE REALISTIC!" Who hasn't received that reprimand? Usually it is an exhortation to be more cynical or more suspicious, to pay more attention to the money or the impossibility of an ideal. Sometimes the rebuke is needed, for our wishes may intoxicate us and clouds of fantasy can surround our heads, obscuring the ground. But "Be realistic" often means, "Don't let your guard down, get what you can; ideals are for suckers and the world is full of wolves. Be practical!"

The successful man of business is the model we are given for being "practical." Politicians come close behind; both scorn "romantic dreamers." The military, the bankers, the public officials, the corporate executives — the men of power — they are The Realists. Although there has been evidence enough that something is missing, that such "realism" produces wars, economic depressions, and a large number of Miniver Cheevys who blow their brains out in one way or another, the man of power has retained his authority as the voice of realism. On the other hand, the ethics and points of view expressed in religious and mystical traditions are regarded as practical only on Sundays, and not really practical, even then: "All that's okay theoretically, but the world is different and you've got to hustle to survive!" These words may be a caricature, but this view has penetrated us so deeply that most people carry around their own interior voice that pounces on deviant thoughts, labeling them "romantic," "impractical," "mystical," "magical," "crazy." The voice of "realism" comes down like a whip, keeping us in line.

We listen to that voice not only because we have been trained to it, but because there is much in our thinking that is magical. The wishes, fears, and passions of our childhood persist and live again in our behavior. And the laws of object logic are needed to survive. No matter how free your spirit, you cannot fly from the tenth floor of a building; you will fall and die. Respond to every outstretched hand and soon your own will be outstretched.

Nevertheless, something is clearly wrong with the old way. The action mode of thought, perception, and activity is no longer realistic by itself; conquering the object world, we stand in the shadow of species death. It is men of business, politics, and war who have led the long march and are now openly confused, uncertain, and frightened; the line of their march is straight for the cliff.

Most scientists have erred, as well. Too arrogant in intellect, they discarded what they could not think, labeling it "unreal." But they have begun to see that error and they speak now in other terms.

The conclusions of a multidisciplinary research group:

"Numerous problems today have no technical solution. Examples are the nuclear arms race, racial tensions, and unemployment. Even if society's technological progress fulfills all expectations, it may very well be a problem with no technical solution, or the interaction of several such problems, that finally brings a disastrous end to population and capital growth."

A professor of electrical engineering, Willis Harman:

"... hardly a task can he imagined for which a technology cannot be developed if resources are devoted to it and sufficient time is allowed. Hardly a task, that is, except solution of the huge societal problems that now confront us, and which seem in considerable measure to be a product of our technological prowess. Perhaps a third frontier is the inward one — the frontier of the vast inner space of consciousness. And perhaps it is here that we must turn to find the eventual resolution of these problems that so perplex us."

No technical solutions! The Western genie hangs his head, his powers of possession, of conquest and control, of building and destruction now useless, worse than useless.

What is needed?

The research group proposes:

"... trading certain human freedoms, such as producing un-limited numbers of children or consuming uncontrolled amounts of resources, for other freedoms, such as relief from pollution and crowding and the threat of collapse of the world's system. It is possible that new freedoms might also arise — universal and unlimited education, leisure for creativity and inventiveness, and, most important of all, the freedom from hunger and poverty enjoyed by such a small fraction of the world's people today."

Hell or paradise would appear to lie within the realm of our choice. Our choice, however, depends on our values, and our values depend upon our outlook, our concepts, on the way we view ourselves and others; it is not a technical problem.

A former physicist, now futurist, J. R. Platt, makes a similar point:

"We may be facing a decade or more of disasters, as our older institutions and nation-state structures are forced to deal with the new global crises. Our ability to handle these crises depends upon leadership and commitment and organizational structure and our ability to make necessary changes fast enough. But it probably also depends in a crucial way on how rapidly we all begin to accept and practice certain concepts about our relation to each other and to the world, concepts that are essential for global cooperation and survival...."

What concepts?

A naturalist, Aldo Leopold, speaking almost thirty years ago:

"We abuse land because we regard it as a commodity belonging to us. When we see land as a community to which we belong, we may begin to use it with love and respect. There is no other way for land to survive the impact of mechanized man, nor for us to reap from it the esthetic harvest it is capable of....

"That land is a community is a basic concept of ecology, but that land is to be loved and respected is an extension of ethics.

That land yields a cultural harvest is a fact long known, but latterly often forgotten."

The concepts are those of community and oneness, based on the perception of oneself in kinship with the earth, rather than as its conqueror; of feeling connected to a thousand generations of human, animal, vegetable, and even mineral forms, stretching far behind us in evolutionary time and with a destiny that stretches far beyond us into the future. In the usual random, mechanistic, aggressive world view, the long-term goal of the evolution of our species hardly seems practical when compared to the need to invest in a retirement plan, or to build a house; anxiety tips the scales forever in the direction of short-term profit. "If I don't do it, the next guy will"; there is truth in that prediction. Yet such "practical" advice is leading us and our children to utter desolation.

J. R. Platt, again:

"We are passing through a philosophical and religious transformation in this generation, a transformation consistent with our new scientific knowledge as well as with our new awareness of inner human meaning and outer global responsibility. It is a transformation that is even more remarkable and more necessary than the astonishing technological transformation and social transformations of our time. It is only on some new philosophical and religious foundation of this kind that any viable society of our children and grandchildren can be built."

A change in our customary world view is now a practical necessity, and that change would seem to require a different experience of one's personal self, of time, of the living world. It is not a matter of technologies, of finding new ways to manipulate the environment, but of a change in perception, leading to a change in values. The values needed are congruent with the assertions of mystics, "romantic dreamers," people ordinarily regarded as impractical.

Mystical perceptions always undergo translation, and translation leads to error, but a consistent message does emerge from many different texts:

- the value of surrender to the natural flow of the world;
- the futility of pursuing material satisfactions;
- the possibility of attaining a mode of existence superior to the one in which we usually live; and
- the unknowable presence or force that is nothing, defined by negatives, since it is not part of the object world and yet is perceptible. That "God," that "Love," is immanent in every man and in everything.

We are waves, mystics say, and like waves not different from the ocean. Yet who knows that this is true? Who knows what these words, derived from objects, mean when applied beyond the object world? It is difficult for us to grasp, centered as we are in the action mode. Thus, "surrender" is distasteful and "no-thing" appears to be a joke.

The course of our learning from womb to adulthood has been a path of adaptation to objects. We learned to use the object world by becoming objects ourselves. Having created an object self, we have defended that same self, and now "surrender" or "selflessness" feels like a loss. To surrender to something other than yourself, as mystics advise, suggests passivity and the threat of slavery.

A thousand tyrants have invited surrender, and history is witness to the perils of relinquishing one's will. China is powerfully self-sufficient, but the Western observer is often chilled, uneasy by what the Chinese, with admirable selflessness, have surrendered. The most precious jewel of modern civilization is the possibility of freedom, the freedom to be what we really are, in its unique form, and to be that with full strength and with our full heritage. Uniqueness and autonomy should not be surrendered.

Our fear of "surrender" arises from a confusion of modes, a judging of one realm by the concepts of another. Our education in the action mode has pre-empted our minds, narrowing our lives; meanwhile, the experience of beyond self is minimal and overbalanced by the action mode. Although that mode has made possible freedom from material needs and from disease, it has also brought us to the edge of disaster. That is understandable: we have lost our organismic balance. The receptive mode, the intuitive mode, the allowing mode, is needed now for our survival. It has always been there, perhaps provided for a time of need — which is now — but we have not used it. We have tolerated living in an odd, abstract world, constructed and maintained by all those forces of indoctrination to which we subscribe, knowingly or not: schools, family training, college, newspapers, job requirements — all flying the flag of self, of acquisition, of socially approved conquest and control. That system is no longer enough; we need a different kind of action, a new realism.

The world ship is sinking. There is no time to free ourselves unless freeing ourselves helps the world at the same time. Can we do that? How?

THE THREE PRISONERS

After the death of Rabhi Uri of Strelisk, who was called the Seraph, one of his hasidim came to Rabbi Bunam and wanted to become his disciple. Rabbi Bunam asked: "What was your teacher's way of instructing you to serve?"

"His way," said the hasid, "was to plant humility in our hearts. That was why everyone who came to him, whether he was a nobleman or a scholar, had first to fill two large buckets at the well in the market place, or to do some other hard and menial labor in the street."

Rabbi Bunam said: "I shall tell you a story. Three men, two of them wise and one foolish, were once put in a dungeon black as night, and every day food and eating utensils were lowered down to them. The darkness and the misery of imprisonment had deprived the fool of his last bit of sense, so that he no longer knew how to use the utensils he could not see. One of his companions showed him, but the next day he had forgotten again, and so his wise companion had to teach him continually.

"But the third prisoner sat in silence and did not bother about the fool. Once the second prisoner asked him why he never offered his help.

"'Look!' said the other. 'You take infinite trouble and yet you never reach the goal, because every day destroys your work. But I sit here and try to think out how I can manage to bore a hole in the wall so that the light and sun can enter, and all three of us can see everything.'" [Buber]

He sits and thinks in isolation: *it is not enough.* The other teaches the fool: it is not enough; the fool does not learn. None of the three works toward escape and freedom. None of the three knows how.

But if they worked together, couldn't they escape? Couldn't the fool provide shoulders on which one wise man could stand, whose own shoulders might be the base from which the third could reach the opening above? Or perhaps they'd share utensils and, together, dig through the wall to freedom. The strength and skill of each need to be combined in the service of the larger goal.

We are blind and crazy most of the time, living in dungeons — although we do not know it. Our abstractions swirl through our heads, creating phantom worlds of their own in which we stumble around enchanted, seeking to escape by constructing more rooms within more mental rooms. The rooms are our theories, theories of all kinds: what is good, what is man, time, death, and god. Most theories were learned so long ago we've forgotten they are theories; we think they're real. Yet every thought we have is unreal, a selection, an abstraction. Inside the abstract rooms we cannot see the world. It is a perceptual problem; the answer is not more thought but more perception.

Watching is the key. Watch what draws you back into the prison rooms. What holds you there, like a spider's thread? "Attachment to objects makes men blind and deaf," said Mohammed. Notice the attachments, see where the strands are stuck to objects (money, youth, approval, pleasure), trace them back inside. There is a place where the web collects. When I look inside and see its shape, I realize that it's the personal self, the phantom built of my desires: my memories, emotions, virtues, skills, the color of my hair — everything I've won and built and call myself, the object I was taught was me. The bonds of attachment, the spider's silk, fan out from "me" to the things of the world.

We have used the action mode to spin the web, and we are caught. Yet action is not bad. The action mode preserves our biological self; with it we preserve others. We need the action mode to play our role in man's journey, but it must give way to action of a different kind. So the Vedas declare: "It is not action that brings suffering but the greediness of the mind for the result, that strengthens our bondage in the world."

Desire sustains the object self and feeds it; desire is the wish to have. To have we must be objects. After all, there must be something that can have what is desired; that object is the personal self. There we stand, object to object; and then the trouble starts. Whatever we desire, we must get and keep; there is disappointment from expectations and there is fear of loss, "me" and "my" object must be preserved. And objects become hated from fear as they are loved from desire. So we suffer from desire; we are objectified.

"I want and so I act. What else can there be?"

Something else. First stop having. Step away from it, as if you were walking through a store, enjoying the sight of all the merchandise, but declining to be encumbered. There is the salesman; he holds out the thing you want. See it glitter! Beautiful! But it is heavy to carry; it becomes a strain. Decline. Let the interior muscles ease, your hands fall to your sides, resting there. Look, admire, and walk away.

"What happens then?"

When you give up having, your problems disappear. Is that a strange idea, impossible, absurd? Try it; you can do it. Step aside.

Give it up. Let it go.

"But what is left? What remains?"

Experiencing. Acting. And something more.

"Why would I want to act at all?"

You will act. The present moment calls us, what is needed can guide our way. The flow of things provides direction if we're aligned. Relinquishing having, we are free to feel the current and, like swimmers, be carried and act at the same time.

The old traditions speak of service: performing of an action without thought of gain. Not because it's Good, but because the thought of gain spins another strand of silk, anchoring you to your object self. You are freed when you serve a task, doing what is needed, what the moment calls for. Working "selflessly," you walk away from the spider's web.

MUDDY ROAD

Tansan and Ekido were once traveling together down a muddy road. A heavy rain was still falling.

Coming around a bend, they met a lovely girl in a silk kimono and sash, unable to cross the intersection.

"Come on, girl," said Tanzan at once. Lifting her in his arms, he carried her over the mud.

Ekido did not speak again until that night when they reached a lodging temple. Then he no longer could restrain himself. "We monks don't go near females," he told Tanzan, "especially not young and lovely ones. It is dangerous. Why did you do that?"

"I left the girl there," said Tanzan. "Are you still carrying her?" [Reps]

Desires, fears, and hatred: with these the object self fastens us to other objects. The strands are invisible. To find them we must feel them. How can we feel them and trace them to their binding post, to cast them off, attaining freedom? Everyday life is our means, for our attachments happen every day. In all the little actions of our life, the self arises and binds us. Everyday life is the path. Our difficulties, our discomforts, our despair are signals that our object self has driven us to clutch a puff of smoke. Such suffering is not our essence, not our "tragic destiny"; it is the wasteful, grotesque product of an abstract world, our unseen insanity. Our everyday pain is a chance to see, and through seeing to become free.

Intuition tells us there is hell, purgatory, and heaven:

Hell is suffering without hope. Ignorant of the cause, we go around and around in a circle of cause and effect of our own making.

Purgatory is suffering through which we become free of suffering. In purgatory we use suffering as an occasion to learn. Understanding the cause of our suffering, we break the circle.

Heaven is freedom, harmony, love. Suffering is a function of self-concern. Having freed ourselves of self-concern. Heaven arises as our new being.

All three realms are present in our everyday life.

Everyday life is the path for us. Everyday life is the path for alleviating the misery of the world. Contemplation on a mountain top won't do. Squatting in one's corner of the dungeon won't do. The world needs you to work in it; you need the world to learn. Sacrifice? No. Somber toil? No. The joy of action; the high pleasure of selfless power; the exquisite, sensual delight of sanity? Yes! So, what do you say?

"What should I do?"

No! Don't say that. It kills it. It kills you. Asking that creates a state of consciousness from which nothing can be done. Experiment and see. Pretend to be asking someone, "What should I do?" Close your eyes and feel what asking that question does to you. Do it now. Stop reading, close your eyes, and ask, "What should I do?" (Try it now.)

WHAT WAS IT LIKE? Did you feel uncertain, a little bewildered, forehead wrinkled slightly, eyes a little pinched, looking upward, plaintively, to someone else — waiting to be told? It's the old dependency poison seeping into every cell, deadening the energy of change.

"What should I do?"

You can always find someone who will reply:

"Join Zero Population Growth."

"Be more honest."

"There's nothing you can do; it's out of your hands!"

"Contribute."

"Boycott!"

"Stock up on food!"

"Buy a farm (don't forget the guns)."

"Move to New Zealand!"

Does that help? Imagine millions of people following those directions, scurrying like ants, swarming back and forth from New Zealand to the grocery store to a rally to a stiff drink to bed. No, it doesn't help.

"So what should I do?" The eyes roll up to heaven, the shoulders shrug, and helplessness, like a warm, soft shawl, wraps itself around the already snoring citizen.

It's a functional matter. "What should I do?" asks for help, and asking for help throws a switch on the organismic engine, readying it for that purpose. Helplessness has a function, and body and mind cooperate in the task of being cared for, of being helped. Being cared for is not bad; it is an activity, like any other. But "What should I do?" cannot lead you to realistic action in the world.

So ask a different question: "Where does my energy want to go?"

For that you turn inside, to yourself. You listen and feel... "Where does my energy want to go?" Unaccustomed to asking, you may not hear an answer. So try a fantasy: Imagine you are free and unafraid, completely unafraid — what would you want to do? Go ahead, close your eyes, imagine that your fear is gone and you are strong — what would you want to do? (Try the fantasy now.)

WHAT CAME TO MIND? What did your energy show you? Was it something unreal? If it showed you pleasure, that's not bad. Pleasing yourself may be the first step, a test to know that you are free. If so, imagine next that you have had the pleasure and can have more, but what else would you want to do? What service is yours? What would be fun to try? What venture would call forth your strength in a joyful pouring out of all you have, the thing you'd want to try to do, if you were free, if you were unafraid? What action is yours?

So ask that question again: "Where does my energy want to go?" Close your eyes. Listen. Feel. Watch what you are shown.

"Before his death Rabbi Zusya said, 'In the coming world, they will not ask me: Why were you not Moses? They will ask me: *Why were you not Zusya?*" [Buber]

CONCLUSION

ALL these things have been true for me, have helped me stay afloat on the wild ocean of my life. They are truths about the human world. Yet they are perishable answers: they help only for a while and they carry me just so far. True as they may be, they have not been enough. For a long time, I continued seeking an end to my restlessness; my dissatisfaction could be lulled for a while but would return saying, "Something is still wrong." I needed solid ground under my feet, not emotions or "experiences" or more abstractions. These past few years my seeking has subsided, for I'm learning what it is I have to do, and as I do it the confusion of this world begins to clear. Let me tell you how this has happened. Realistically, you ought to know so you won't be misled. And it might apply to you.

I've been learning by reading teaching stories, like the ones I've shown you here. They've been prepared by a modern Sufi named Idries Shah. They're not secret; you can buy the books in many stores. The stories themselves are strange. Some are simple, some fantasy; some are rich, some are sparse. All are strangely powerful. They infiltrate invisibly, disappearing from my mind. Then a moment comes when they reappear, spring to sight, and show the motive of my thought and action in the everyday. They show me myself.

The stories are changing my life, my world. They seem to be templates, patterns that mirror patterns of deceit, subtle self-deceit that has clogged my vision so I cannot see. Bit by bit, vision improves and my life is clarified, like a foggy day clearing in patches, revealing glimpses of the sky.

There is a Teaching, the stories say, a science for knowing what we are and what we're for. It has worn a thousand costumes, to fit cultures of the past. The Teaching moves on, but its costumes remain behind, colorful shells, the life force gone. At present, old and interesting costumes abound, good for playing games, creating confusion. But the Teaching is still alive and here today, the stories say, invisible in contemporary clothes, specific for the time, the place, and the right people.

The stories work. I've been reading them three years, and I haven't met Idries Shah. It doesn't seem to matter. He's written his books for the Western mind that's bred to literature and intellect; he says our minds need preparation and the mode of teaching must be different from the mode that suited a peasant in Japan, an Arab in the Middle Ages, or a Jew in ancient Rome.

My life has been changing. Something is happening that is different from what went before, more direct, more powerful, freeing me in ways I do not notice at the time. Not "spiritual" in any sense I thought I knew that word. Yet it feels like land after a shipwreck. Hard work — more hard than what has gone before. The effort my own; the subject my behavior and my thought; independence of a different kind. Hard work. The only kind that seems to meet the need for waking from our strange world dream.

THE MAGIC MONASTERY

A certain quiet dervish used often to attend the weekly meals given by a cultivated and generous man. This circle was known as "The Assembly of the Cultured."

The dervish never took part in the conversation, but simply arrived, simply shook hands with all present, seated himself in a corner, and ate the food provided.

When the meeting was over, he would stand up, say a word of farewell and thanks, and go his way. Nobody knew anything about him, though when he first appeared there were rumors that he was a saint.

For a long time the other guests thought that he must indeed he a man of sanctity and knowledge, and they looked forward to the time when he might impart some of his wisdom to them. Some of them even boasted of his attendance at their meetings to their friends, hinting at the special distinction which they felt in his presence.

Gradually, however, because they could feel no rela-Tionship with this man developing, the guests began to suspect that he was an imitator, perhaps a fraud. Several of them felt uncomfortable in his presence. He seemed to do nothing to harmonize himself with the atmosphere, and did not even contribute a proverb to the enlightened conversation which they had come to prize as a necessary part of their very lives. A few, on the other hand, became unaware that he was there at all, since he drew no attention to himself.

One day the dervish spoke. He said:

"I invite all of you to visit my monastery, tomorrow night. You shall eat with me."

This unexpected invitation caused a change in the opinions of the whole assembly. Some thought that the dervish, who was very poorly dressed, must be mad, and surely could provide them with nothing. Others considered his past behavior to have been a test. At last, they said to themselves, he would reward them for their patience in bearing with such dreary company. Still others said to one another:

"Beware, for he may well be trying to lure us into his power."

Curiosity led them all, including their host, to accept the hospitality.

The following evening the dervish led them from the house to a hidden monastery of such size and magnificence that they were dazed.

The building was full of disciples carrying out every kind of exercise and task. The guests passed through contemplation halls filled with distinguished-looking sages who rose in respect and bowed at the dervish's approach.

The feast which they were given surpassed all powers of description.

The visitors were overwhelmed. All begged him to enroll them as disciples forthwith.

But the dervish would only say, to all their entreaties: "Wait until the morning."

Morning came and the guests, instead of waking in the luxurious silken beds to which they had been conducted the night before, clad in gorgeous robes, found themselves lying stiff and stark, dispersed on the ground within the stony confines of a huge and ugly ruin, on a barren mountainside. There was no sign of the dervish, of the beautiful arabesques, the libraries, the fountains, the carpets.

"The infamous wretch has tricked us with the deceits of sorcery!" shouted the guests. They alternately condoled with and congratulated one another for their sufferings and for having at last seen through the villain, whose enchantments obviously wore off before he could achieve his evil purpose, whatever that might be. Many of them attributed their escape to their own purity of mind.

But what they did not know was that, by the same means which he had used to conjure up the experience of the monastery, the dervish had made them believe that they were abandoned in a ruin. They were, in fact, in neither place.

He now approached the company, as if from nowhere, and said: "We shall return to the monastery."

He waved his hands, and all found themselves back in the palatial halls.

Now they repented, for they immediately convinced themselves that the ruins had been the test, and that this monastery was the true reality. Some muttered: "It is as well that he did not hear our criticisms. Even if he only teaches us this strange art, it will have been worthwhile."

But the dervish waved his hands again, and they found themselves at the table of the communal meal — which they had, in fact, never left.

The dervish was sitting in his customary corner, eating his spiced rice as usual, saying nothing at all.

And then, watching him uneasily, all heard his voice speak as if within their own breasts, though his lips did not move. He said:

"While your greed makes it impossible for you to tell self-deceit from reality, there is nothing real which a dervish can show you — only deceit. Those whose food is self-defeat and imagination can be fed only with deception and imagination."

Everyone present on that occasion continued to frequent the table of the generous man. But the dervish never spoke to them again.

After some time the members of the Assembly of the Cultured realized that his corner was now always empty. [Shah]

My intellect has helped to show me the bars of my cage of dreams, which it has helped create. It has not shown me the key in my hand with which I lock myself in, which I need to cease turning. The stories show me that. What may come next I do not know. I feel more sane and would not go back for any amount of "bliss" that I had felt before. Sanity is the finest pleasure I have known. So I work on myself, to reduce greed, vanity, and fear.

EXCLUSION

Rais El-Aflak, "The Lord of the Skies," who suddenly appeared in Afghanistan and then disappeared after giving a number of cryptic lectures, said:

"Almost all of the men who come to see me have strange imaginings about man. The strangest of these is the belief that they can progress only by improvement. Those who will understand me are those who realize that man is just as much in need of stripping off rigid accretions to reveal the knowing essence, as he is of adding anything.

"Man thinks always in terms of inclusion into a plan of people, teachings and ideas. Those who are really the Wise know that the Teaching may be carried out also by exclusion of those things which make man blind and deaf."
[Shah]

No need to "improve" yourself, no need to accept stoically your "existential despair." No need to drink the poison of "Each person is alone." No need to swear allegiance to the strange world that you've been taught and learned: the road of time, isolation, meaninglessness, and the confinement of your consciousness to the little box, labeled with your name, out of which you peer. No need to push aside your inner sense that says, "Something is wrong."

The truth is very hopeful. Very strong. Very real.

"There is no cause for fear. It is imagination, blocking you as a wooden bolt holds the door. Burn that bar...."

Printed in Great Britain
by Amazon

30869545R00179